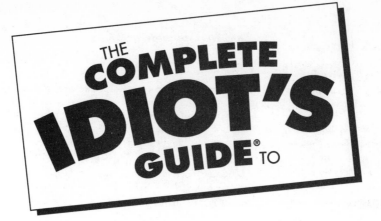

THE
COMPLETE IDIOT'S GUIDE® TO

Cooking— for Guys

by Tod Dimmick

D1377101

ALPHA

A member of Penguin Group (USA) Inc.

For Spencer and Kurt, the little guys.

Copyright © 2004 by Tod Dimmick

All rights reserved. No part of this book shall be reproduced, stored in a retrieval system, or transmitted by any means, electronic, mechanical, photocopying, recording, or otherwise, without written permission from the publisher. No patent liability is assumed with respect to the use of the information contained herein. Although every precaution has been taken in the preparation of this book, the publisher and author assume no responsibility for errors or omissions. Neither is any liability assumed for damages resulting from the use of information contained herein. For information, address Alpha Books, 800 East 96th Street, Indianapolis, IN 46240.

THE COMPLETE IDIOT'S GUIDE TO and Design are registered trademarks of Penguin Group (USA) Inc.

International Standard Book Number: 1-59257-269-3
Library of Congress Catalog Card Number: 2004108623

06   05   04   8   7   6   5   4   3   2   1

Interpretation of the printing code: The rightmost number of the first series of numbers is the year of the book's printing; the rightmost number of the second series of numbers is the number of the book's printing. For example, a printing code of 04-1 shows that the first printing occurred in 2004.

Printed in the United States of America

Note: This publication contains the opinions and ideas of its author. It is intended to provide helpful and informative material on the subject matter covered. It is sold with the understanding that the author and publisher are not engaged in rendering professional services in the book. If the reader requires personal assistance or advice, a competent professional should be consulted.

The author and publisher specifically disclaim any responsibility for any liability, loss, or risk, personal or otherwise, which is incurred as a consequence, directly or indirectly, of the use and application of any of the contents of this book.

Most Alpha books are available at special quantity discounts for bulk purchases for sales promotions, premiums, fund-raising, or educational use. Special books, or book excerpts, can also be created to fit specific needs.

For details, write: Special Markets, Alpha Books, 375 Hudson Street, New York, NY 10014.

Publisher: *Marie Butler-Knight*
Product Manager: *Phil Kitchel*
Senior Managing Editor: *Jennifer Chisholm*
Senior Acquisitions Editor: *Renee Wilmeth*
Development Editor: *Christy Wagner*
Production Editor: *Megan Douglass*
Copy Editor: *Nancy Wagner*
Illustrator: *Chris Eliopoulos*
Cover/Book Designer: *Trina Wurst*
Indexer: *Brad Herriman*
Layout: *Becky Harmon*
Proofreading: *Donna Martin*

Contents at a Glance

Contents

What the recipe symbols mean:

▲ Fast

● One-pot meal

■ Make-ahead

Foreword

I have been in the restaurant business all my life, and I constantly describe food and cooking procedures to employees and guests. I thought I was good, but with Tod Dimmick's entertaining and practical new book, you can't go wrong!

Tod takes you through food and recipes as if he was there in your kitchen, through real-life analogies answering all your questions before you even ask them. Most recipe books assume one knows what a teaspoon is or how to make a marinade (or knowing what a marinade is!). This book never makes these assumptions. Key elements are listed that are vital in any kitchen, from prep time to equipment. In everyday language, with entertaining humor that makes you want to read on, Tod presents recipes in a manner that will make anyone (even the guy who has trouble pouring a bowl of cereal) feel confident cooking a meal. He writes in such a way that you are learning without even trying.

Tod shows us how to make a meal in "real life"—using what is in our cabinet. He shows us, at the same time, how to save time and money with ingredients and methods. The "variation" tips he adds to many of his recipes make each meal interesting and delicious. The food for date night chapter is fun and ingenious, while the food and wine chapter is a nice overview for buying great wine at reasonable prices and matching them with your masterpiece. Tod even includes a mini suggested wine list at the end, for those of you who don't really want to "figure wine out" but want to enjoy wine just the same.

Although this book is written for the "guy" who doesn't feel comfortable in a kitchen, who doesn't like to clean, or who doesn't like to do a lot of planning, this book will also appeal to anyone (yes, women, even some of you!) who knows how to cook, but would like to take the monotony out of the menu with new, appetizing, and easy dishes.

How many guys thought cookbooks talk a different "language" that makes cooking complicated and time-consuming? How many of us never really tried to understand food and cooking techniques because we thought we had to go to cooking school to make a great meal? How many of us have friends who like to keep their "cooking secrets" to themselves—knowing darn well the only secret is that cooking *can* be simple, quick, and easy if you know the basics, a few rules of thumb, and some tricks?

If I have just described you—let me proudly present *The Complete Idiot's Guide to Cooking—for Guys*. With Tod Dimmick's new book in your kitchen, people will be asking you where you learned *your* secrets.

Daniel Mastrangelo
Restaurateur
New York City

New York City restaurateur Daniel Mastrangelo has been the founder and/or general manager of several well-known restaurants, including The Steakhouse at the Monkey Bar, Sorriso Ristorante, Finch Tavern (Stanley Tucci's restaurant in Westchester, New York), Coco Pazzo 74th Street, and Le Madri.

Introduction

Guys have a reputation for being food-challenged, not in eating—we do that fine—but in cooking. As a guy who used to avoid the kitchen like the plague, I know.

For a variety of reasons, though, many guys find themselves driving the stove. To find out just how many, I went out on the road. Wherever I went, whether a worksite or a firehouse, I found men more than willing to talk turkey. *It's funny that guys today have a reputation for not being cooks*, I thought, as I scribbled down recipe after recipe from a carpenter who is as passionate about food as he is about finish work. That reputation is also ironic when you consider that the history of fine food is filled with great chefs … who also happen to be guys.

I verified some things you already know. Guys hate kitchen cleanup (priority number one from everyone). We want great flavor, but we're not interested in spending all day or a lot of money. When we're in mixed company, guys like to do it right: We want to make a meal with class, but *still* one that doesn't take a long time to prepare.

These ground rules shape everything in this book, from ingredients to cooking methods to directions.

I cover a few other ground rules later, but you get the idea. My hope is to show that cooking for guys, even the most certifiable I've-never-been-in-a-kitchen-in-my-life guy, is not only possible—it's fun.

Each chapter in this book has two general types of recipes. The first are those recipes, generally called "fast," that make good use of basic building block foods, such as canned meats and vegetables. These recipes often use only 4 or 5 ingredients and often enable you to have dinner ready in 15 minutes or less. Think of skillet-cooked meats, savory pasta dishes, and seafood.

The second are recipes, also fast by any standard, that are just a bit more "home-made" in look and feel. These might take 20 minutes of your time. Some, such as slow cooker recipes, benefit from time gently cooking while you watch the game or engage in some other productive activity. In this corner, we have dishes like meat loaf, home-made pasta sauce, casseroles, and more.

Is it possible to cook and have fun at the same time? Of course! That's the whole point.

How This Book Is Organized

The recipes in this book cover just about every type of dish you can imagine, from appetizers to desserts and from pasta to chicken wings. They are organized, however, by themes, such as type of cooking (stove top), or type of occasion (date night). Methods are all early in the book, so that once you've tried a few similar recipes, you might start to get comfortable enough with them to start experimenting (like roasting beef instead of chicken).

But be careful! Do that too many times, and someone is going to call you a cook.

Throughout, you'll find tips and suggestions to make cooking a meal more of a pleasure than a pain. My not-so-secret mission is to show that once you're comfortable with the basic methods (stove top, broiler, oven, etc.), you'll then feel like you have a *license to grill*, so to speak. Then the fun really starts.

We divided the book into four parts:

Part 1, "Starting Line Basics," covers cooking basics from a guy's perspective, from explanation of equipment ("power tools and hand tools") to ingredients and methods. We start with a favorite guy topic—the "secret sauce" (every guy seems to has one.) You'll find recipes for favorite dishes from meat loaf to pork chops. Finally, we'll hold our own pasta sauce competition. (Question: Can a guy live on pasta alone?)

Part 2, "Method and Madness," explores a range of recipes within general cooking methods, such as using the grill, stove top, oven, and more. To keep you healthy, there's a chapter on vegetables, and to keep you happy, there's a chapter on desserts that even a guy can make.

Part 3, "Survival Rations," keeps a guy alive during the week. We look at quick, tasty weeknight meals and at big leftover-oriented batches that will pay dividends later in the form of "instant" meals with zero cleanup. We'll play with our food in the chapter on kid-friendly fare and polish things a bit with food the ladies will love (then regress with food the ladies will hate). And how could this part be complete without serving up a helping of nachos and other south-of-the-border–inspired foods?

Part 4, "Big Games and Big Themes," offers fun, flavor-packed recipes oriented around themes such as The Big Game, firefighter food, date night, and more. You'll also find a food and wine guide and a wine-buying checklist. I'll do my best to make you look good, no matter what the occasion.

Need-to-Know Info

In each chapter, you'll find helpful hints in the form of small boxes with information related to the topic at hand. Here's what to look for:

 End Run

These are tips on how to make something simpler, faster, or easier.

 Menu Manual

These contain words and phrases used in cooking or in recipes.

 Food Fumble

These are alerts about a common misunderstanding, mistake, or potential hazard.

Acknowledgments

This work would not have been possible without a crew of guys (including some women!) who care about food, including:

From the Fire Department (Food Division), thanks to Richard Adams, Barry Forrest, Mike Haigis, Tommy Topham, and Captain Mike Lentini of the Natick, Massachusetts Fire Department, and Jim Herbert of Station 6 of the Newton, Massachusetts Fire Department. Thanks also to Blake Allison, David Bachman, Roger Bridgeman, Andrew Dimmick, Warren Dimmick (yes, they are my brothers), Edward Evantash, Sara Flaherty, Andy Frankenfield, Bruce Hain, Walter Horning, Rob Levinson, Eric Lundblad, John Marchiony, John Naatz, Muffi O'Brien, Sandy Richardson, Fred Surr, Barry Friedman, Frank Manzi, Italo DeMasi, and many others for inspiration, recipe suggestions, and support.

I am indebted to Renee Wilmeth, senior acquisitions editor at Alpha Books, and to John Woods of CWL Publishing Enterprises for their enthusiastic support of this project and invaluable guidance and feedback throughout.

Finally, thanks to my sons Spencer and Kurt (small guys with large opinions), who serve as an ongoing testing panel for supposedly kid-friendly food. ("Dad, I'm not eating that, it's yucky!") To my parents, Dave and Freddie Dimmick, and my mom-in-law, Elaine Early, who all helped pick up the wreckage along the way. And to my wife, Jen, who made it possible for me to spend so much time focusing on the subtleties of gourmet guy food. I love you.

And to Lexie the hairy-scruffy-friendly dog, who tested a lot of guy food leftovers. She told me everything was great, if one can judge by a clean plate.

Special Thanks to the Technical Reviewer

The technical reviewer for *The Complete Idiot's Guide to Cooking—for Guys* was Ellen Brown, a Providence, Rhode Island–based cookbook author, caterer, and food authority. The founding food editor of *USA Today*, she has written 10 cookbooks, including *The Complete Idiot's Guide to Slow Cooker Cooking* and *The Complete Idiot's Guide to Cooking with Mixes*. Her articles have appeared in more than two dozen publications, including *Bon Appétit*, *The Washington Post*, and *The Los Angeles Times*. *The Gourmet Gazelle Cookbook* won the IACP award in 1989, and she is a member of the prestigious "Who's Who of Cooking in America."

Trademarks

All terms mentioned in this book that are known to be or are suspected of being trademarks or service marks have been appropriately capitalized. Alpha Books and Penguin Group (USA) Inc. cannot attest to the accuracy of this information. Use of a term in this book should not be regarded as affecting the validity of any trademark or service mark.

Part 1

Starting Line Basics

Part 1 is designed to get us all on the same page. If you're brand new to cooking, start with Chapter 1, where you'll find an introduction to cooking methods, equipment (power tools and hand tools), and a grocery list of basic foods you should have in your cabinet and your fridge. With all this info under your belt, you'll be well equipped to hit the ground (or the stove) running.

Then the fun starts. We'll look at seasonings and what I call "secret sauces"—flavorful sauces and marinades that lift ordinary food to a higher level. We'll review top guy-favorite recipes—those things you love but might think are too hard to make. Finally, we'll tip our hat to one of those foods critical to guy survival—pasta (and the sauce that goes on top).

Chapter 1

Ingredients, Tools, and Ground Rules

In This Chapter

- Kitchen tools of the trade
- KP duty: essential appliances
- Working with recipes: cooking methods and terminology
- Simple ingredients for delicious results

In this chapter, you'll find kitchen basics to help you get started, from tools and appliances to how to use the recipes in this book. To get started, let's first look at cooking priorities. I'll bet we're on the same page.

Rules of the Game

In preparing for this book, I spoke with a lot of guys about cooking. It turns out we all have similar priorities. "Easy cleanup" was the message I heard again and again. Many others stated that they have real trouble following recipes. They'd rather use "a little of this, a little of that." These are guys after my own heart. But before diving in, it's important to know some basics (as in what "a little" means, or what can be substituted for what). That's what this chapter, and this book, is about.

So before anything else, let's go over the ground rules to every recipe and piece of advice in this book:

- **Cleanup should be minimal.** If there's a choice between one bowl or two, we'll stick with one.

- **It has to taste great!** If there were a "guy-tested-and-approved" seal, you'd find it here. Take a look at the recipes in this book, and I think you'll agree that you're in for a taste treat.

- **Keep the ingredients basic.** I'll focus on ingredients you might already have in your pantry or refrigerator. I'll also suggest a shortlist of "secret weapon" ingredients that can turn something ordinary into something fun and delicious.

- **I don't have all day!** Neither do you. Recipes in this book focus on making the best use of your time, with emphasis on quick prep and, of course, minimum cleanup.

- **Spare the expense.** A great meal does not have to cost an arm and a leg. No recipe in this book will break your budget.

- **It's gotta be convenient.** One-pot meals, even portable meals, rated high on my informal "Cooking for Guys Survey," so I aim to please. Throughout these pages, you'll find dishes that follow you wherever you go—uh, in a good way, of course.

- **Keep it simple!** I know you don't want multi-stage kitchen projects and recipes with 25 steps, 2 pages of text, and hours of prep. So I'll give you simple-but-good recipes you can actually use.

End Run

If cleaning up isn't your favorite pastime, you're not alone. Almost every guy I spoke with listed "I hate to clean" (or a variation of that theme song) as one of their kitchen commandments.

What do these ground rules mean when the rubber hits the road?

- We'll make smart use of basic seasonings, sauces, and "secret weapons" that add flavor without confusion.

- We'll make good use of cooking in quantity, because leftovers can be delicious with zero prep and cleanup.

- We'll look to ingredients such as pasta that lend themselves to flavorful, quick dishes.

- One-pot meals featuring all the food groups find their way into these pages, too.

- We'll make it classy when we need to impress, casual when we're looking to relax, and throughout keep an eye toward fun. If we find the chance to get all three attributes in one dish or one meal, that's a bonus.

Cookware: Now You're Cooking

You don't need expensive or fancy pots and pans to make any of the recipes in this book. You *do*, however, need practical, quality cookware that will do the job without requiring a home equity loan.

Here's a basic cookware shortlist:

- A large (10-inch) skillet with a lid and spatter screen
- A large (4-quart) saucepan with a lid
- A large stockpot (that holds 2 to 3 gallons of water)
- A large (4-quart) casserole or baking dish with a lid
- A roasting pan with a lid

Let's take a look at these in a little more detail (in case you're wondering what the heck a stockpot is and how it differs from a roasting pan).

Skillets

I could make a decent case that a big skillet or frying pan could be the only item a basic cook needs. It can fit a whole meal but can also be used for simply cooking onions. If it's cast iron (which I recommend), that ol' skillet can be used on the stove top, inside the oven, or under the broiler (or all three, if you want to get fancy). I even used to take mine camping with me, until I got in trouble for all the soot. Choose a nice big one, say 10 inches or more across (and a separate one for camping).

End Run

For more value for your money, go for sturdy cast iron when you're buying a frying pan. It's inexpensive and will last indefinitely. It also has the attribute touted by its fancy cousins: mass. This heft enables even cooking, which is invaluable no matter what you're making.

A new cast iron skillet will last indefinitely, but you should "season" it by spreading a thin coating of cooking oil on the skillet and baking it for about an hour in a 350°F oven. This creates a smooth cooking surface in the skillet, making food less likely to stick and making the skillet easier to clean!

Saucepans

A saucepan is another must-have, whether you're heating up pasta sauce or cooking vegetables. Buy a 4-quart one and a 2-quart one, too, if you want to cover the bases. Don't necessarily get the cheapest saucepan you see. Look for one with a substantial bottom that will distribute heat evenly so food doesn't scorch in the middle.

> **End Run**
>
> To go with that large saucepan, consider getting a steamer insert. This is a folding perforated metal device that opens like a flower inside the saucepan and holds foods over the bubbling water. An insert will hold anything that needs steaming, most often vegetables, and can save you the expense of purchasing a whole separate vegetable steamer.

Stockpots

Stockpot, cooking pot, stew pot—whatever you call it, every kitchen needs one of these. The tradition of the never-ending stew is appealing to guy-types, and lucky for us, there's a wealth of history and tradition that centers on the stockpot. This big stove-top container should hold at least 2 gallons of liquid, preferably more. When we get to dishes like beef stew, chili, soups, and chowders, the stockpot is the place where it all happens. (And don't forget boiled foods such as lobster and corn on the cob. You'll need a stockpot for those, too.)

Casserole Dishes

These ceramic or glass heatproof containers with lids are terrific for oven (the large dishes) and microwave cooking (the smaller dishes). In this book, you'll find a number of recipes that call for a "large" (4-quart) casserole dish, which is big enough to make a big meal that will either feed a group or keep you alive for the week. Casserole dishes enable carefree cooking in the oven while you channel surf. Don't touch that dial.

> **End Run**
>
> For those of us who don't like to clean, your grocery or hardware store will have disposable foil roasting pans. Use it once, then chuck it (uh, recycle it). Can't beat that for cleanup.

Roasting Pans

A roasting pan is useful for this cooking shortlist. Roasts are an easy ticket to a great meal, and you'll find some really easy recipes here for roasts. This same roasting pan can serve double duty as an ovenproof container for other foods as well (other cuts of meat, baked potatoes, vegetables, etc.). Get one that is at least 9×13 inches with sides at least 4 inches high. Roasting pans come with a rack that suspends your roast over any liquid in the pan.

Other Stuff

You could fill your kitchen with a ton of other cooking implements if you catch the cooking bug: Baking trays and muffin pans are useful; a wok is great if you like stir-frying; a fish poacher is great if you're a fish fan, etc.

To minimize cleanup, also get a spatter screen for your skillet. Next time you pan-fry something juicy, you'll be quite happy you didn't have to wipe grease off the counter.

Hand Tools: For the Kitchen, Not the Garage

This *is* a cookbook, remember? So to get the food ready for the pots and pans I've just described, you need some hand tools.

Here are the essentials:

- ◆ Can opener
- ◆ Measuring cups
- ◆ Measuring spoons
- ◆ Knives
- ◆ Spoons and spatulas
- ◆ Corkscrews and gadgets
- ◆ Cutting board
- ◆ Salad spinner

Now let's take a closer look at each.

Can Openers

You could spring for the power version, but a manual can opener is very reliable and you can take it to the campground (without the really long extension cord).

End Run _____

A glass measuring cup is microwave-safe, so you can heat up the sauce or liquid you're measuring right in the measuring cup. You just saved some cleanup time!

Measuring Cups

Even the most die-hard, never-measure-anything cook occasionally has to use measuring cups. Get a set of cups with ¼ cup, ⅓ cup, ½ cup, and 1 cup sizes for dry ingredients (baking mix, flour, etc.), and another glass 2 cup for liquid ingredients (beer, cream, melted butter, etc.).

Measuring Spoons

In the recipes in this book, I've minimized the measurement requirement, but even so, you'll need measuring spoons. A set usually includes ⅛ teaspoon (abbreviated tsp. in the recipes), ¼ teaspoon, ½ teaspoon, 1 teaspoon, ½ tablespoon (abbreviated TB.), and 1 tablespoon (although many don't include the ⅛ teaspoon and ½ tablespoon sizes).

End Run _____

Spend an extra few bucks to get a decent, balanced chef's knife. It will have satisfying, balanced weight in your

Jack's Knives

A fancy kitchen could have a dozen different knives. I've found, however, that I use two knives for most everything: a chef's knife (get started with an 8-incher) and a paring knife (two would be even better; I always seem to lose one).

Spooning, Scooping, Scraping, and (Cork)Screwing

When you go to the store to get that knife, pick up a few other things to make the job easier:

◆ **A pasta spoon,** with those big teeth all around the edge, is great for serving spaghetti and all kinds of pasta.

◆ **Wooden spoons** are good for stirring soups, sauces, and other simmering stuff.

◆ **Rubber spatulas** help you scrape every last bit of hot fudge out of the jar (they're also useful for real cooking).

◆ **Regular (metal) spatulas** are a must for fry-pan cooking. You need to have something to flip pancakes and sausages. A metal spatula is perfect for a cast iron skillet, but if you've got nonstick cookware, better get a plastic one, too.

◆ **A melon scoop,** which is like an ice-cream scoop but smaller, is a useful tool to have in a kitchen drawer. Kids and adults like scoops of food, from melons to little balls of ice cream.

- **A peeler** for vegetables (cucumbers, potatoes, etc.) is also on the must-have list.
- **A bottle opener and corkscrew** are probably already in your kitchen, right? If not, better get them.
- **A wire whisk,** for easy mixing.
- **A colander,** for rinsing foods and draining pasta and cooked vegetables.
- **A big ladle,** for serving up bowls of soups, chowders, stews, and chili.
- **Tongs,** so you don't have to get third-degree burns on your fingers while turning bacon in the skillet.

Kitchen Patrol: Appliances and Power Tools That Love Guys ... and Vice Versa

Ah, power tools. In the garage or in the kitchen, whatever room they're in, guys love 'em. Some you probably already have (a microwave, an oven, a stove, and a fridge); others, if you don't have, you should consider getting. Each item here can save time and add fun ... and isn't that the reason we're here?

- Oven
- Stove
- Microwave oven
- Refrigerator and freezer
- Outdoor grill
- Indoor electric grill
- Slow cooker
- Toaster/toaster oven
- Food processor
- Timer (stand alone or on your microwave)

Food Fumble

With opportunity comes risk, even in the kitchen. That high heat will cook quickly, so when using the broiler, keep an eye on your meal to prevent forage fires. When using oven heat, on the other hand, you can go play foosball while things are cooking.

Crack the Code: The Recipe Is the Key to Edible Success

A single recipe can fill multiple pages and have dozens of steps, but you won't find those lengthy, complicated recipes in this book. What do the recipes in this book look like? Let's take a look. Here's a basic recipe and its parts:

Tex-Mex Bean Dip

Prep time: 5 minutes • Cook time: 4 minutes • Serves: 6 guys as an appetizer

1 (15-oz.) can fat-free refried beans

1 (16-oz.) tub sour cream or light sour cream

1 cup shredded Mexican-style or Monterey Jack cheese

1 cup salsa (your favorite)

Scrape beans into a microwave-safe serving bowl and microwave for 2 minutes to make them easier to mix. Stir in sour cream, cheese, and salsa and heat in the microwave for another 2 minutes. Stir one more time and serve with tortilla chips.

Variation: Add 1 (4-ounce) can chopped green chilies for even more flavor.

That doesn't seem too hard, does it? Now let's take a look at each of the parts and see how easy this really is:

◆ **Title.** *Tex-Mex Bean Dip:* The title will be descriptive of the dish, including the main theme (beans!) and a hint as to what it's for (dip!).

◆ **Recipe key:** *("Fast"):* These codes you'll see in the Contents include "Fast" (a triangle), "One-Pot Meal" (a circle), and "Make-Ahead" (a square). Most everything in this book (because that's our whole objective) falls into the "fast" category.

◆ **Recipe features.** *Prep time, Cook time (if applicable), Serves:* This info tells you how much to make and how much time you'll need to plan for.

◆ **Ingredients.** *1 (15-oz.) can fat-free refried beans …:* This is a list of what you'll need to make this recipe, how much you'll need of it (1 can, 1 cup, 1 tablespoon, etc.), and the order in which you'll need them. Some ingredients, such as canned foods, come packed in liquid. The ingredient list will tell you whether to throw out that liquid, use it, or save it in case you need it later (that's "reserve" in recipe-speak).

◆ **Directions.** *Stir, or in a food processor …:* These are the specific directions or methods for how to use the ingredients to make your dish. These directions will be in order, with first steps first.

> **End Run**
>
> With all recipes, it's a good idea to read through the ingredient list before you start, just to be sure you don't do a lot of work and then get to lizard gizzards and—*oops!*—don't have any. I keep ingredient lists short, so that shouldn't be too much of a problem.

◆ **Variations or notes.** If I can give you useful information, such as common ways to make this recipe using different ingredients (a *substitution*), I'll often give that information here. If the notes are especially interesting, they might also be in a box on the side of the recipe, such as an "End Run." Variations might make a recipe low-fat or suggest other ingredients (adding chilies) to change the flavor.

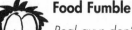

Food Fumble

Real guys don't ask for directions … but still, it's nice to make something edible for a change. Follow a basic recipe once, but after that, don't be a slave to directions. The point is that you understand the method, what goes first, what goes second, etc. After that, follow the basic method and have fun.

Menu Manual

A **substitution** in sports takes one player out and replaces him with another. In cooking, we use substitutes for some of the same reasons. I might get tired of one player (chicken) and send in another (pork). Don't be afraid to substitute; just use common sense. Pork and chicken, for example, are both meats with similar flavor (mild) and cooking characteristics (quick cooking). Follow the rule of replacing *like with like* and you'll usually be okay. If you look in your fridge and see that you have no chicken but you do have tuna, give it a try. (Obviously, don't substitute onions for chicken, or you'll get a completely different dish.)

Now for the Fun Part: Favorite Ingredients

To get a sense of their favorites, I talked to a lot of guys about this book. If I had a buck for every pasta recipe and chicken dish I heard about, I could be retired by now. But these ingredients say a lot about the priorities guys have: quick preparation; satisfying, even comfort-food flavors; and easy cleanup. You'll find these ingredients and themes reflected loud and clear throughout this book. We'll take these ideas and have some fun with them. We'll check out how, with slightly different preparation or maybe a simple new ingredient, you'll meet an old friend and not even recognize him.

So what key ingredients do you need to have in your cabinet /pantry and in the fridge? Obviously you don't need to have all these on hand all the time, but with a good selection of the following, you'll be able to prepare many of the dishes in this book with ease.

In the Cabinet

First up, canned soups:

◆ Chicken and beef broth

◆ Condensed cream soups (mushroom, celery, and chicken)

Next, canned meats and seafood:

◆ White tuna fish packed in water

◆ Chicken and turkey packed in water

◆ Chunk ham (in 5-ounce cans in the canned food section)

◆ Salmon packed in water

And some more essentials of the canned vegetables and grains variety:

◆ Sliced mushrooms

◆ Green chilies (4-ounce cans of spicy peppers)

◆ Diced tomatoes

◆ Tomato sauce

◆ Sliced white potatoes

◆ Corn

◆ Black beans

◆ Kidney beans

◆ Cannellini beans

◆ Refried beans

◆ Chickpeas (sometimes called garbanzo beans)

◆ Chopped garlic (available in jars at your grocery store)

◆ Split peas

◆ Sauerkraut

◆ Water chestnuts

◆ Canned pasta

◆ Crushed pineapple

◆ Canned spaghetti

End Run

A lot of guys I spoke with mentioned healthful eating as a priority. We all love wings (you'll find them here, too), but we'll occasionally eat our vegetables, as well. This book is definitely not about counting calories, but I want healthy readers who will live a long time.

End Run

I list several staples here, but, of course, a lot of other ingredients add fun to your food. Under canned seafood, for example, you could also add canned shrimp and canned crabmeat—two ingredients that enable delicious meals.

And every pantry must contain pasta and starches:

- Spaghetti
- Linguini
- Shells
- Angel hair
- Rotelle
- Macaroni
- Lasagna
- White quick-cooking rice
- Brown rice

Food Fumble

When you open anything stored in a can or a jar but don't finish it, put the rest in the fridge for short-term storage. You'll avoid mold, nasty smells, and other unappetizing science experiments.

End Run

Don't forget canned pasta and spaghetti! We'll use these traditional classics to create

The Fridge Is Your Friend

You probably already have juice, milk, beer, etc. in your refrigerator. What else do you need? Here are some of the main ingredients for recipes you'll find in this book:

- Sour cream
- Mayonnaise
- Cheddar cheese (shredded and in a block)
- *Horseradish*

Menu Manual

Horseradish is the sharp, spicy root that forms the flavor base in many condiments from cocktail sauce to sharp mustards. It is a natural match with roast beef. The form generally found in grocery stores is prepared horseradish, which contains vinegar and oil, among other ingredients, and you'll need to keep it in your fridge. If you come across pure horseradish, use it much more sparingly than the prepared version, or try cutting it with sour cream.

- Bottled lemon juice
- Mozzarella cheese
- Stick butter
- Eggs
- Chicken and other poultry (from boneless, skinless breasts for quick cooking to whole roasters for week-long eating)

- Beef (ground beef, beef roasts, steak—your favorite cut)
- Pork (tenderloin, chops, ground pork)
- Seafood (all kinds)

Food Safety!

Germs are everywhere. Always prepare food on clean surfaces, using clean equipment, and wash your hands before handling food. It's just plain sad when someone makes themselves sick by handling food with dirty hands. Those are the headlines you read about in the paper that you'd just as soon not have anything to do with you.

Also read expiration dates. Foods, especially perishable foods such as meats and milk, come from the store with "sell by" or "use by" dates. Plan your cooking so you'll use these foods prior to that date. Some foods (such as seafood) should be eaten immediately, others (such as some cheeses) will last for many days in the fridge. Keep your freezer in mind if you buy extra steak.

And please don't set your house on fire. Keep clutter away from the stovetop especially. A kitchen fire doesn't have the same romance as a fire in the fireplace.

As much as guys hate waste, there are times when food goes bad, and for your own safety you should chuck it.

With the equipment listed in this chapter on hand, a fridge full of tasty ingredients, and your new expertise at following a recipe, the rest of this book is going to be like a visit to an all-you-can-eat buffet of your favorite foods. Have fun!

The Least You Need to Know

- You only need a shortlist of kitchen tools to get started—fast.
- Don't focus on how much time it takes to cook something (a slow cooker, for example, can take all day). Instead, focus on how much of *your time* is needed (that same slow cooker recipe only takes 5 minutes of your time and the rest can be spent mowing the lawn).
- Recipes are the assembly instructions for a dish. Follow a basic recipe once, and you'll know how to make it next time without even looking.
- Test cooking with the oven, broiler, and microwave. These easy methods will have you amazed with what you can do.
- You don't need a supermarket-size pantry, but you do need some basic ingredients as a starting point to create many of the recipes in this book.

Chapter 2

The Appeal of the Meal: Seasoning, Secret Sauces, ... and Secret Weapons

In This Chapter

- ◆ A punch-list of sure-win seasonings
- ◆ Secret sauces: every guy has one
- ◆ "Secret" weapons to win friends and influence people
- ◆ Seasoning mixes that make life easy
- ◆ What's the rub?

In this chapter, we take a quick look at herbs, spices, and blends (both store-bought and homemade), including a shortlist of individual seasonings you should have in your cabinet. You'll also find a list of what I call "secret weapons": ingredients—many of which you probably already have—that add excitement to a meal.

Then we'll tinker with these flavorful building blocks to make some secret sauces—something every guy seems to have. We'll start with some of the easy classics (sauces from ready-made bases) and also look at some easy from-scratch sauces.

Herbs and Spices and Everything Nice

When you like a dish, such as pasta, chili, or pork chops, chances are, a big part of what you like is the flavor of the seasonings used in the dish. These flavors often come from *herbs*, *spices*, and blends of these seasonings, often with salt. Change just one spice in your pasta sauce, and you'll notice a big difference.

Your grocery store has dozens of herbs and spices. But don't get overwhelmed; pick up the blends and individual seasonings I give you in the following sections, and you'll be good to go.

Seasoning Blends

These seasoning blends are the cheater's shortcut to flavorful dishes. Even just a dash adds layers of flavor.

Menu Manual

Herbs are edible plants characterized by fresh aromas and flavors, such as parsley, sage, rosemary, oregano, and thyme. The leaves are used either fresh or dried in cooking. **Spices** are pungent seasonings also of vegetable origin, often seeds such as mustard, pepper, or cloves.

Food Fumble

Some seasoning blends are on the mild side; others will make your hair stand on end. Start with a little, then add more to get to the flavor level you like. It doesn't work to add a lot and then try to remove some!

- **Italian seasoning** is sitting on your grocery store shelf. The blend includes basil, oregano, rosemary, and thyme and is a useful seasoning for quick flavor that evokes the "old country" in sauces, meatballs, soups, and vegetable dishes.

- **Cajun seasoning,** great on stews and meats, includes garlic, salt, paprika, red pepper, and other herbs and spices.

- **Chili powder** is not one spice, but a seasoning blend that includes chili pepper, cumin, garlic, and oregano. Proportions vary among different versions, but all offer a warm, rich flavor.

- **Curry powder** is a rich blend of Indian-style seasonings including hot pepper, nutmeg, cumin, cinnamon, pepper, and turmeric.

- If you're a fan of salt, pick up a **basic seasoning mix** such as Jane's Crazy Mixed-Up Salt. This salt-based mix contains onion, garlic, pepper, and other seasonings thrown into the mix. If you want to add salt separately, consider a mix such as Mrs. Dash, which includes onion, pepper, celery seed, basil, and a whole bunch of other flavorful ingredients. Adding either of these to many dishes will add just the touch of flavor you want.

These are just a few basic spice blends. Many others vary from end-purpose (steak seasoning) to flavor theme ("Southwest") to specific ingredients (lemon-pepper).

Individual Herbs and Spices

You can get away with using spice blends in your cooking, but if you want to go a bit further, pick up some of these individual herbs and spices for your shelf or fridge:

- Basil
- Cinnamon
- Cloves
- Cumin
- Dill
- Marjoram
- Nutmeg

- Minced onion
- Oregano
- Paprika
- Red pepper flakes
- Rosemary
- Sage
- Thyme

End Run

Your dry herbs will last a long time in a dark, dry, and preferably cool place. If you have a choice, avoid that cabinet over the stove, which tends to get hot and accelerate flavor loss. Also, periodically sniff your dried herbs. If they get to the point of smelling musty, it's time to replace them.

Fresh herbs bring even better flavor, but you must use them right away. If you're going fresh, the amounts needed are different, too, because you'll need more of the fresh stuff. In this book, I specify dried herbs to keep things simple, but if herbs are your thing, try the fresh!

Secret Weapons

I call the items on this list "secret weapons" because they work their magic in the background of any dish. Chances are you'll never know they're there; you'll just wonder why the meal you just made tastes so good. You can find all these on your grocery store shelves.

- **Balsamic vinegar** is an Italian vinegar. It is heavier, darker, and sweeter than most vinegars and adds a touch of easy class to recipes.
- **Bouillon** in its dried form from chicken, beef, vegetable, etc. stock (not the actual broth Mom used to serve you when you were sick) is a popular starting

ingredient for soups because it adds flavor (and often a lot of salt). A jar of bouillon powder in the cabinet is a definite secret weapon.

♦ **Dijon-style mustard** is a sharp, spicy mustard that works like a dream with many meats and vegetables as well as in spicy-sweet sauces.

♦ **Hoisin sauce** is probably something you've had if you've had Chinese food. This sweet sauce, made from sugar, soy sauce, vinegar, fruit, garlic, and spices, adds secret magic to all kinds of dishes.

♦ **Hot pepper sauce** can be used in everything from marinades to vegetables, stews, and pasta sauces. There are a zillion hot pepper sauces, so choose your favorite. Tabasco is one common name on the grocery store shelves. These sauces vary from mildly spicy to call-911 hot.

♦ **Italian dressing** is one of the top-secret weapons because it can be used as a flavorful base in sauces and marinades. You can even use it alone as a marinade for meats, and your diners will be impressed. Most Italian dressings include oil, vinegar, salt, garlic, and herbs such as basil and oregano.

End Run

One of the advantages of secret weapons is novelty appeal, otherwise known as "variety is the spice of dinner." We've all had chicken, but you'll be blown away by that same old bird dressed up in hoisin. It's enough to make me look forward to dinner.

♦ **Ketchup** you know, of course, but you might be surprised how it can be used over and above squirting on a burger. Ketchup includes tomatoes (no kidding), vinegar, sugar, onion, and other stuff.

♦ **Olive oil** is a fragrant liquid produced by crushing or pressing olives. Olive oil makes for a rich base in marinades and coatings for meats and vegetables. You can even use it alone as a dip for bread in place of butter. Your doctor will tell you it's good for your heart, too.

♦ **Pesto** is a thick spread or sauce made with fresh basil leaves, garlic, olive oil, pine nuts, and Parmesan cheese. Other new versions are made with other herbs. You can make rich and flavorful pesto at home or purchase it in a grocery store and use it on anything from appetizers to pasta and other main dishes. You'll find pesto both on the pasta sauce shelf and in the refrigerated section in many grocery stores. For flexibility, go for the one by the pasta sauces. It will last on your shelf until you need it.

♦ **Salsa** is more than just a dip for your tortilla chips. These chopped spicy vegetable and fruit sauces can be a sauce for cooked meats (check out Chicken Salsa in Chapter 7)—it'll make you look like you spent a lot of time cooking! You can also add salsa to other sauces or in chili with magical effect. Just keep in mind that some salsas are mild and others are really hot, so pick the one that suits your taste.

- **Sour cream** (yeah, I know you know what sour cream is) as a secret weapon can serve as the base for a range of easy, quick, velvet-smooth sauces that are so good you'll be licking the plate. "Light" (as in low-fat) sour cream is a good substitute in many cases where you'd like to reduce the fat in your recipe.

- **Soy sauce** is a delicious, dark, Asian-style sauce made from fermented soybeans, grains, and salt. Soy sauce is delicious as a marinade by itself and as a component in many dishes.

- **Teriyaki** is another delicious, Asian-style sauce made of soy sauce, rice wine, ginger, and sugar. It works beautifully with seafood as well as most meats.

- **Worcestershire sauce** was originally developed in India and contains tamarind. This spicy sauce is used as a seasoning for many meats and other dishes.

End Run

Don't have space in your pantry for everything on this list? Get the following five first (you probably already have half of them):

- Dijon mustard
- Italian dressing
- Hot pepper sauce
- Soy sauce
- Ketchup

These are essential in a lot of the recipes in this book, and you'll be swimming in flavor. Check out how they are used in some of the secret sauces in the next section.

The Secret Sauce

For many of us, the appeal of a meal does not necessarily come from the main ingredient, but rather it's the seasoning that gives the dish its flavor. Whether you like spicy flavors such as hot peppers, chili, or cumin or sweet flavors from honey, sugar, or molasses, those attributes often come from the spices you add rather than the main ingredient in the dish. The sauce enhances the natural flavors of the steak, the chicken, or the fish to create something new. There are as many sauces as there are cooks out there. I've picked some of the classics—easy to make and delicious—to share with you here.

End Run

For a foolproof twist on store-bought barbecue sauce, pour about 1 cup store-bought stuff into a bowl and stir in ⅓ cup soy sauce and ¼ cup molasses or sugar. Presto sauce.

Menu Manual

Most recipes in this book will tell you how many it serves (for example, Serves: 4 guys or 6 regular people). Because most of us don't eat sauce for dinner, I give yield measurements here instead. Yield is a measure of how many cups of sauce you'll make.

For those of you who actually *do* eat sauce for dinner, one of these recipes will serve one, antacid not included. (That was a *joke*.)

Eric's Italian Marinade and Sauce

Prep time: 2 minutes • Yield: About 2½ cups

½ (12-oz.) can Coca-Cola

1 cup ketchup

⅔ cup Italian dressing

Mix together Coca-Cola, ketchup, and Italian dressing. Use marinade aggressively on chicken, pork, ham, steak tips, or breakfast cereal. Well … maybe not breakfast cereal.

Menu Manual

A **marinade** is a seasoned sauce usually high in acid content. The acid breaks down the muscle of the meat, making it tender, while the seasonings add flavor. Italian dressing can be used as a marinade because it has both the seasoning and the acid (vinegar). To marinate a food such as meat, seafood, or other food is to soak it in a marinade. Putting food in a zipper bag or a bowl, covering it in marinade, and sticking it in the fridge—a guy can do that.

Warm Honey-Mustard Sauce

Prep time: 2 minutes • Yield: About 1 cup

¼ cup canola or other cooking oil

¼ cup honey

½ cup Dijon-style mustard

1 TB. balsamic or other vinegar

Mix together oil, honey, mustard, and vinegar in a microwave-safe measuring cup and heat for 1 minute. Use to smother ham, chicken, and pork.

South S-Easy Marinade

Prep time: 2 minutes • Yield: About 2½ cups

1 (8-oz.) can crushed pineapple in juice, drained

½ cup teriyaki sauce

¼ cup chopped garlic

1 TB. sugar

Mix together pineapple, teriyaki sauce, garlic, and sugar in a bowl. As an example of use, pour ½ sauce over chicken breasts in a bowl, cover the bowl, and set in the fridge for a couple hours or more until you're ready to cook. Use remaining marinade as a relish to serve with chicken.

Food Fumble

Avoid contaminated marinades and sauces by keeping any that come in contact with raw meat separate from sauce you want to use for dipping.

Beerbecue Sauce

Prep time: 2 minutes • Yield: About 1¾ cups

1 cup ketchup

¼ cup beer

¼ cup firmly packed dark brown sugar

2 TB. vinegar

1 TB. Worcestershire sauce

Dash hot pepper sauce or *to taste*

Mix together ketchup, beer, brown sugar, vinegar, Worcestershire sauce, and hot sauce in a 1-pint measuring cup or a bowl. Heat for 1 minute in the microwave, stir again, and use as a marinade, to brush on meat before cooking, and as a dipping sauce.

Menu Manual

A **dash** refers to a few drops, usually of a liquid, that is released by a quick shake of, for example, a bottle of hot sauce. **To taste** means to use as much as you like to get to the level of flavor you want from that ingredient.

Grampy's Spicy-Sweet Barbecue Sauce

Prep time: 5 minutes • Yield: About 1⅓ cups

1 cup ketchup	½ tsp. cumin
2 TB. vinegar	½ tsp. ground ginger
3 TB. molasses	¼ tsp. ground red pepper
1 TB. dry mustard powder	¼ tsp. ground black pepper

In a bowl or pint measuring cup, mix together ketchup, vinegar, molasses, mustard, cumin, ginger, red pepper, and black pepper. Use as a marinade, to brush on meat before cooking, and as a dipping sauce.

End Run

This version, adapted from my recipe in *The Complete Idiot's Guide to 20-Minute Meals,* is a sweet-spicy sauce that will keep you coming back.

To save time and cleanup with sauces, measure and mix them right in a 2-cup (1-pint) measuring cup. Then use that measuring cup to pour the sauce where you need it.

Covers Anything Marinade

Prep time: 2 minutes • Yield: About ¾ cup

⅓ cup olive oil	1½ tsp. ground cumin
¼ cup lemon juice	1 tsp. salt
1 TB. Italian seasoning	½ tsp. ground black pepper

Mix together olive oil, lemon juice, Italian seasoning, cumin, salt, and black pepper in a 1-pint measuring cup or a bowl. Use as a marinade and to brush on everything from chicken to chops before cooking.

End Run

If you have lemons handy, squeeze them to get fresh lemon juice. The bottled stuff will work, but fresh lemon juice is better. You can squeeze that juice the old-fashioned way (with your hands), or with a nifty device like a lime squeezer.

Cocktail Sauce

Prep time: 2 minutes   •   Yield: About 1¼ cups

1 cup ketchup

2 TB. chili powder

2 TB. prepared horseradish

1 TB. lemon juice

Mix together ketchup, chili powder, horseradish, and lemon juice in a 2-cup measure or a bowl. If you've got time, make this ahead and put the cup, covered, in the fridge for a couple hours to let the flavors blend.

Spiced Homemade Ketchup

Prep time: 5 minutes   •   Yield: About 1½ cups

1 cup (8 oz.) tomato sauce

2 TB. tomato paste

2 TB. Worcestershire sauce

1 TB. soy sauce

1 TB. molasses or brown sugar

1 TB. vinegar

½ tsp. ground black pepper

Dash hot pepper sauce

Thoroughly whisk or mix together tomato sauce, tomato paste, Worcestershire sauce, soy sauce, molasses, vinegar, black pepper, and hot pepper sauce in a 1-pint measuring cup or a bowl. You want the result to be smooth, like, well, ketchup. Use as a marinade, to brush on meat before cooking, and, of course, on french fries.

Spicy Mayonnaise

Prep time: 2 minutes   •   Yield: About 1¼ cups

1 cup mayonnaise

1 TB. chopped garlic

1 TB. lemon juice

1 TB. olive oil

½ tsp. dried dill

¼ tsp. ground black pepper

Dash hot pepper sauce

Mix together mayonnaise, garlic, lemon juice, olive oil, dill, black pepper, and hot sauce in a 1-pint measuring cup or a bowl. Great on a main course of chicken or fish; you can even use this as a dip.

Raspberry Mustard Sauce

Prep time: 2 minutes • Yield: About 1 cup

½ cup Dijon-style mustard

¼ cup seedless raspberry jelly

2 TB. canola or other cooking oil

1 TB. balsamic or other vinegar

Mix together mustard, jelly, oil, and vinegar in a pint measuring cup or a bowl. Serve on ham, turkey, pork chops, sausages, etc.

Variation: Use a different fruit jelly or, for a festive change of pace, cranberry sauce.

That's the Rub

A rub is a dried seasoning mix that is rubbed onto meats to add flavor and tenderize prior to cooking. Sealed in a jar, dry rubs will last a long time in your cabinet. Do try these on all cuts of pork, chicken, beef, and fish.

Tex-Mex Rub

Prep time: 3 minutes • Yield: About ¼ cup

1 TB. garlic salt	1 tsp. dried oregano
1 TB. chili powder	1 tsp. paprika
1 tsp. ground cumin	1 tsp. ground black pepper

Mix together garlic salt, chili powder, cumin, oregano, paprika, and black pepper in a small jar with a lid.

Cajun Rub

Prep time: 3 minutes • Yield: About ¼ cup

5 tsp. garlic salt	2 tsp. crushed red pepper
2 tsp. ground cumin	1 tsp. ground black pepper

Mix together garlic salt, cumin, red pepper, and black pepper in a small jar with a lid. Put this on your wings and you've got Bourbon Street ... kind of.

The Least You Need to Know

♦ Seasonings can make a dish. Lucky for you, I've given you a seasoning punch list.

♦ Flavorful "secret" sauces can be fast, easy to make, and enable delicious, unusual meals.

♦ Keep "secret weapons" (ready-made sauces and seasonings) on standby in your cabinet and fridge, and use them to change an ordinary meal into something extraordinary.

♦ Ready-made delicious, balanced seasoning blends can get you on the way quickly.

♦ For a savory shortlist, keep Dijon mustard, Italian dressing, ketchup, soy sauce, and hot pepper sauce on hand to create multiple flavorful meals.

♦ Herbs and spices, such as oregano and cumin, are distinctive, easy-to-use seasonings that add personality to any dish.

Chapter 3

Need-to-Know Recipe Basics

In This Chapter

- ◆ Recipes every guy should know
- ◆ Winners have a "can-do" attitude!
- ◆ Homemade is not only delicious, but quick and easy, too
- ◆ Secrets to dressing up store-bought meals

In this chapter, I'll give you some of the most popular dishes for guys. These recipes don't take much of your time, and with the smart use of canned and frozen foods, the results are magic! You just might be surprised how easy homemade can be after trying the recipes in this chapter.

You "Can-Do" These Tasty Dishes

These recipes make smart use of canned ingredients, but don't sacrifice any flavor. *You* don't have to tell anyone you used ingredients from a can.

Sloppy Joes with Mushrooms

Prep time: 5 minutes • Cook time: 15 minutes • Serves: 4 guys or 6 regular people

1 lb. lean ground beef

1 (15-oz.) can Sloppy Joe sauce or Emergency Sloppy Joe Sauce (recipe follows)

1 (4-oz.) can mushroom stems and pieces, drained

Dash hot pepper sauce

6 or 8 hamburger buns or sandwich rolls

Cook beef in a skillet over medium heat, stirring, for 8 to 10 minutes until meat is browned and there's no red in sight. Drain fat from skillet, holding back meat with a spoon or a lid so you don't lose dinner. Stir in Sloppy Joe sauce, mushrooms, and hot pepper sauce. Cook for 1 minute, then spoon equal amounts Sloppy Joe mixture onto each bun bottom, top, and serve.

Variation: Use ground pork or turkey in place of ground beef. A slice of cheese is a nice addition, too.

For more stove top recipes, check out Chapter 6.

Emergency Sloppy Joe Sauce

Prep time: 2 minutes • Serves: 4 guys or 6 regular people as part of a Sloppy Joe recipe

1 (14.5-oz.) can diced tomatoes (drain some liquid by holding the lid on and tipping the can over the sink)

¼ cup ketchup

1 (4.5-oz.) can chopped green chilies

1 TB. Worcestershire sauce

Mix together tomatoes, ketchup, chilies, and Worcestershire sauce in a bowl. Use as the sauce in the recipe for Sloppy Joes with Mushrooms.

Ham and Bean Dinner

Prep time: 5 minutes • Cook time: 5 minutes • Serves: 4 guys or 6 regular people

2 (¾-lb.) ham steaks, cut into ½-inch *cubes*

2 (16-oz.) cans baked beans

½ cup barbecue sauce (your favorite)

Dash hot pepper sauce

Mix together ham steaks, baked beans, barbecue sauce, and hot pepper sauce in a large saucepan and heat, stirring, over medium heat for 5 minutes or until hot. Serve in bowls with green beans alongside to balance the meal (and to complete the all-beans, all-the-time diet).

Variation: Microwave in a microwave-safe bowl for 3 to 5 minutes.

For more stove top recipes, check out Chapter 6.

Menu Manual

To **cube** a food is to cut it into small squares or rectangles. In the case of a ham steak, all you do is cut it in ½-inch-wide strips, then cut across those strips to get cubes.

Mac and Cheese I: Dressed-Up Store-Bought

Prep time: 5 minutes • Cook time: 20 minutes • Serves: 4 guys or 6 regular people

1 (14.5-oz.) box or 2 (7.25-oz.) boxes macaroni and cheese

2 (5-oz.) cans chunk ham, drained

1 (14.5-oz.) can diced tomatoes

Dash hot pepper sauce (optional)

Prepare mac and cheese according to the package directions. Add ham, tomatoes, and hot pepper sauce (if using), mix thoroughly, and heat for another 3 to 4 minutes over low heat.

Chili Con Carne

Prep time: 5 minutes • Cook time: 20 minutes • Serves: 4 guys or 6 regular people

1 lb. lean ground beef	2 TB. chili powder
1 (16-oz.) can *refried beans*	1 TB. ground cumin
1 (16-oz.) jar medium salsa	1 cup shredded Monterey Jack or other cheese
1 (15-oz.) can red kidney beans, drained	1 cup sour cream

Cook ground beef in a large skillet, stirring over medium heat for 8 to 10 minutes or until meat is browned and there's no red in sight. Drain the fat. Stir in refried beans, salsa, kidney beans, chili powder, and cumin and cook, stirring, over low heat for 10 minutes or until heated through. Add a little beer or water if it's too thick. Distribute to serving bowls, top with cheese and sour cream, and serve.

Variations: Use ground pork or turkey in place of ground beef.

For more stove top recipes, check out Chapter 6.

Menu Manual

Refried beans are twice-cooked beans—most often pinto beans—softened into a thick paste and often seasoned with peppers and spices. Label descriptions commonly include "green chili" or "spicy," "traditional," and "fat-free." Pick your poison, but if you're not crazy about lard (rendered pork fat), consider the fat-free or vegetarian versions. If your refried beans resemble a brick, microwave them in a bowl for a minute to loosen before mixing into the chili.

Oh, and **con carne** means "with meat."

Fast Nachos

Prep time: 5 minutes • Cook time: 3 minutes • Serves: 4 guys or 6 regular people

1 (16- or 18-oz.) bag plain tortilla chips

2 (8-oz.) bags shredded Mexican-style or Monterey Jack cheese

1 TB. chili powder

2 (2.25-oz.) cans sliced ripe olives, drained

1 (4.5-oz.) can chopped green chilies

2 cups (16 oz.) sour cream

Arrange chips in a thick single layer on four or six plates (you will have chips left over). Sprinkle cheese over each plate, then sprinkle chili powder over cheese. (Whether you have cheese left over depends on how thick you like it on your nachos. A thin layer = more crispy chips.) Finally, spread olives and chilies among the plates. Microwave each plate for 1 minute on high or until cheese melts—but only until the cheese melts or you'll end up with chewy, leathery chips. Serve with a *dollop* of sour cream on each.

For more microwave recipes, check out Chapter 7. For more on the Southwest theme, see Chapter 15.

Menu Manual _____

A **dollop** (thoroughly unscientific) is a spoonful of something creamy and thick, like sour cream or whipped cream. Just to make things confusing, a dollop can also be the same thing as a dash when you're talking about liquids, like hot sauce. In this book, a dollop is sour cream, a dash is hot sauce (remember, keep things simple).

Can-Do Beef Stew

Prep time: 10 minutes   •   Cook time: 1 hour, 5 minutes   •   Serves: 5 guys or 8 regular people

3 TB. olive or canola oil

1½ lb. beef stew meat, cut into ½-inch cubes

1 (14.5-oz.) can diced tomatoes with garlic (or with onions and garlic)

1 (15-oz.) can sliced white potatoes, drained

1 cup water

2 TB. Worcestershire sauce

1 TB. beef bouillon granules

Dash hot pepper sauce

2 (9-oz.) pkg. frozen peas and pearl onions, thawed

Heat oil in a large skillet over medium heat and cook beef, stirring, until browned or about 5 minutes. Stir in tomatoes, potatoes, water, Worcestershire sauce, bouillon, and hot pepper sauce. Heat until mixture begins to bubble. Turn down the heat to low, cover, and go surf bad movies for an hour. Come back, add peas and onions, and cook for another 5 minutes. Ladle stew into bowls and carefully carry your bowl over to the TV. Try not to spill it on yourself; it's hot.

Variation: For an alternative to frozen-pea-pearl-onion mixture, use a canned peas-and-carrots mix (drained).

For more stove top recipes, check out Chapter 6.

Homemade Never Looked So Good

These comfort food classics rate a 10 on the nostalgia scale for guys.

Meat Loaf

Prep time: 10 minutes • Cook time: 90 minutes • Serves: 6 guys or 8 regular people

2 lb. lean ground beef	1 TB. Italian seasoning
1½ cups Italian-style *breadcrumbs* (or plain)	2 TB. Worcestershire sauce
2 eggs, lightly beaten	¼ cup ketchup
1 cup (4 oz.) shredded cheddar cheese	Salt and ground black pepper to taste
2 TB. chopped garlic	

Preheat the oven to 350°F. Wash your hands (no kidding). In a big bowl, use your hands to mix ground beef, breadcrumbs, eggs, cheese, garlic, Italian seasoning, and Worcestershire sauce. The mixture should cling together. If it doesn't, add a little beer or milk until it does. Line a baking dish or tray with aluminum foil. Place mixture on the foil and form it into a loaf. Wash your hands again. Pour ketchup over the top of the loaf and spread it around with the back of a spoon. Slide meat loaf into the oven and cook, uncovered, for about 90 minutes. When done, a meat thermometer will read 160°F for beef. To serve, slice with a butter knife and put pieces on serving plates. Peas alongside are a natural, as is more ketchup. Finish beer.

Variation: Use ground pork or turkey in place of ground beef.

For more oven recipes, check out Chapter 7.

> **Menu Manual**
>
> You can find **breadcrumbs** on your grocery store's shelves. You can also use plain old bread, cut up into small pieces and added to the mix. In that case, double the amount you use (store-bought breadcrumbs are more dense).

Wilbur Burgers

Prep time: 5 minutes • Cook time: 10 minutes • Serves: 2 guys or 4 regular people

1 lb. ground pork

¼ cup breadcrumbs

1 egg, lightly beaten

1 tsp. Worcestershire sauce

Salt and ground black pepper to taste

Toasted hamburger buns

Food Fumble

Getting your hands dirty in the kitchen is not the same thing as handling food with dirty hands! Nobody wants to eat unnecessary germs, so wash your hands before handling any raw meat. And of course, wash afterward as well to get rid of that raw smell (unless you like having neighborhood dogs following you).

Wash your hands (no kidding). In a bowl, mix ground pork, breadcrumbs, egg, and Worcestershire sauce. Form the mixture into patties about ½-inch thick and 4 inches across and cook in a large skillet (or on a grill) over medium heat about 4 minutes per side or until cooked through. Place each burger on a toasted bun and dress as you like.

Variation: Use ground beef or turkey in place of ground pork.

For more stove top recipes, check out Chapter 6.

Pork Chops and Spicy Applesauce Cream

Prep time: 5 minutes • Cook time: 20 minutes • Serves: 4 guys or 6 regular people

8 chops (about 2 lb.)

Salt and ground black pepper to taste

3 TB. olive oil

1 cup applesauce

1 cup sour cream

¼ cup Dijon-style mustard

Sprinkle chops with salt and pepper on both sides. Heat oil in a skillet over medium heat and cook chops for 6 minutes each side or until cooked through. (Unless you've got a monster frying pan, you'll have to do these 3 or 4 at a time.) Remove chops to serving plates, add applesauce, sour cream, and mustard to the skillet, and cook, stirring, for 2 minutes or until heated through. Pour some applesauce mixture over each chop and serve. Some bread and a salad make this a meal.

For more stove top recipes, check out Chapter 6.

Six-Minute-Gorgeous Garlic Bread

Prep time: 5 minutes • Cook time: 3 minutes • Serves: 4 guys as a snack, one guy for an unbalanced meal (it has been done)

1 long loaf French or Italian bread, sliced lengthwise along the side

½ cup olive oil

3 TB. chopped garlic

1 TB. dried oregano

1 tsp. salt

¼ cup shredded Parmesan cheese

Preheat the broiler. Set out two halves of bread on a baking tray, cut side up. In a bowl, mix olive oil and garlic and, using a spoon, spread mixture generously on both cut sides of bread. Sprinkle bread with oregano, salt, and Parmesan cheese. Slide under the broiler (set the rack at the next-to-highest level). Broil for 3 minutes or until garlic bread is sizzling and beginning to brown. Cut into slices and serve.

For more broiler recipes, check out Chapter 7.

Mac and Cheese II: Easy Homemade

Prep time: 5 minutes • Cook time: 20 minutes • Serves: 4 guys or 6 regular people

1 lb. dried macaroni

4 TB. (½ stick) butter

1 cup (8 oz.) sour cream

1 cup Italian-style breadcrumbs

1 (8-oz.) pkg. shredded cheddar cheese

1 cup shredded Parmesan cheese

Dash hot pepper sauce (optional)

Cook macaroni according to package directions, drain, and return to the cooking pot. In a 2-cup measuring cup, melt butter in the microwave for 30 seconds (it will not completely melt, but it will start to soften and hot noodles will do the rest). Add butter, sour cream, breadcrumbs, cheddar cheese, Parmesan cheese, and hot sauce (if using) to macaroni and mix well. Serve with a salad, and you've got a thing of beauty.

Roast Chicken Dinner

Prep time: 5 minutes • Cook time: 3 hours • Serves: 4 guys or 6 regular people

Chicken:

1 (5- to 7-lb.) whole "oven stuffer/roaster" chicken

¼ cup olive oil

2 TB. lemon juice

2 TB. chopped garlic

1 TB. Italian seasoning

1 tsp. ground cumin

Salt and ground black pepper to taste

½ cup water

Vegetables:

3 large baking potatoes, scrubbed and cut into 2-inch-square pieces

3 onions, peeled and quartered

5 big carrots, peeled and cut into 2-inch pieces

Preheat the oven to 325°F. Rinse chicken under cold running water and pat dry with paper towels. Chuck the towels (along with raw-chicken germs). In a bowl, mix olive oil, lemon juice, and garlic. Place chicken in a large roasting pan without the grill or a large casserole dish. Drizzle olive oil mixture all over chicken—and even get a little on the inside. Sprinkle chicken with Italian seasoning, cumin, salt, and pepper—get some on the inside, too. Pour water into the pan around but not on chicken (you don't want to wash off the seasoning) and slide chicken into the hot oven. Cook for about 2 hours, then add potatoes, onions, and carrots around chicken, adding a little more water if the pan is dry. Cook for another hour (total cooking time will be about 30 minutes per pound of weight) or until chicken is fully cooked. If you have a meat thermometer, the meat should be 185°F in the thigh.

Pull that masterpiece out of the oven and let it cool for a few minutes. For a pretty chicken, lift it out of the juices (and grease) and set it on a carving platter or tray. Carve off slices to serve with cooked carrots, onions, and potatoes alongside. Drumsticks and legs are darker, richer meat; breast meat is white. Of course, you can just carve it right in the cooking dish.

For more oven recipes, check out Chapter 7.

End Run

A roast chicken takes only minutes of prep and then it roasts by itself in the oven. It will either feed a big group all at once or feed a few for days. Perhaps best of all, it's got class. Bring out a roast chicken for a dinner for a group of people, and everything is right with the world.

The cook-time rule of thumb for roast chicken is about 30 minutes per pound or 3 hours for a 6-pound bird. To make the chicken, and the vegetables, taste even better, open the oven every now and then and spoon some of the juice in the pan over the chicken and vegetables (this is called *basting*). If you're watching a game, do this during commercial breaks and you'll be a master chef.

The Least You Need to Know

- With some basic recipes in your kitchen toolbox, you'll know some of the most-requested favorites.
- Many of these recipes are not only easy, but they offer a balanced one-pot meal as well.
- Canned foods can be fast, easy, building blocks for a tasty meal.
- Cooking a homemade meal can be quick and painless.

Chapter 4

The Great Pasta Sauce Competition

In This Chapter

- The Sauce Doctor takes on store-bought sauce
- The secrets of homemade tomato sauce
- More than just tomatoes: creamy sauces

Pasta makes an easy, tasty, and satisfying meal, and it's no big surprise that so many of us survive on pasta. One measure of pasta's popularity is a look at your grocery store's sauce and pasta shelves. It feels like half the store (well, it's big, anyway).

This chapter recognizes our saucy reality in two ways. We'll tinker with store-bought sauce, and we'll spoon into several easy and satisfying homemade sauces. Nothing impresses the family like serving them a homemade sauce.

The Sauce Doctor Is In!

Plain pasta sauce is the starting point for most of these easy, delicious sauces. At the end I'll give you a few other sauces, still all simple and all delicious.

Note: These recipes assume you'll be cooking 1 pound dry pasta to serve with the sauce. Note, too, there will be pasta left over on many of the recipes. Let your own cooking style dictate how much pasta you cook. For me, that leftover spaghetti is the perfect quick meal tomorrow night. If, on the other hand, you are more likely to lose those shells in the back of the fridge until they have to be thrown out, then just cook less to begin with.

End Run

There are enough different types of pasta sauce at your grocery store to be confusing. In this chapter, we start from a simple base, plain sauce. Another option is to start with a *marinara* sauce base (marinara is more highly seasoned than plain pasta sauce—usually with garlic and oregano) or one of the many sauces flavored with vegetables, meats, cheeses, etc.

Italian Chicken Pasta Sauce

Prep time: 2 minutes • Cook time: 10 minutes • Serves: 4 guys or 6 regular people as part of a pasta and sauce meal

2 (5-oz.) cans water-packed chunk white chicken meat, drained

1 (26-oz.) jar plain pasta sauce

1 TB. Italian seasoning

½ tsp. ground black pepper

Put chicken in a saucepan, breaking up any large chunks with your stirring spoon. Pour pasta sauce in the pan and add Italian seasoning and black pepper. Thoroughly mix sauce, turn the heat to between low and medium and *simmer*, stirring, for 10 minutes. Serve over cooked pasta.

Menu Manual

To **simmer** is to boil a liquid gently so it barely bubbles. In the case of sauce, simmering heats it, but doesn't cause it to aggressively boil. A rapid boil will cause enthusiastic sauce bubbles that will burst all over the stove top and countertop and force you to consider an annual cleaning (remember, thou shalt clean as little as possible). It might also burn the sauce, unless you're stirring it constantly.

Spicy Meat Sauce

Prep time: 2 minutes • Cook time: About 15 minutes • Serves: 4 guys or 6 regular people as part of a pasta and sauce meal

1 lb. lean ground beef

1 (26-oz.) jar plain pasta sauce

2 tsp. ground cumin

Dash hot pepper sauce

Parmesan cheese

Cook ground beef in a large skillet over medium heat, breaking meat into small pieces and stirring with your spatula until meat is cooked, about 8 minutes. Drain excess fat from beef. Pour pasta sauce over meat, add cumin and hot pepper sauce, turn the heat to between low and medium and simmer, stirring, for 5 minutes. Serve over cooked pasta and top with Parmesan.

Food Fumble

Draining hot fat takes care because it must cool before you can dispose of it permanently. One option is to drain the fat into an empty food can, then dispose of the can after the fat cools and solidifies. Don't pour it into anything plastic, or you'll get a fatty, melty mess. That might be another kitchen ground rule: Thou shalt not injure thyself unnecessarily.

Seafood and Olive Sauce

Prep time: 2 minutes • Cook time: 10 minutes • Serves: 4 guys or 6 regular people as part of a pasta and sauce meal

2 (10.5-oz.) cans white clam sauce

2 (6-oz.) cans water-packed chunk white tuna, drained

2 (2.25-oz.) cans sliced ripe olives, drained

1 TB. Italian seasoning

Dash hot pepper sauce

Pour clam sauce into a saucepan and add tuna, olives, Italian seasoning, and hot pepper sauce. Break up any big pieces of tuna. Thoroughly mix sauce and simmer over medium heat, stirring, for 10 minutes or until bubbling. Serve over cooked pasta and top with Parmesan cheese.

Variation: Use canned minced clams (drained) in place of the tuna.

End Run

Clam sauce comes both white and red (tomato-based) and is a terrific change of pace when it comes to pasta sauces. You'll find it on the grocery store shelf near the other pasta sauces.

Hot Sausage 'n' Pepper Sauce

Prep time: 5 minutes • Cook time: 25 minutes • Serves: 4 guys or 6 regular people as part of a pasta and sauce meal

2 TB. olive oil	1 (26-oz.) jar plain pasta sauce
³/₄ lb. "hot" Italian sausages	2 dashes hot pepper sauce
2 green bell peppers, stems and seeds removed, and cut into 1-inch pieces	

Heat oil in a large skillet over medium heat. Cook sausages about 5 minutes. While sausages are cooking, cut peppers in half lengthwise. Using a small sharp knife, cut out and discard stems and seeds, then chop the remaining pepper flesh into 1-inch chunks. Add green pepper pieces to skillet, turn over sausages, and cook for another 5 minutes or until meat is cooked and all pink has disappeared from the center. Remove the skillet from heat and, using a knife and fork, cut sausages into 1-inch pieces. Pour pasta sauce over meat, add hot pepper sauce, put the skillet back over medium-low heat and simmer, stirring, for 10 minutes. Serve over cooked pasta.

Variation: To tone down the spice, omit hot pepper sauce. For a mellow sausage sauce, use sweet Italian instead of hot sausage.

End Run

Now for some pasta physics. If you want a meal where you get a bit of everything in each bite, use components that are roughly the same size and shape. For example, a pasta sauce with sausage and pepper pieces each, say, about 1 inch across, would go well with a pasta in the same size ballpark, for example, penne, shells, or bow ties (farfalle).

Spaghetti with Meatballs

Prep time: 2 minutes   •   Cook time: 15 minutes   •   Serves: 4 guys or 6 regular people as part of a pasta and sauce meal

1 lb. frozen precooked meatballs or Easy Homemade Meatballs (recipe follows)

1 (26-oz.) jar plain pasta sauce

1 TB. Italian seasoning

1 TB. Worcestershire sauce

½ tsp. ground black pepper

Put meatballs in a saucepan and pour pasta sauce over. Add Italian seasoning, Worcestershire sauce, and black pepper. Thoroughly mix sauce and simmer over medium-low heat, stirring, for 15 minutes. Serve over cooked pasta and sing the "On top of spaghetti …" song.

Variation: If you're using homemade (unfrozen) meatballs, you'll only need to heat the sauce for 5 minutes.

Easy Homemade Meatballs

Prep time: 10 minutes   •   Cook time: 25 minutes   •   Serves: 4 guys or 6 regular people as part of a pasta and sauce meal

1 lb. ground turkey, pork, or beef

1 TB. chopped garlic

1 TB. Worcestershire sauce

1 TB. Italian seasoning

1 tsp. salt

½ tsp. ground black pepper

2 dashes hot pepper sauce

Preheat the oven to 350°F. In a bowl, thoroughly mix ground meat, garlic, Worcestershire sauce, Italian seasoning, salt, pepper, and hot pepper sauce and shape mixture into golf ball–size balls. Arrange meatballs in a roasting baking pan so they don't touch each other and cook in the oven for 25 minutes or until cooked through.

These meatballs are a beautiful sight on top of spaghetti, but don't be afraid to put them in a submarine sandwich or even—*gasp*—eat them alone.

Variation: You can also make these with lamb or other poultry.

End Run

For a terrific appetizer, serve a plate of hot meatballs with toothpicks and a bowl of thick blue cheese dressing alongside for dipping. Include plates or plenty of napkins. You're going to make a mess, but it's worth it.

Italian Shrimp and Shells

Prep time: 2 minutes • Cook time: 10 minutes • Serves: 4 guys or 6 regular people as part of a pasta meal

1 (16-oz.) box uncooked pasta shells

½ cup Italian dressing

2 (6-oz.) cans tiny cocktail shrimp, drained

Dash hot pepper sauce

⅓ cup shredded Parmesan cheese

Menu Manual

Toss does not mean throw your food. It means to mix everything so the sauce evenly coats the food.

Cook pasta, drain it, and return it to the cooking pot. Pour in Italian dressing, shrimp, and hot pepper sauce and *toss* to coat pasta. Distribute to serving plates and sprinkle aggressively with Parmesan cheese.

Use shells or another pasta with a similar size and shape. The sauce is very flavorful, so a little goes a long way.

Clean-Out-the-Fridge Pasta Sauce

Prep time: 5 minutes • Cook time: 20 minutes • Serves: 4 guys or 6 regular people as part of a pasta and sauce meal

3 TB. olive oil

½ head broccoli, stems peeled and cut into ½-inch pieces

1 cup baby carrots, cut into ½-inch pieces or 2 large carrots, peeled and cut into ½-inch pieces

1 (26-oz.) jar plain pasta sauce

½ cup pepperoni slices (about ⅓ [6-oz.] pkg.)

Heat oil in a large skillet over medium heat. Add broccoli and carrots and cook, stirring, for 10 minutes or until vegetables are beginning to soften (I like a bit of a crunch, but not too much). Add sauce and pepperoni. Thoroughly mix sauce and simmer over medium heat, stirring, for 10 minutes or until bubbling. Serve over cooked pasta.

Food Fumble

This catch-all sauce is a convenient way to use those strays hanging out in the fridge, but you still need to address whether some things need pre-cooking. Most fresh vegetables (carrots, broccoli, etc.) should be cooked first, then added to the sauce. Otherwise your sauce will be crunchy. Cooked meats are fine, but raw meats should be cooked before being added to the sauce.

Quick and Easy Homemade Sauces

Many guys make their own tomato sauce for use on pasta, pizza, and as a base for many other dishes. It's not hard, and there's a pride of ownership that the contents of a jar just can't match. As for taste, there's no comparison. I've included two of my favorites here, one using canned tomatoes and the other using fresh tomatoes.

Homemade Tomato Sauce

Prep time: 5 minutes   •   Cook time: 20 minutes   •   Serves: 4 guys or 6 regular people as part of a pasta and sauce meal

3 TB. olive oil

1 large onion (baseball size), peeled and chopped into ¼- to ½-inch pieces

1 TB. chopped garlic

1 (28-oz.) can plum tomatoes, chopped, liquid reserved

2 TB. tomato paste

1 TB. Italian seasoning

1 TB. Worcestershire sauce or soy sauce

1 tsp. salt

½ tsp. sugar

Dash hot pepper sauce

Heat oil in a large skillet over medium heat and cook onion for 5 minutes, stirring a couple times. Add garlic and cook another 2 minutes. Pour in chopped tomatoes with juice, tomato paste, Italian seasoning, Worcestershire sauce, salt, sugar, and hot sauce. Cook, stirring, for 10 minutes and serve over pasta. Delicious.

Use this sauce on pasta, but also keep it in mind as a secret weapon to add to chili and stews or use as a sauce for pizza.

Food Fumble

I'm aggressive with onions, and these recipes show it. That sharp onion flavor becomes sweet and rich after cooking. All that said, however, if you like onions but onions don't like you, use ½ onion or even omit it altogether from these recipes.

Fettuccini Alfredo

Prep time: 5 minutes • Cook time: 20 minutes • Serves: 4 guys or 6 regular people as part of a pasta meal

1 lb. fettuccini or other pasta

1 cup light sour cream

1 cup shredded Parmesan cheese

½ stick (4 TB.) butter, melted

½ tsp. salt

½ tsp. ground black pepper

Cook and drain fettuccini and place it back in the cooking pot. Immediately add sour cream, Parmesan cheese, melted butter, salt, and pepper. Toss to coat and serve.

Mushroom-Romano Pasta Sauce

Prep time: 5 minutes, including making Homemade Tomato Sauce base • Cook time: 20 minutes • Serves: 4 guys or 6 regular people as part of a pasta and sauce meal

1 batch Homemade Tomato Sauce recipe (earlier in this chapter)

2 cups (about 8 oz.) sliced white mushrooms (available in your grocery store produce section)

½ cup shredded Romano cheese

Prepare Homemade Tomato Sauce as recipe indicates. About 5 minutes after you add tomatoes and seasonings in Homemade Tomato Sauce recipe, add mushrooms. When the "done" bell on your timer goes off, stir in Romano. You'll have mushrooms that still have a bit of texture, and your sauce will be a cheese- and mushroom-lover's dream.

Spaghetti Carbonara

Prep time: 5 minutes   •   Cook time: 20 minutes   •   Serves: 4 guys or 6 regular people as part of a pasta meal

1 lb. spaghetti

2 eggs, lightly beaten

½ cup sour cream

½ cup shredded Parmesan cheese

½ lb. cooked bacon, drained on paper towels and crumbled into ¼- to ½-inch pieces

Salt and ground black pepper to taste

Cook and drain spaghetti and place it back in the cooking pot. Immediately add eggs and mix so hot pasta will cook eggs. Add sour cream, Parmesan cheese, and bacon. Toss to coat and serve with salt and pepper on the side.

Easy Pesto Sauce

Prep time: 15 minutes   •   Serves: 4 guys or 6 regular people as part of a pasta meal

1 cup tightly packed chopped fresh basil leaves

2 TB. chopped garlic

½ cup *pine nuts* or walnuts

½ cup grated or shredded Parmesan cheese

¾ cup olive oil

½ tsp. salt

Put basil, garlic, pine nuts, Parmesan cheese, olive oil, and salt in a food processor and give it a whirl until you've got a thick paste. If it needs help processing, add some more olive oil. Stir about ½ into your cooked pasta (a little more if you like extra flavor). Save the rest.

End Run

Freeze any extra pesto in a spare ice-cube tray wrapped in plastic wrap. For a pasta dish, pry out 3 to 4 cubes, thaw them in the microwave for 1 minute, and you're good to go.

Menu Manual

Pine nuts really are from a type of pine tree. They are a traditional component of pesto, and they add a rich crunch to many other recipes. In the case of pesto, walnuts can easily work instead.

Chicken Marsala Pasta

Prep time: 10 minutes • Cook time: 20 minutes • Serves: 6 guys or 8 to 10 regular people as part of a pasta meal

3 TB. butter

6 boneless, skinless chicken breasts (about 2 lb.)

Salt and ground black pepper

½ cup flour

3 TB. olive oil

1 (14.5-oz.) can (about 2 cups) chicken broth

¾ cup *Marsala* cooking wine

2 cups (about 8 oz.) sliced white mushrooms

3 TB. lemon juice

Melt butter in a large skillet over medium heat. Sprinkle both sides of chicken breasts with salt and pepper and roll breasts in flour so that each is coated. Cook breasts in a single layer in the skillet for about 4 minutes per side or until cooked through. Remove cooked breasts from the skillet and keep warm in a warm oven or on a plate covered with foil.

Turn the heat under your skillet to high and add olive oil, chicken broth, and Marsala. Cook, stirring, for 10 minutes. Add mushrooms and lemon juice and cook for another 2 to 4 minutes. Sauce will *reduce* and thicken.

Distribute cooked pasta to serving plates, place a piece of chicken on top (or to the side), and pour sauce over each serving. This sauce has great concentrated flavor, so a little will go a long way.

Thanks to Mike Lentini, of the Natick, Massachusetts Fire Department, for the inspiration for this.

Menu Manual

Marsala is a sweet, strong (in alcohol) wine. The "cooking" version is available at your grocery store, or get it from your local package store—both are fine. There is also a dry Marsala, but it isn't what you want for this dish.

To **reduce** is to heat a broth or sauce to remove some of the water content, resulting in more concentrated flavor.

Pasta e Fagioli

Prep time: 10 minutes • Cook time: 20 minutes • Serves: 6 guys or 8 to 10 regular people as part of a pasta and sauce meal

1 batch Homemade Tomato Sauce (recipe earlier in this chapter)

2 (15.5-oz.) cans cannellini beans, drained and rinsed

1 (10-oz.) pkg. frozen spinach, thawed and squeezed dry (optional)

½ cup dry white wine

¼ tsp. hot pepper sauce

4 (14.5-oz.) cans chicken broth

½ (16-oz.) box uncooked macaroni (or other pasta)

1 tsp. salt

¼ tsp. ground black pepper

½ cup shredded Parmesan cheese

Mix Homemade Tomato Sauce, cannellini beans, spinach (if using), wine, hot pepper sauce, and chicken broth in a large saucepan over medium heat until just beginning to boil. Add macaroni and cook for 10 minutes or until pasta is cooked to your liking. Serve with salt, pepper, and a generous spoonful of Parmesan cheese.

End Run

A jar of store-bought marinara sauce will do the trick in place of Homemade Tomato Sauce if you're in a hurry.

The Least You Need to Know

♦ Store-bought sauce is a terrific starting point for easy, tasty sauces you can dress up to suit your tastes.

♦ Whether you're considering tomato sauce, a creamy alfredo, or a traditional Italian-style sauce, homemade sauces are actually quick and easy.

♦ Sauces are appealing because they are so flexible. Do you have a favorite ingredient? Within reason, try it in a sauce.

♦ Pasta comes in wondrous varieties. If you are looking for something new for dinner, try different shapes, different colors, or even different flavors from pasta made with different ingredients.

Part 2

Method and Madness

The fun continues with a review of basic cooking methods in Part 2. We start with grilling (seems right, because all cooking started over fire). We'll head next to the stove top to prepare tasty skillet and one-pot meals. Next, the oven, broiler, and our old friend the microwave beckon as we prove that a guy can even roast something (and it's easier than you think).

We'll explore how to achieve great slow-cooked flavor with minimum effort with stews, soups, chowders, and, of course, slow cooker meals. After all these main courses, we'll check out simple, delicious vegetable dishes that make the meal complete. And finally, we'll show off a set of delicious desserts even a guy can make.

Chapter 5

A License to Grill

In This Chapter

◆ Easy, delicious grill recipes for beef, chicken, and pork
◆ Secrets of successful searing
◆ A grilling guide for seafood fanatics
◆ Grilled vegetables make the meal complete

Where there's smoke there's fire, and the grill is where it all started. When we think of a guy cooking, we can usually picture him wearing an oversize apron that says "Warning: Guy playing with fire." He's got his game face on, and he's poking at something unrecognizable on a furiously smoking grill.

There's some truth to that cliché. As guys, we're attracted to fire, and, let's face it, the "direct" heat is easy to understand. As the famous comedian says, "There's no low, medium, or high. Either it's off, or it's on." (Expletives deleted.)

We'll make good use of that basic understanding in this chapter as we check out both indoor and outdoor grilling methods.

Fasten your seat belts. This is where it all starts.

Meat on the Grill

Unless otherwise noted, you can make the recipes in this chapter using both indoor and outdoor grills. Outdoor charcoal grilling takes longer because of the time it takes to bring the charcoal to cooking temperature, but this method also imparts the most flavor. An outdoor gas grill heats up faster, and for that reason, can be more convenient. Outdoor grilling also means easy cleanup (remember our ground rule: "Cleanup should be minimal"). Indoor electric countertop grills such as the George Foreman Grill are convenient and fast to use, and they provide a terrific alternative when there's a hurricane outside or you live in an apartment.

End Run

For fast, clean charcoal fires, get a "charcoal chimney" at your hardware store (or most places that sell charcoal grills). You pour charcoal in the top, stuff newspaper in the bottom, and light the newspaper. It's usually faster than the lighter fluid method, and you don't have to worry about whether you're getting lighter fluid taste on your food.

Spiced Pork Chops

Prep time: 15 minutes if you include charcoal grill heating, less for other grilling methods • Cook time: 10 minutes • Serves: 4 guys or 6 regular people

3 TB. olive oil	1 tsp. salt
2 TB. lemon juice	½ tsp. ground black pepper
1 tsp. ground cumin	2 lb. pork chops, about ¾ inch thick
1 tsp. hot pepper sauce	

Preheat the grill. Mix olive oil, lemon juice, cumin, hot pepper sauce, salt, and pepper in a bowl. Place chops on a platter or in a bowl, pour olive oil mixture over, and turn each chop to coat both sides. Place chops on the grill and cook for 10 minutes, turning at the 5-minute mark, or until cooked through.

Variation: Try boneless chicken breasts in place of pork chops.

Marinated Ham Steaks

Prep time: 15 minutes if you include charcoal grill heating, less for other grilling methods (not including marinating time)   •   Cook time: 6 minutes   •   Serves: 3 guys or 4 regular people

2 ham steaks (about ¾ lb.)

1 cup Eric's Italian Marinade and Sauce (about ½ batch; keep the rest in your fridge) (recipe in Chapter 2)

To set up marinade, place ham steak in a large zippered plastic bag or plastic container with a lid. Pour marinade over steak, cover or seal, and shake to make sure ham is coated. Stick that bad boy in the fridge (if possible, do this in the morning before you go to work and it will be nicely flavored when you get back).

At cooking time, preheat the grill. When the grill is at the temperature you like, place marinated ham over the center where the heat is highest. Cook with the grill covered for 3 minutes and turn over ham. Pour some marinade on the cooked side, close the lid, and grill for another 3 minutes. Remove and serve.

Baked beans, green beans, and fresh bread make nice sides for this dish.

End Run

The ham is already cooked, so don't feel the need to grill it for long. Your objective here is to get the steak hot, but keep it juicy and not dry it out.

End Run

A ham steak is convenient, but a full ham in your fridge is even better. Talk about a thing of beauty! Slice off steaks, and you've got dinner—you don't even have to heat it if you don't want to. Cut off chunks, and you've got the key ingredient in a baked ham dish. The ham bone goes into Barely Work Split-Pea Soup (recipe in Chapter 8). Put the whole darn thing in the oven with a sauce, and you've got impressed guests. *Ham ... it's what's for dinn ...* uh, I think that's been said before about another meat.

Perfect Steak

Prep time: 15 minutes if you include charcoal grill heating, less for other grilling methods   •
Cook time: 10 minutes   •   Serves: 4 guys or 6 regular people

2 TB. kosher salt

2 tsp. ground cumin

1 tsp. coarsely ground black pepper

3 lb. steak, such as tenderloin, Delmonico, sirloin, rib eye, porterhouse, and London broil

In a cup or a small bowl, mix salt, cumin, and pepper. Set out steaks on a large plate or a dish that you can cover. Sprinkle ½ salt mixture on steaks and use the back of a big spoon to press pepper into flesh. Turn steaks, sprinkle remaining salt mixture evenly over, and press that in, too. Cover the plate or dish until you're ready to cook.

At cooking time, preheat the grill. When ready, place steaks over the center where the heat is highest. Cook with the grill covered for 1 minute to *sear* steaks, then turn them over and cook for 5 minutes. Turn steaks again and cook for 4 minutes or to your desired level of *doneness*. Remove and serve.

Salad and fresh bread make nice sides for steak. Of course, a baked potato is a steak tradition, too.

Menu Manual

To **sear** is to quickly brown the exterior of a food over high heat to preserve interior moisture (that's why many meat recipes involve searing). **Doneness** refers to whether you like your meat *rare* (red in the middle), *medium* (pink in the middle), or *well done* (gray all the way through). Test by making a 1-inch cut through the edge of the steak with a sharp knife and examining the inside.

Most of these recipes use the quick *direct* method (meat straight on top of heat). One notable exception is Beer Can Chicken, which uses the *indirect* method (heat on the sides but not directly below), a method perfect for longer, slower, and gentler cooking.

Beer Can Chicken

Prep time: 20 minutes • Cook time: 45 minutes to 1 hour • Serves: 4 guys or 6 regular people

1 (12-oz.) can beer (you pick)

1 (5-lb.) whole chicken

¼ cup Covers Anything Marinade (recipe in Chapter 2)

Preheat the grill. While your hands are clean, pop open beer and take a couple swallows so about ¼ is left. Set beer aside. Unwrap chicken, take out giblets (the little paper package of kidney, liver, neck, and other beauties inside the body cavity) for another use. Rinse chicken inside and out with cold water and dry it with a paper towel. Get out your roasting pan and put chicken in the pan to catch drips as you cover it with marinade. Spread marinade all over the outside and as best you can on the inside. Pour leftover marinade into the beer can, gently swirl it to mix, and pour out about ½ into the roasting pan. Place the can with the remaining beer marinade upright in the center of the roasting pan, lift chicken (careful, this bird is slippery now), and lower chicken over the beer can (opened side up), so the can slides up into the body cavity. The chicken should stand up with its beer can base, with the can and the two legs acting as a kind of three-legged stool in the center of the pan.

Go to the grill. If it's charcoal, divide the glowing coals so there are piles on two sides of the grill. If it's gas and you have three burners, light only the two side burners. Place chicken in its pan in the center of the grill (the heat from the sides is called "indirect" heat) and cover. Grill for 45 minutes to 1 hour, replacing coals as necessary. Cooking time will vary depending on how much heat your grill is generating and the size of the bird. To test for doneness, either insert a meat thermometer in the thigh and breast (the temperature should be 165 to 170°F) or cut into these same places (the juices should be clear).

Remove chicken in its pan from the grill. Carefully remove chicken from the can—this is a two-man-with-hot-mitts job and beer will be hot, so be careful. Set chicken on a platter that can hold juices that will run out when you cut the meat.

Serve with salad, bread, and, uh, beer.

Variation: Beer Can Chicken will also work in the oven. It will *not* work on an electric countertop grill!

For an even simpler seasoning, use ¼ cup olive oil, 1 teaspoon salt, and ½ teaspoon ground black pepper in place of Covers Anything Marinade. Drizzle the chicken inside and out with the oil and sprinkle with salt and pepper. Flavor is more mild than the marinade.

For a terrific sauce, pour the flavored beer juices from the can and any remaining juices from the pan into a saucepan and boil for a few minutes until the liquid reduces. Use that sauce to pour over sliced beer can chicken.

Barbecued Chicken

Prep time: 15 minutes if you include charcoal grill heating, less for other grilling methods   •
Cook time: 15 minutes   •   Serves: 4 guys or 6 regular people

3 lb. chicken parts (breasts, thighs, drumsticks, or your favorite parts)

¼ cup Grampy's Spicy-Sweet Barbecue Sauce (recipe in Chapter 2) or your favorite store-bought sauce

Preheat the grill. Place chicken parts in a large, microwave-safe bowl or a casserole dish with a lid, cover, and microwave on high for 5 minutes, rearranging the parts after 2½ minutes to allow even cooking. Remove the bowl from the microwave—careful, it's hot—and pour some barbecue sauce over chicken, turning the pieces to coat. Lay chicken pieces on the grill and cook, covered, for 10 minutes, turning halfway through and brushing with additional barbecue sauce from the bowl. Test to be sure chicken is done and remove to the serving plates, serving any remaining sauce from the bowl (that did not come into contact with raw meat) for extra dipping.

Variation: Add 5 to 10 minutes grill time if you don't want to use the microwave.

Food Fumble

For the record, *never* attempt to use outdoor grills indoors, because the resulting gases can kill you. The desire to grill indoors is why the electric grill was invented.

While we're on reminders, don't forget to keep the sauce used on raw meat completely separate from the sauce for dipping. Raw meats can contain bacteria that can make you very sick. No trips to the ER today, thanks.

Kebabs

Prep time: 15 minutes if you include charcoal grill heating, less for other grilling methods   •
Cook time: 8 minutes   •   Serves: 4 guys or 6 regular people

Wooden or metal kebab skewers (available in grocery stores; see the following End Run on soaking wooden skewers!)

1½ lb. sirloin tips, cut into 1-inch chunks

2 large bell peppers, seeded and ribs removed, and cut into about 1-inch-square pieces

1 (8-oz.) pkg. small white mushrooms (or large mushrooms, cut in half lengthwise)

1 large sweet onion (baseball size), such as Vidalia, peeled and cut into pieces about 1-inch square

⅓ cup Italian dressing

Preheat the grill. Assemble kebabs on the skewers, alternating pieces of steak, peppers, mushroom, and onion, repeating as necessary to fill skewer. Arrange kebabs on a plate and drizzle with dressing. Place kebabs on the grill and cook for 8 minutes, turning once, or until sirloin tips are cooked through.

Serve with rice and you're done.

Variation: Use cubes of chicken breast or pork and try out other vegetables, like grape tomatoes or spicy peppers.

End Run

When assembling kebabs, cut all ingredients in pieces about the same size and choose ingredients that cook at about the same rate. For example, mushrooms, onions, and peppers will cook nicely in about the same time as a similar-size piece of steak. A chunk of carrot, however, will still be unpleasantly hard (not to mention hard to skewer), and a slice of tomato might turn to mush over that same period of steak-grilling time.

If you're using wooden skewers, soak them first in water to minimize the chance of burning them. Metal skewers don't need soaking, but then you have to clean them afterward if you want to keep them. You can toss the wooden skewers.

Blue Cheese Burgers

Prep time: 15 minutes if you include charcoal grill heating, less for other grilling methods •
Cook time: 12 minutes • Serves: 2 guys

1 lb. lean ground beef

2 tsp. Worcestershire sauce

2 tsp. soy sauce

1 tsp. barbecue sauce

½ cup crumbled Gorgonzola or other crumbled blue cheese

Toasted hamburger buns

In a bowl, mix together ground beef, Worcestershire sauce, soy sauce, and barbecue sauce. Roll Gorgonzola into 4 balls and separate hamburger into 4 patties. Spread patties until they are longer on two opposite sides and put 1 cheese ball in the middle of each patty. Roll hamburger around cheese and press to flatten. Grill for 1 minute on each side, then turn and cook about 5 minutes per side or until cooked through. Place each burger on a toasted bun and dress each burger as you like.

Apple Ribs

Prep time: 15 minutes if you include charcoal grill heating, less for other grilling methods •
Cook time: 20 minutes • Serves: 4 guys or 6 regular people

½ cup apple butter (with jellies and jams in your grocery store)

2 TB. canola oil

2 TB. honey

2 TB. cider vinegar (or wine vinegar)

2 tsp. ground cumin

1 tsp. salt

½ tsp. ground black pepper

3 lb. pork ribs

Preheat the grill. Mix apple butter, oil, honey, vinegar, cumin, salt, and pepper in a bowl. Place ribs in a big baking or casserole dish (big enough to hold the ribs), pour apple butter mixture over, and turn ribs to coat. (If you have time, marinate the ribs for an hour or two before cooking.) Place ribs on the grill and cook 10 minutes per side or until cooked through.

With a sunny day, coleslaw, and bread or biscuits (depending on where you live), you've got the fixings for a perfect barbecue.

Grilled Seafood

Some people might be surprised to hear it, but seafood on the grill is a natural—as long as you're careful to pick ingredients that will hold up to grill cooking.

Grilled Southwest Salmon

Prep time: 15 minutes if you include charcoal grill heating, less for other grilling methods   •
Cook time: 8 to 10 minutes   •   Serves: 2 guys or 3 regular people

2 big salmon steaks (about 1½ lb.)	½ tsp. ground cumin
2 TB. lime juice	½ tsp. paprika
3 TB. olive oil	¼ tsp. ground black pepper
1 tsp. seasoned salt	

Preheat the grill. Put fish steaks in a bowl and *drizzle* first with lime juice, then olive oil, turning pieces to be sure they are coated. In a small bowl, mix salt, cumin, paprika, and pepper and sprinkle spice mixture with a spoon over steaks, again turning to coat. Place steaks on the grill and cook for 4 minutes. Turn and drizzle with any remaining juices from the bowl and grill for another 4 minutes or until fish is just barely cooked (it will continue to cook for a minute after you take it off the heat).

Serve with lemon wedges, a salad, and warm bread and imagine that it's summertime on Cape Cod.

Menu Manual

To **drizzle** is to lightly sprinkle drops of a liquid over food.

End Run

When it comes to grilling, there are two kinds of fish. Grill-ready "steak" fish, such as salmon steaks, shark, and swordfish, can be placed straight on the grill and will hold together when turned. Some sturdy fillets (bass comes to mind) also work if you're careful. Delicate fish, such as flounder, sole, bluefish, and other fillet fishes, will fall apart, causing Grill Anger Syndrome (GAS). You can protect these delicate fishes by dressing them as you like and cooking them in a special fish basket designed for grill use. You can also cook them by wrapping them in foil before placing them on the heated grill for cooking. This cuts down on grill flavor (and GAS), but you won't have to watch your food slide through the grill.

Swordfish with Herb Butter

Prep time: 15 minutes if you include charcoal grill heating, less for other grilling methods • Cook time: 8 to 10 minutes • Serves: 4 guys or 6 regular people

¼ cup (½ stick) butter

1 TB. Italian seasoning

½ tsp. dried rosemary

¼ tsp. ground black pepper

3 TB. olive oil

2 TB. lemon juice

4 swordfish steaks (about 2 lb.)

Preheat the grill. Place butter, Italian seasoning, rosemary, and pepper in a heatproof measuring cup and melt butter in the microwave. Allow melted butter to stand with herbs and seasonings for a few minutes for the flavor to spread. Heat butter for another few seconds if it is hardening and stir in olive oil and lemon juice.

Place swordfish in a bowl, pour some sauce over each side, and spread it around with the back of a spoon (don't stick the spoon that touched raw fish into butter sauce because you're going to use that sauce again). Grill fish for 4 minutes, then turn and grill for another 4 minutes or until fish is just cooked. Divide fish to serving plates and drizzle pieces with remaining herbed butter.

Serve with lemon wedges, buttered green beans, and a baked potato.

Variation: Use another sturdy steak fish, such as tuna or shark, in place of swordfish.

> **End Run**
>
> Unless otherwise noted, you can swap indoor vs. outdoor grilling methods as you like (take an electric grill section recipe and use it on a charcoal grill instead and vice versa).

Lemon-Mayo Bluefish

Prep time: 15 minutes if you include charcoal grill heating, less for other grilling methods •
Cook time: 8 to 10 minutes • Serves: 4 guys or 6 regular people

¼ cup mayonnaise

3 TB. olive oil

¼ tsp. ground black pepper

2 bluefish fillets (about 2 lb.)

1 lemon, sliced thinly into about 12 wheel
cross-sections

Preheat the grill. Mix mayonnaise, olive oil, and pepper in a bowl. Line a big plate or platter with a
large piece of aluminum foil. (The piece of foil should be big enough that it can be folded over the
top of the fish and the edges crimped to keep those juices inside.) Arrange fish in a single layer,
skin side down, on aluminum foil. Spread mayo mixture over exposed fillets and arrange lemon
slices over the top. Carefully fold over the foil and fold in all the edges to minimize chances of
self-destructing dinner. Using a spatula or two, carefully slide foil-wrapped fish onto the grill
and cook for 4 minutes per side. Remove fish from
grill, open the foil by folding back one of the
edges, and test to be sure it's done.

Serve with lemon wedges, buttered green beans,
and a baked potato.

Variation: Substitute another fillet fish such as
trout, salmon, or bass.

End Run

Bluefish is often a bargain
compared to the more trendy
fishes in the market.

Grilled Veggies

The grill works the same flavor magic on your vegetables as it does on the main course. These are a few of my favorites.

Cheesy Asparagus

Prep time: 15 minutes if you include charcoal grill heating, less for other grilling methods   •
Cook time: 6 minutes   •   Serves: 2 guys or 3 regular people as a side dish

1 lb. fresh asparagus	¼ tsp. ground black pepper
3 TB. olive oil	¼ cup shredded Parmesan cheese

Preheat the grill. Rinse asparagus under cold water and cut off and discard the tough bottom inch of each spear. Place asparagus spears on a plate and drizzle with olive oil, turning to coat all sides. Sprinkle with pepper. Place spears on the grill in a single layer and cook for 6 minutes, turning once. Remove from the grill to serving plates, sprinkle with Parmesan cheese, and serve.

Variation: This method also works well with long slices of zucchini.

Grilled Mixed Vegetables

Prep time: 15 minutes if you include charcoal grill heating, less for other grilling methods •
Cook time: 6 minutes • Serves: 4 guys or 6 regular people as a side dish

3 small zucchini, ends trimmed, and sliced lengthwise into quarters (4 long pieces per squash)

2 large red or green bell peppers, seeded and stems removed, and cut into ½-inch-thick cross-sections

1 large sweet onion (baseball size), such as Vidalia, peeled and cut crosswise into ¼-inch slices

½ cup extra-virgin olive oil

2 TB. chopped garlic

Dash hot pepper sauce

2 tsp. dried basil

Salt and ground black pepper

Preheat the grill. Put zucchini, bell peppers, and onion in a large bowl. Mix olive oil, garlic, and hot pepper sauce in a cup, pour mixture over vegetables, and stir to coat. Sprinkle basil over everything. Spread veggies on the grill and cook for 6 minutes, turning once. Serve, seasoning to taste with salt and black pepper.

Food Fumble

To prevent Grill Anger Syndrome, lay skinny vegetables (zucchini spears, asparagus, etc.) across the grill bars so they won't fall through. You can grill even smaller vegetables, but to do so, first pick up a grill basket at your hardware store. This nifty device will keep small ingredients safe and unsacrificed.

The Least You Need to Know

◆ Hamburgers might be where it all started, but the grill offers a lot more.

◆ Grilled beef, pork, and poultry dishes are fast, easy, and delicious.

◆ Seafood on the grill opens an ocean of possibilities.

◆ Grilled vegetables are delicious and can round out the complete grill meal.

Chapter 6

Stove Top 101

In This Chapter

- ◆ Stove top cooking provides both speed and flavor
- ◆ Use the skillet for easy, tasty meals
- ◆ Beef meals, pork recipes, poultry delicacies, and seafood dishes that will make your mouth water
- ◆ Frying, sautéing, and other magic methods

Cooking on the stove top is another natural for guy cooks. Like grilling, we've got direct heat below and the food we want to cook on top (usually in a skillet), so everything makes sense. One big difference from grilling is that we have the opportunity to add moisture to the skillet, such as sauces and oils—juicy additions that just don't work on the grill. Stovetop cooking tends to be a quick method because of the direct heat—another bonus for the guy who doesn't have all day.

Fast and Flavorful

These stove top recipes are not only delicious, but they'll also help you get dinner on the table fast.

Pan-Fried Rueben

Prep time: 5 minutes   •   Cook time: 5 minutes   •   Serves: 4 guys or 6 regular people

2 TB. butter

½ lb. sliced corned beef (available at your grocery store or deli)

8 to 12 slices pumpernickel or rye bread

½ lb. sliced Swiss cheese

½ (14.5-oz.) can (1 cup) sauerkraut, drained and rinsed

½ cup Russian or Thousand Island dressing

Melt butter in a large skillet over medium heat. Place a slice of corned beef on a piece of bread, followed by a slice of cheese and, if you like thick sandwiches, another slice of corned beef and another slice of cheese. Top with a big spoonful of sauerkraut and a spoonful of Russian dressing (spread around with the back of the spoon). Top sandwich with another slice of bread and place sandwich in the skillet. Cook for 3 minutes per side or until cheese melts (the thicker version will take longer).

Variation: A dab of spicy mustard adds additional flavor to this delicious sandwich.

Chicken Sausage Sautéed with Onions and Peppers

Prep time: 5 minutes   •   Cook time: 9 minutes   •   Serves: 4 guys or 6 regular people

2 TB. olive oil

1 large sweet onion (baseball size), such as Vidalia, peeled and cut into ½-inch chunks

2 large green bell peppers, stems and seeds removed, and cut into ½-inch chunks

2 tsp. Italian seasoning

1 lb. fully cooked chicken sausage, cut into ½-inch–thick slices

1 (5-oz.) can sliced black olives, drained

Dash hot pepper sauce

Salt and ground black pepper

End Run

Check your package of sausage to be sure it says "fully cooked." If the sausage is not fully cooked, cook it thoroughly first.

Heat oil in a large skillet over medium heat. Add onion, bell peppers, and Italian seasoning and cook, stirring, for 5 minutes or until pieces begin to soften. Add sausage, olives, and hot pepper sauce and cook, stirring, for 4 minutes or until heated through. Serve, seasoning to taste with salt and pepper.

Variation: Mix with cooked rice or shaped pasta for a complete meal.

Ham and Pineapple Stir-Fry

Prep time: 5 minutes • Cook time: 9 minutes • Serves: 3 guys or 4 regular people

3 TB. olive oil

1 small onion (about the size of a golf ball), peeled and chopped into ¾-inch–wide chunks

½ head broccoli, stems peeled, and broken into 1-inch–wide *florets*

2 ham steaks (about ¾ lb. each), cut into ¾-inch–wide chunks

1 (8-oz.) can chunk pineapple in water, drained

2 TB. teriyaki sauce

Heat oil in a large skillet, add onion and broccoli, and cook for 5 to 6 minutes, stirring, until onion is browned and broccoli is *crisp-tender.* Stir in cubed ham steak and pineapple and cook for another 3 minutes or until heated through. Pour teriyaki sauce over mixture, stir, and serve as is, or put it on top of cooked rice.

Variation: Use 4 scallions in place of 1 onion for added color. Rinse scallions, cut off the roots and dark green leaves, and cut the rest into ½-inch chunks.

Menu Manual

A **floret** is the flower or bud end of broccoli or cauliflower.

Crisp-tender is an appetizing point in vegetable cooking when the vegetable is just cooked enough to enjoy but still has some crunch left to it. Cook vegetables too long and you get mush.

Skillet Ham and Egg Dinner

Prep time: 5 minutes • Cook time: 20 minutes • Serves: 2 guys or 3 regular people

3 TB. olive oil

1 small onion (golf ball size), peeled and chopped into ¾-inch-wide chunks

3 eggs

½ cup (4 oz.) sour cream

¼ cup milk

1 cup (4 oz.) shredded Swiss cheese

½ (¾-lb.) ham (1 cup), cut into ½-inch–square chunks

Salt and ground black pepper

Heat oil in a large skillet, add onion, and cook for 5 minutes, stirring, until onion is browned. While onion is cooking, use a fork to thoroughly mix eggs, sour cream, milk, and shredded cheese in a bowl. Add egg mixture to the skillet and cook, stirring, for 2 minutes. Stir in cubed ham and cook for another 3 minutes or until eggs are *set*. Distribute to plates and serve, seasoning to taste with salt and pepper.

Menu Manual

In egg-cooking language, **set** means the eggs have firmed from the heat.

A salad and bread alongside make this a quick, nutritious meal.

Creamed Chicken and Noodles

Prep time: 5 minutes • Cook time: 20 minutes including pasta cooking time • Serves: 4 guys or 6 regular people, with leftovers

1 (16-oz.) pkg. egg noodles

1 (10.7-oz.) can condensed cream of chicken soup

1 (9-oz.) pkg. frozen peas and pearl onions, or 1 (10-oz.) pkg. frozen peas

1 (5-oz.) can water-packed chunk chicken meat, drained

½ cup (4 oz.) light sour cream

Dash hot pepper sauce

Cook noodles according to package directions. While noodle water is heating, set a saucepan on another burner and add cream of chicken soup (don't use extra water called for on the can), peas, chicken meat, sour cream, and hot sauce and cook, stirring, over medium heat for 5 minutes or until heated through.

Distribute noodles to serving plates, top with creamed chicken, and serve.

Variation: Use canned peas and carrots, drained, instead of frozen vegetables. The dish will not need to be heated as long because the vegetables won't need to be heated from frozen.

Shrimp and Garlic Penne

Prep time: 5 minutes • Cook time: 20 minutes • Serves: 4 guys or 6 regular people

1 (16-oz.) pkg. penne pasta

⅓ cup olive oil

3 TB. chopped garlic

1 TB. Italian seasoning

Double dash hot pepper sauce

1 lb. *(51 to 70 count)* cooked shrimp, *peeled, and deveined, with tail off,* defrosted and drained

½ lemon

Salt to taste

Shredded Parmesan cheese

Cook pasta. Meanwhile, heat oil in a skillet over medium heat, add garlic, Italian seasoning, and hot pepper sauce. Cook, stirring, for 2 minutes. Add shrimp and cook, stirring, for just 1 minute or until shrimp is heated through. Distribute pasta to serving plates and top with shrimp. Squeeze some lemon juice over each serving, season to taste with salt, and top with Parmesan cheese.

Menu Manual

Shrimp is sold according to size, and the label will also tell you how much of the work has been done for you (whether it's cooked already, shelled, with or without tail, etc.). Size is measured in the number per pound (**51 to 70 count** means there are that many in 1 pound). **Cooked, peeled, and deveined, with tail off** means you're ready to go. This means you'll pay more, but it also means you have less work to do. If the seafood section doesn't have this kind of shrimp, check out the frozen section.

Beergoggle Fried Fish

Prep time: 5 minutes • Cook time: 4 to 6 minutes • Serves: 4 guys or 6 regular people

2 lb. whitefish fillets, such as haddock, flounder, or catfish

½ cup beer

1 egg

1 cup Italian-style breadcrumbs or plain breadcrumbs with 1 tsp. Italian seasoning

1 tsp. salt

½ tsp. ground black pepper

⅓ cup canola oil

End Run

The amount of time required to cook fish depends on how thick the fillets are because, as you might guess, thicker fillets require more time. As a rule of thumb, remove the fish when the inside is almost cooked and opaque, as it will continue to cook from residual heat after you take it out of the skillet.

Rinse fillets under cold water and pat dry with paper towels. Whisk beer and egg in a bowl. Mix breadcrumbs, Italian seasoning, salt, and pepper in a baking dish or a wide bowl. Heat oil in a large skillet over medium heat. One by one, dip fish fillets in beer mixture and then breadcrumbs, turning to coat both sides. Place fillets in a single layer in the skillet and cook for 2 minutes per side or until done, turning the fillets gently with a slotted spatula.

Serve with lemon wedges, bread, and salad and you've got a great meal.

Stove Top Classics

Some of these meals are famous and rightly so. Simple and delicious, they are likely to become your kitchen standbys.

Creamed Chipped Beef on Toast

Prep time: 5 minutes • Cook time: 20 minutes • Serves: 4 guys or 6 regular people

½ stick (4 TB.) butter

¼ cup all-purpose flour

2½ cups milk, heated for 2 minutes in the microwave

2 (8-oz.) jars dried beef or 6 (2½-oz.) pkg. beef or corned beef slices, cut into ½-inch strips

Double dash hot pepper sauce

8 slices toast

Melt butter in a large skillet over medium heat. When butter is melted, use a *whisk* or a fork to stir in flour to form a thick paste. Cook over low heat for 2 minutes, stirring constantly. Then slowly whisk in milk. Keep stirring as milk heats and thickens. When milk starts to boil, add beef and hot pepper sauce and cook, stirring, until heated through. Serve on toast, two slices per plate, for a big meal.

Food Fumble

Whenever the words *boil* and *milk* appear in the same sentence, as in this recipe, that means pay close attention. Milk easily boils over into a frothy mess.

Menu Manual

A **whisk** is a handy kitchen tool. It's basically round wires with a handle (it looks kind of like those wire gutter protectors that keep leaves out of the downspout). Use it to rapidly mix things like eggs, pancake batter, and gravy. We like these kinds of foods, so a whisk is not a bad thing to have in the drawer.

Don't be scared, but that paste you just made with butter and flour is, in cook-speak, called a **roux** (pronounced *roo* as in *kangaroo*). Won't that impress the girls!

Pork and Pea Pod Stir-Fry

Prep time: 8 minutes • Cook time: 10 minutes • Serves: 4 guys or 6 regular people

1½ lb. boneless center-cut pork chops, cut into ½-inch pieces

3 TB. teriyaki sauce

1 TB. olive oil

1 medium onion (pool ball size), peeled and chopped into ½-inch pieces

1 (9-oz.) box frozen snow peas or sugar snap peas

Place cut pork in a bowl and stir in teriyaki sauce. Heat oil in a large skillet over medium heat. Add onion and pork and sauté, stirring, for 5 minutes. Add frozen pea pods and cook for an additional 5 minutes or until pork is cooked through.

Serve over cooked rice.

Curried Pork

Prep time: 8 minutes • Cook time: 8 to 10 minutes • Serves: 4 guys or 6 regular people

3 TB. olive oil

1½ lb. boneless center-cut pork chops, cut into ½-inch pieces

1 medium onion (pool-ball size), peeled and chopped into ½-inch pieces

2 tsp. curry powder

½ cup chicken broth

½ cup raisins

1 crisp apple, such as Granny Smith or Gala, cored and cut into ¼-inch pieces

½ cup plain yogurt or sour cream

1 tsp. salt

¼ tsp. ground black pepper

Heat oil in a large skillet over medium heat and sauté pork, onion, and curry powder for 5 minutes, stirring every now and then. Add chicken broth, raisins, and apple and cook for 3 minutes longer or until pork is cooked through. Stir in yogurt or sour cream, sprinkle with salt and pepper, and heat for another minute, stirring. Serve over rice.

Variation: I like the peels on the apples (not to mention it saves time), but you can peel the apple if you like.

Hot Pepper Shells with Chopped Ham

Prep time: 5 minutes   •   Cook time: 15 minutes   •   Serves: 4 guys or 6 regular people
(There will probably be leftovers.)

1 (16-oz.) box uncooked pasta shells

¼ cup olive oil

2 TB. chopped garlic

1 TB. crushed red pepper

1 large green bell pepper, stem and seeds removed, cut into ¾-inch chunks (about the size of the cooked pasta shells)

1 large yellow or red bell pepper, stem and seeds removed, cut into ¾-inch chunks (about the size of cooked pasta shells)

1 (¾-lb.) ham steak, cut into ½- to ¾-inch chunks

½ tsp. ground black pepper

¼ cup shredded Parmesan cheese

Cook pasta shells. While pasta is cooking, heat oil in a large skillet over medium heat. Add garlic, red pepper, and bell pepper chunks to the skillet and cook, stirring, for 5 minutes or until bell pepper pieces begin to soften. Add ham and black pepper and cook for 1 minute longer. When pasta is done, drain cooking water and return pasta to its pot. Dump cooked pepper-ham mixture over pasta and mix with a spoon. Serve in bowls or on plates, topped with a healthy sprinkling of Parmesan cheese.

Skillet Fish Chowder

Prep time: 10 minutes • Cook time: 25 minutes • Serves: 4 guys or 6 regular people

3 strips bacon

1 large onion (baseball size), peeled and chopped into ½-inch pieces

4 large (8-oz. or larger) potatoes, scrubbed and cut into ½-inch chunks

2 cups milk

2 cups light cream

2 lb. whitefish fillets, such as cod, haddock, or flounder, cut into bite-size chunks

½ tsp. ground black pepper

Salt to taste

End Run

Current health literature suggests that fish fats offer a number of health benefits, including lower cholesterol. So have seconds.

Cook bacon in a saucepan over medium heat for 3 minutes per side or until crisp and brown. Remove bacon to use as a garnish and add onion to the skillet. Cook onion for 5 minutes, stirring, or until onion softens. Add potatoes, milk, and cream and cook, stirring now and then, 15 minutes or until potatoes are soft enough to stab with a fork. Add fish to chowder and cook for 5 minutes or until fish is cooked through. (You'll be able to tell because fish pieces will break apart easily.) Add pepper and salt (if using) and serve in bowls topped with crumbled bacon.

The Least You Need to Know

- ◆ Stove top cooking can be fast and simple.
- ◆ From seafood to poultry, pork to chicken, skillet recipes include all your favorite foods.
- ◆ Simple combinations of meat, vegetables, and seasonings enable you to make delicious stove top meals.
- ◆ Many classic stove top dishes will take you right down kitchen memory lane.

Chapter 7

You *Can* Stand the Heat: Microwave, Oven, and Broiler 101

In This Chapter

- ♦ Simple, tasty meals you can make tonight
- ♦ Be a microwave menu master
- ♦ Your oven: more than a kitchen ornament
- ♦ Easy broiler recipes: high heat never tasted so good

This chapter spotlights easy dishes made with the microwave, oven, and broiler. We're probably all well acquainted with the microwave, but you might be surprised at the range of dishes you can prepare using that little box. Then there's your regular oven, a misunderstood appliance that can become one of your best friends. And don't forget the broiler, which enables you to make quick, high-flavor cooking—sometimes while you mow the lawn or take a nap or watch the game … Give some of these recipes a try, and you'll find that yes, you *can* stand the heat.

Microwave Menu Mania

How did we ever live without the microwave? Using the microwave oven as the only heat source, you can prepare a number of dishes (here and throughout the book). And if we're talking leftovers, where would we be if we couldn't nuke that plate of lasagna or bowl of chili?

Nuclear Chicken-Chunk Stew

Prep time: 4 minutes • Cooking time: 4 minutes • Serves: 4 guys or 6 regular people

2 (5-oz.) cans water-packed white chicken meat, drained

1 (10.75-oz.) can condensed cream of mushroom soup

1 (15-oz.) can mixed peas and carrots, drained

1 (6-oz.) can sliced mushrooms, drained

1 cup milk

Food Fumble

The directions on a soup can often tell you to add a full can water or milk. For this recipe, you only add 1 cup milk, which works out to be about ½ can. Any more will make your stew a bit on the soupy side.

Mix together chicken, cream of mushroom soup (don't use any extra water), peas and carrots, mushrooms, and milk in a large, microwave-safe dish with a lid. Cover mixture and microwave for 4 minutes or until stew is hot and soup is mixed in. If your microwave does not have a turntable, stir a couple times to ensure even cooking. Ladle stew into bowls and serve.

Variations: Substitute your favorite canned vegetables. A few drops of hot sauce works wonders, too. Healthful versions of cream soups will also work.

End Run

I barely need to say this, but for the one guy out there who doesn't have a bottle of hot pepper sauce in the fridge, *go get one*. With common names like Red Hot and Tabasco and more exotic names like Scorned Woman (I'm not kidding), hot pepper sauce is a great way to jazz up the simplest recipe, but experiment carefully with quantities. Most people use just a few drops. A spoonful could hurt.

Tuna on the Waves

Prep time: 3 minutes • Cooking time: 25 minutes including watching *Star Trek* while the water boils • Serves: 4 guys or 6 regular people

1 (12-oz.) pkg. egg noodles

2 (6-oz.) cans water-packed white tuna, drained

1 (10.75-oz.) can condensed cream of mushroom soup

1 (15-oz.) can corn kernels, drained

1 cup milk

½ cup light sour cream

Prepare noodles using package directions, drain, and set aside. Mix tuna, cream of mushroom soup (don't use any extra water), corn, milk, and sour cream in a microwave-safe dish with a lid. Cover and microwave for 4 minutes or until everything is hot. If your microwave does not have a turntable, stir a couple times to ensure even cooking. While tuna mixture is cooking, spread noodles on serving plates. Then spoon tuna mixture over noodles and serve.

Scalloped Potatoes with Ham

Prep time: 2 minutes • Cooking time: 5 minutes • Serves: 4 guys or 6 regular people

2 (15-oz.) cans sliced new potatoes, drained

1 cooked ham steak (about ¾ lb.), cut into ½-inch cubes

1 cup milk

3 TB. butter, cut into 1 tsp.-size pieces

½ tsp. onion salt or salt

Ground black pepper to taste

Arrange potato slices and ham in a microwave-safe baking dish. Pour milk over mixture. Dot top of potatoes with pieces of butter and microwave for 5 minutes or until heated through. Serve with additional salt (you might not need this if the ham is salty) and pepper.

Variation: Instead of canned potatoes, use "real" potatoes you slice yourself. "New" (thin-skinned) or red potatoes can be cleaned and sliced with the skin on. Baking potatoes can be used, but only if you like those thick skins. Otherwise, you'll have to peel them, and that's work (remember our ground rule: "Keep it simple!").

Teriyaki Salmon

Prep time: 3 minutes   •   Cooking time: 4 minutes   •   Serves: 4 guys or 6 regular people

1½ lb. salmon fillets with skin, rinsed under cold water and patted dry with paper towels

2 TB. canola oil

2 TB. teriyaki sauce

1 TB. lemon juice (fresh if possible, as you've already got the lemon wedges out, but bottled juice will also work)

2 TB. butter, cut into 1-tsp.–size pieces

Lemon wedges to garnish

Arrange salmon fillets in a single layer in a microwave-safe casserole or a baking dish with a lid. Pour oil, teriyaki sauce, and lemon juice over fish, turning fillets to coat both sides. Turn so skin side is down, dot salmon with pieces of butter, put on the lid, and microwave for 4 minutes or until fish is cooked. If your microwave does not have a turntable, turn fish pieces a couple times to ensure even cooking. To serve, place servings of fish on each plate and spoon any remaining liquid from the baking dish over each piece. Garnish with lemon wedges and serve with rice or fresh bread.

Variation: If you're not crazy about teriyaki sauce, omit it and add 1 extra tablespoon lemon juice. You could also try 1 teaspoon Cajun seasoning, chili powder, or Italian seasoning or a pre-made sauce that sounds good to you.

Food Fumble

Microwaves vary in power, so watch delicate foods (such as fish) carefully. Cook it too long, and you've got fish jerky—which is what your significant other will call you, too. Check to see if it's cooked at the recommended time. If not, cook for another minute, check it again, and so on. Fish should be just barely opaque (white—or in the case of salmon, pink). It will actually keep cooking for a minute after you take it out of the microwave, too.

Micro-Baked Spuds

Prep time: 2 minutes   •   Cooking time: 9 minutes   •   Serves: 4 guys or 6 regular people

4 baking potatoes, cleaned and poked with a
fork to allow hot gas to escape

Place potatoes on a microwave-safe casserole or baking dish (preferably with a lid) and nuke for 7 minutes or until potatoes are soft. If your microwave does not have a turntable, turn the plate halfway through the cooking time. Serve with butter and/or sour cream, salt, and pepper. Served with beer, some people would call this a meal.

Food Fumble

Potato grenade alert! When nuking whole potatoes, either slice them or pierce their skins several times with a fork before heating. This allows the steam to escape and avoids a messy explosion. Believe me, I've skipped doing this, and then I've had to clean the microwave (remember our ground rule: "Cleanup should be minimal").

Micro-Mash

Prep time: 4 minutes   •   Cooking time: 10 minutes   •   Serves: 4 guys or 6 regular people

4 large potatoes, peeled and cut into 1-inch
cubes

½ cup milk

4 TB. butter

½ tsp. garlic salt or salt

Arrange potato pieces in a microwave-safe baking dish with a lid. Pour milk over potatoes, drop in butter, and sprinkle with salt. Cover and microwave for 10 minutes or until pieces are soft. If your microwave does not have a turntable, stir potato pieces a couple times. Then, using a fork or one of those potato-masher tools, mash potatoes to the consistency you like—for me, some lumps are perfect; others want to get out a hand beater to make those spuds really creamy. That part is up to you. Serve on a cold night with snow falling on the unraked lawn outside and all will be right with the world.

Chicken Salsa

Prep time: 3 minutes • Cooking time: 7 minutes • Serves: 4 guys or 6 regular people

1½ lb. boneless, skinless chicken breasts

2 TB. canola oil

2 TB. water

½ tsp. salt

Pinch ground black pepper

1 cup salsa (your favorite)

1 cup shredded Mexican-style or Monterey Jack cheese

Arrange chicken breasts in a microwave-safe baking dish with a lid. Pour oil and water over chicken, turning the pieces to coat. Sprinkle with salt and pepper. Put on the lid and microwave for 7 minutes or until chicken is cooked. If your microwave does not have a turntable, turn the pieces a couple times to ensure even cooking. Remove chicken to serving plates, microwave salsa in a microwave-safe container for 1 minute, and spoon salsa over each piece of chicken on the serving plates. Sprinkle each serving with shredded cheese and you're done.

Variation: Substitute chutney for salsa for a more exotic flavor.

Food Fumble

Don't microwave foods that need a crispy skin to taste good. Crisp is one thing a microwave doesn't do very well (that's why these recipes use skinless breasts). Plus, if you're watching your weight or cholesterol, remember that the reason the skin on the chicken is so tasty is because that's where the fat lives. Skinless chicken breasts already have the skin and the fat layer underneath removed.

The Oven Is Too Easy

With guys, the oven often gets a bad rap. Maybe it's the image of Grandma spending the whole week by the oven during the holidays. The fact is, it's really less work than the stove top. You can slide in your meal and go watch the game until you hear the buzzer (on the oven timer, not on the game). Here are some examples.

End Run

Some recipes call for canned meat, such as chicken. If you've got leftover chicken in the fridge, that's just as good. In fact, just finding those leftovers can be the inspiration for making some of these dishes.

Hawaiian Chicken Dinner Loaf

Prep time: 4 minutes • Cooking time: 25 minutes • Serves: 4 guys or 6 regular people

2 (5-oz.) cans water-packed white chicken meat, drained

1 (15-oz.) pkg. cornbread and muffin mix

1 (8-oz.) can crushed pineapple in juice, drained

1 (4.5-oz.) can chopped green chilies

¾ cup milk

1 egg, lightly beaten

Preheat the oven to 375°F. Mix together chicken, cornbread mix, pineapple, chilies, milk, and egg in a bowl and scoop mixture into a *greased* 2-quart casserole dish. Slide the dish into the oven and cook for about 25 minutes or until loaf is nicely tan on top. Remove from the oven, slice into squares, and serve. A salad alongside makes a meal.

Menu Manual

If you haven't used the oven much (or at all), one of the secrets is **preheating.** When you preheat the oven, you give it time to heat up to the right temperature, so when you put your food in it starts cooking right away. Most ovens will take about 10 minutes to preheat to 375°F.

Greased (or **oiled**) does not mean 10W-40. It means spraying the inside of the pan with cooking spray or rubbing it with a paper towel that has butter or oil on it so your food won't stick and the pan will be easier to clean.

Barbecue Chicken Pizza

Prep time: 5 minutes • Cooking time: 10 minutes • Serves: 2 guys or 3 regular people

2 (5-oz.) cans water-packed white chicken meat, drained

½ cup barbecue sauce

1 (14-oz.) pkg. pre-baked prepared pizza crust

½ cup (4 oz.) pasta or pizza sauce

1 cup shredded mozzarella cheese

Preheat the oven to 450°F. Dump chicken meat into a bowl, crush larger pieces with the back of a spoon, and mix in barbecue sauce. Set pizza crust on a baking tray. Pour pasta sauce on crust, spread it around with the back of the spoon, and sprinkle cheese over sauce. Spread barbecue chicken mixture around on crust and bake pizza for about 10 minutes or until crust is crispy and cheese is melted. Slice into wedges on a cutting board and serve. Make a bunch of these for a casual dinner party.

Variation: Use pineapple with your chicken on this pizza.

Potato, Cheese, and Ham Bake

Prep time: 4 minutes • Cooking time: 25 minutes • Serves: 4 guys or 6 regular people

2 (15-oz.) cans sliced new potatoes, drained

2 (¾ lb. each) cooked ham steaks, cut into ½-inch cubes

2 eggs

⅓ cup milk

1 (8-oz.) pkg. shredded Monterey Jack cheese

Salt and ground black pepper

Preheat the oven to 400°F. Mix potato slices and ham in a greased 2-quart casserole dish. In a bowl, mix eggs and milk with a fork until yolks are broken and everything is blended. Pour egg-milk mixture over ham and potatoes and cover with cheese. Bake for 20 minutes or until eggs have set (cooked solid). Serve with additional salt (you might not need this if the ham is salty) and pepper.

Variation: If you've got onion flakes in your cabinet, shake a bunch over potatoes before you spread cheese to add flavor.

Tuna Bake

Prep time: 4 minutes   •   Cooking time: 30 minutes   •   Serves: 4 guys or 6 regular people

2 (6-oz.) cans water-packed white tuna, drained

2 cups cooked pasta such as spaghetti or small-size pasta such as ziti, elbows, etc.

1 (10.75-oz.) can condensed cream of mushroom soup (or other cream soup)

1 (15-oz.) can whole-kernel corn, drained

⅓ cup sour cream

1 (4.5-oz.) can chopped green chilies

1 (8-oz.) pkg. shredded Monterey Jack cheese

Salt and ground black pepper

Preheat the oven to 375°F. In a bowl, mix tuna, pasta, cream of mushroom soup (don't use extra water called for on the can), corn, sour cream, and chilies. Scrape mixture into a greased 3-quart casserole dish and top with shredded cheese. Bake for 30 minutes. Serve, seasoning to taste with salt and pepper. A salad alongside and you've got a great meal.

Beak in a Blanket

Prep time: 10 minutes   •   Cooking time: 20 minutes   •   Serves: 4 guys or 6 regular people

1 (5-oz.) can water-packed chunk chicken, drained

½ (8-oz.) tub whipped chive cream cheese

2 tsp. Italian seasoning

1 (16-oz.) can biscuit dough (in the chilled food section of your grocery store)

Preheat the oven to 375°F. In a bowl, mix chicken, cream cheese, and Italian seasoning until well blended. Open can of biscuit dough (there's a tab on one end that you pull, then you press the seam with a spoon until the side pops open). Separate biscuits. One by one, stretch each to about twice its size. Spread some cream cheese mixture on each biscuit half, fold over other half to form a half-circle shape, and arrange on a baking tray. Bake for 20 minutes or until dough is nicely browned. Serve to appreciative clucking.

Roast Beef

Prep time: 10 minutes • Cooking time: About 90 minutes for a 3-pound roast • Serves: 4 guys or 6 regular people

1 (3-lb.) top boneless round beef roast

1 tsp. ground black pepper (freshly ground if you've got a grinder)

1 small onion (golf ball size), peeled and sliced

Preheat the oven to 450°F. Place roast on a roasting pan or a casserole or baking dish. Sprinkle pepper and spread onion slices over roast. Slide roast into the oven on the center rack and cook for 10 minutes at 450°F. Then turn down the heat to 325°F, set the timer for 80 minutes, and go watch the second half of the game. Check for doneness either by using a *meat thermometer* or by cutting with a knife. (Juices will run clear when roast is well done, pink if rare or medium.) Serve with potatoes and buttered green beans and you've got a meal.

Variations: Use a rolled rib eye instead of round. If you have time, pour the marinade over the meat several hours before you cook it.

Menu Manual

A **meat thermometer,** a useful and inexpensive kitchen tool for any meat-eater, removes any doubt about whether your meat is "done" or not. All you do is insert the thermometer into the center of your meat. Most are labeled so the little dial tells you what you want to know. If it points to "Beef, medium" and that's where you want to be, you're done. For beef, the general temperature vs. doneness range is:

130 to 140°F	Rare
140 to 150°F	Medium
150°F and above	Well done

Tan Your Food Under the Broiler

Using the broiler is a lot like grilling, with high heat, quick cooking, great flavor, and all the attributes of a great meal. You will find a few broiler classics here—as well as a lot more in the rest of the book.

End Run

The high, dry heat of broiling (and grilling) is fast but drying for your food. For this reason, broiling recipes often call for protective moisture (sunscreen, if you will) such as oil to keep that chicken from getting sunburned.

Chicken with Pesto Cream Dip

Prep time: 3 minutes • Cooking time: 8 minutes • Serves: 4 guys or 6 regular people

1½ lb. boneless, skinless chicken breasts

2 TB. olive or canola oil

Salt and ground black pepper

½ cup low-fat sour cream

¼ cup prepared *pesto sauce* (available in the pasta sauce section of your grocery store)

Preheat the broiler. Put chicken breasts in a bowl and drizzle with olive oil, turning pieces to coat. Arrange chicken in a baking tray and sprinkle with salt and pepper. Slide the tray under the broiler on the next-to-highest rack and cook for 8 minutes, turning after 4 minutes, or until chicken is cooked (meat will be white all the way through when cut with a knife). Remove chicken to serving plates. Dump sour cream and pesto sauce into a bowl, stir, and microwave for 1 minute. Spoon equal amounts of this pesto–sour cream dip next to each piece of chicken for dipping. Season chicken with additional salt and pepper, if desired, and head for the table (or the couch).

Menu Manual

Pesto sauce is a seasoning secret weapon. Made with fresh basil leaves, garlic, olive oil, pine nuts, and Parmesan cheese, you can make pesto at home or purchase it in a grocery store. Use it on anything from appetizers to pasta and other main dishes.

Turkey Melts

Prep time: 8 minutes • Cooking time: 3 minutes • Serves: 4 (1 melt each, double recipe for more)

1 (5-oz.) can water-packed chunk turkey, drained

¼ cup mayonnaise

½ cup chopped celery

1 TB. Italian dressing

4 slices toasted bread

4 slices Swiss cheese (or your favorite)

Preheat the broiler. In a bowl, mix turkey, mayonnaise, celery, and dressing, mashing any big chunks of meat. Spread equal amounts of turkey mixture on each piece of toast, cover each piece with a slice of cheese, place toasts on a baking tray, and slide the tray under the broiler on the next-to-highest rack. Cook for 3 minutes or until cheese is melted. Serve and gobble.

Variation: You can also use chunk chicken, turkey, or even ham.

Broiled Halibut

Prep time: 5 minutes • Cooking time: 8 minutes • Serves: 4 guys or 6 regular people

1½ lb. halibut steaks

Juice of ½ lemon

2 TB. olive oil

2 tsp. dried rosemary

Salt and ground black pepper to taste

Lemon wedges

Preheat the broiler. Rinse halibut steak in cold water, pat dry with a paper towel, and put in a bowl. Pour lemon juice and olive oil over steak, turning to coat. Sprinkle with rosemary and pepper on both sides and place fish on a baking tray. Slide under the broiler on the next-to-highest rack and cook for 8 minutes, turning halibut over halfway through or until fish is cooked (the fish will be just barely white all the way through). Serve with lemon wedges for drizzling.

Add bread and a salad and you've got a feast.

End Run

To impress that special someone, serve Broiled Halibut with a glass of chilled white wine (Chardonnay or Sauvignon Blanc), and you'll be a hero.

The Least You Need to Know

- ◆ The microwave is not only for heating leftovers. Use it for making the main meal.
- ◆ Keep your "can-do" attitude. Canned and ready-to-use foods lend themselves perfectly to a number of microwave and oven recipes.
- ◆ The oven is easier than you think—and takes less time, too.
- ◆ When it comes to quick cooking and great flavor, make good use of your broiler.

Chapter 8

Thick as Pea Soup: Soups, Stews, Chowders, and Slow Cooker Recipes

In This Chapter

- ◆ Soups that will have you singing
- ◆ Stews hearty enough for the biggest appetite
- ◆ Chowders that will make you a seafood convert
- ◆ Slow cooker recipes good enough to wait all day for
- ◆ New entries for the ongoing chili competition

According to my brother Warren, a comfort-food addict, guys don't like the word *soup*. He says it sounds too light and watery. The hearty soups in this chapter should change his opinion. As for stew and chowder, there's no doubt about their appeal. Thick, rich, and satisfying, that's what this chapter is all about. And because slow cooking uses a lot of the same methods, those hearty dishes are ladled up here, too.

With many soup, stew, chowder, and slow cooker recipes, quick preparation is the name of the game. Then we go do something for a couple hours or the whole day, and when we return, appetizing smells fill the house and make us believe that someone has been busy in the kitchen all day. It will be our secret.

Soups, Stews, and Chowders

In this section, you'll find many variations of the liquid meal, from mild to spicy, and from quick prep to slow cook. They'll all, however, be on the thick, rich, and flavorful end of the soup spectrum. And even if they can cook for a while, they'll only take you a few minutes.

Farmhouse Chicken Noodle Stew

Prep time: 10 minutes • Cook time: 40 minutes • Serves: 4 guys or 6 regular people

3 TB. olive or canola oil

1 medium onion (pool-ball size), peeled and chopped into ½-inch pieces

2 large carrots, scraped and cut into ½-inch slices, or 2 cups baby carrots, each carrot cut in half

2 large celery stalks with leaves, trimmed, washed, and cut into ½-inch slices

3 (14.5-oz.) cans low-sodium chicken broth

1 lb. leftover chicken, cut into ½-inch chunks, or 3 (5-oz.) cans water-packed chunk chicken meat, drained

½ tsp. ground black pepper

½ (8-oz.) box uncooked elbow macaroni or other small-shape pasta

Salt

Heat oil in a large saucepan or skillet over medium heat and cook onion, stirring, for 5 minutes. Add carrots, celery, broth, meat, and pepper. Stir and heat until soup begins to bubble. Reduce heat to low and watch a *M*A*S*H* rerun for 15 minutes. During the commercial break (after 15 minutes), add pasta, stir, and go finish the show and let your soup simmer. After the show, salt soup to taste, stir, and ladle into bowls. Rotate the TV toward the table, butter a slice of bread, and have dinner. Be sure to blow on the soup because it'll be hot.

Variations: There are lots of variations you can make with chicken soup. Instead of adding uncooked pasta, add a can of sliced white potatoes (or chunks of potato) with the vegetables for an even heartier stew. Or stir in cooked pasta or rice 5 minutes before you want to serve.

≈∽

Beef 'n' Beer Chili

Prep time: 10 minutes • Cook time: 40 minutes • Serves: 4 guys or 6 regular people

2 TB. olive or canola oil

1 medium onion (pool-ball size), peeled and chopped into ½-inch pieces

1 lb. lean ground beef or pork

1 (15.5-oz.) can red kidney beans, drained and rinsed

1 (15-oz.) can whole kernel corn, drained

1 (14.5-oz.) can diced tomatoes with juice

½ (6-oz.) beer

2 TB. chili powder

2 TB. *bittersweet chocolate* chips

2 TB. Worcestershire sauce

2 TB. *tomato paste*

1 cup (½ [8-oz.] pkg.) shredded cheddar cheese

1 cup sour cream

Heat oil in a large saucepan over medium heat, add onion, and cook, stirring, for 2 minutes. Add ground beef and cook, stirring, for 5 minutes or until meat is cooked and there's no red around. Drain fat, holding back onion and beef with a big spoon. Stir in beans, corn, tomatoes, beer, chili powder, chocolate chips, Worcestershire sauce, and tomato paste. Cook for 30 minutes, stirring occasionally.

Serve in big bowls and top with shredded cheese and sour cream. The longer this chili simmers, the better it tastes. Leftovers are terrific.

Variation: Chili is tasty served over rice for a one-bowl meal.

Menu Manual

Bittersweet chocolate is chocolate primarily used for baking. It has very little sugar but a ton of rich chocolate flavor. If you don't have bittersweet (or semi-sweet), just skip it in the recipe. Regular chocolate chips are too sweet. Unsweetened cocoa powder can also be used in place of the chocolate chips.

Tomato paste is a thick paste made from concentrated tomatoes. It adds both flavor and a thick richness to sauces and, in this case, chili.

Pork and Apple Stew

Prep time: 10 minutes • Cook time: 40 minutes • Serves: 4 guys or 6 regular people

3 TB. olive or canola oil

1 medium onion (pool-ball size), peeled and chopped into ½-inch pieces

2 lb. boneless pork chops, cut into ½-inch chunks

1 large celery stalk, trimmed, washed, and cut into ½-inch slices

2 (14.5-oz.) cans *vegetable broth*

2 cups apple cider

½ tsp. ground thyme

½ tsp. ground black pepper

¼ tsp. ground cloves

2 (14.5-oz.) cans cut green beans, drained

2 baking apples (such as Granny Smith), washed, cored, and cut into ½-inch pieces (Don't bother to peel them unless you have a thing against peels.)

Salt

Menu Manual

Vegetable broth is, just like it sounds, a broth made from the essence of vegetables. It's in your grocery store next to the chicken broth. You can also use vegetable bouillon cubes and water or chicken broth in this recipe.

Heat oil in a large saucepan or skillet over medium heat and cook onion and pork, stirring, for 8 minutes or until pork is cooked. Add celery, broth, cider, thyme, pepper, and cloves. Stir and heat until stew begins to bubble, then reduce heat to low and cook for 20 minutes. Add green beans and apple pieces and continue cooking for 10 minutes. Salt to taste and serve in bowls with pieces of toasted crusty bread. Delicious!

Steak, Macaroni, and Vegetable Stew

Prep time: 15 minutes • Cook time: 50 minutes • Serves: 4 guys or 6 regular people

¼ lb. bacon

1 medium onion (pool-ball size), peeled and chopped into ½-inch pieces

1 TB. chopped garlic

1 lb. sirloin tips, sliced into ⅓-inch strips

3 (14.5-oz.) cans beef broth

3 TB. sherry (optional)

3 celery stalks, rinsed, trimmed, and chopped into ¼-inch pieces

1 tsp. dried rosemary

1 tsp. dried mustard

½ tsp. dried thyme

½ (16-oz.) box elbow macaroni

½ bunch kale, torn into 1½-inch pieces, rinsed, and stems removed

Salt and ground black pepper

Cook bacon in a large skillet over medium heat for 3 to 4 minutes per side or until crisp and fat is *rendered*. Remove bacon to paper towels. Cook onion in fat for 5 minutes and pour out most of fat, holding onion back with a big spoon. Add garlic and cook another 1 minute. Add beef strips, arranging in a single layer. Cook for 3 minutes per side or until cooked through. Add broth, sherry (if using), celery, rosemary, mustard, and thyme. Heat to a simmer and cook, uncovered, for 25 minutes. Stir in macaroni and spread kale leaves across the top of the stew so the steam from the stew can cook the leaves. Cover and cook for 12 minutes or until macaroni is done to your taste. Stir and ladle into large bowls, seasoning with salt and pepper and sprinkling with crumbled bacon.

Menu Manual

In cooking terms, to **render** means to cook something to the point where it releases its fats and juices. When you cook bacon, for example, the result is crisp bacon and rendered fat.

Clam Chowder

Prep time: 15 minutes   •   Cook time: 30 minutes   •   Serves: 4 guys or 6 regular people

3 slices bacon

1 medium onion (pool-ball size), peeled and chopped into ½-inch chunks

2 (15-oz.) cans sliced new white potatoes, drained and chopped into ¾-inch pieces

2 (8-oz.) bottles clam broth

1 (15-oz.) can whole kernel corn, drained

¼ cup (4 TB.) butter

2 cups chopped clams, or 2 (6½-oz.) cans chopped clams

2 cups light cream

Salt and ground black pepper

Cook bacon in a large saucepan or skillet over medium heat for 3 to 4 minutes per side or until bacon is crispy and fat is rendered. Remove bacon and save it on a paper towel–covered plate. Add onion and cook, stirring, for 5 minutes. Drain excess bacon fat, holding back onions. Add potatoes, clam broth, corn, and butter. Heat to a low boil and add clams. Cook for 5 minutes or until clams are cooked through. Stir in cream, heat for 1 minute, season with salt and pepper, and serve in big bowls with oyster crackers.

Serve with corn on the cob and salad and you've got a picnic. Of course, you can add anything you want to this feast—lobsters, burgers, hot dogs …

Italian Seafood Stew

Prep time: 10 minutes • Cook time: 20 minutes • Serves: 4 guys or 6 regular people

5 TB. olive oil

2 medium onions (pool-ball size), peeled and chopped into ½-inch pieces

2 TB. chopped garlic

2 tsp. Italian seasoning

½ tsp. crushed red pepper

1 cup arugula or fresh parsley, rinsed and coarsely chopped (in the produce section of your grocery store)

1 (15-oz.) can sliced new white potatoes, drained

1 cup dry white wine

1 cup water

1 lb. whitefish, such as cod or haddock, cut into 1-inch chunks

1 cup scallops, rinsed

1 cup cooked small shrimp, peeled with tails removed

Salt and ground black pepper

Heat oil in a large saucepan or skillet and cook onions, stirring, for 5 minutes. Add garlic, Italian seasoning, and crushed red pepper and cook for 1 minute longer. Add arugula, potatoes, wine, and water. Bring to a low boil. Add fish, cook for 5 minutes, then add scallops. Cook for another 3 minutes. Finally, add shrimp, heat for 1 minute or until shrimp is heated through. Serve in bowls by itself, with bread alongside, or atop rice. Season to taste with salt and pepper when serving.

Variation: Raw shelled shrimp can be used in place of cooked shrimp. Add them at the same time as scallops.

Slow Cooker Recipes

Guys like food that can be prepared in a hurry, but we also appreciate savory, rich dishes that are only possible through long, slow cooking. A slow cooker makes quick prep and slow cooking easy.

Potato Vegetable Stew

Prep time: 12 minutes • Cook time: 8 to 10 hours on low or 4 to 5 hours on high •
Serves: 4 guys or 6 regular people

2 lb. (about 4 large) potatoes, peeled and cut into ½-inch chunks

1 very large onion (softball size, or equivalent amounts of smaller onions), peeled and chopped into ½-inch pieces

1 (15-oz.) can corn, drained

2 celery stalks, with leaves, trimmed, washed, and cut into ½-inch slices

2 (14.5-oz.) cans chicken broth

½ tsp. ground black pepper

1 cup light cream

Salt to taste

Mix potatoes, onion, corn, celery, chicken broth, and pepper. Cook on low for 8 to 10 hours or on high for 4 to 5 hours. Add cream 30 minutes before serving and salt to taste. Serve in big bowls.

Variation: Don't peel potatoes (but be sure you scrub them well and cut out any unappetizing parts). You save effort and get added "farmhouse" flavor.

Barely Work Split-Pea Soup

Prep time: 8 minutes • Cook time: 6 to 8 hours on low or 3 to 4 hours on high • Serves: 4 guys or 6 regular people

1 lb. dry split green peas

3 (5-oz.) cans water-packed chunk ham, drained

3 stalks celery with leaves, trimmed, washed, and cut into ¼-inch slices

1 medium onion (pool-ball size), peeled and chopped into ½-inch pieces

½ tsp. ground black pepper

4 cups water

Rinse split peas, then add to the slow cooker along with ham, celery, onion, pepper, and water. Turn the heat to low, stir everything to mix, put on the cover, and head to the back woods for 6 to 8 hours. When you come back, stir the soup again and serve in big bowls with hunks of crusty bread alongside.

Variation: Use ¾-pound ham steak, cubed, or—even better—a meaty ham bone.

Food Fumble

A large (4-plus quart) slow cooker is a good idea if you have a large ham bone for your pea soup. I used a 2-quart one for my last batch, and I had to take the ham bone outside to break it with my wood-splitting maul so it would fit. If any neighbors were watching, I'm sure they were wondering about me …

We like our teeth, and even a slow cooker will not soften a rock. Rinse split peas (and other dried beans) in a sieve or a colander and be sure there are no evil pebbles lurking.

Corned Beef and Cabbage

Prep time: 8 minutes   •   Cook time: 10 to 12 hours on low or 5 to 6 hours on high   •
Serves: 4 guys or 6 regular people, with plenty of leftover corned beef for sandwiches

2 cups baby carrots, rinsed and cut in half
lengthwise

2 large onions (baseball size), peeled and
quartered

3 lb. corned beef brisket

2 cups water

5 peppercorns or ½ tsp. ground black pepper

½ head cabbage, cut into 2-inch chunks

4 large potatoes, scrubbed and cut into 2-inch
chunks

Add carrots and onions to the slow cooker, then corned beef, water, and peppercorns. Cook on
low for about 5 hours, add cabbage and potatoes, and cook for another 5 hours.

Menu Manual

Quartered means to cut
something into four equal
pieces. For this recipe, cut
the peeled onions from end
to end into lengthwise halves,
then cut each of those halves in
half lengthwise.

If your slow cooker won't hold all the ingredients, put
cabbage and potatoes in a saucepan on the stove
instead. Ladle about 1 cup broth from the slow cooker
over vegetables, cover, and cook over medium heat for
30 minutes or until potatoes are done.

To serve, distribute a chunk of corned beef to each
plate along with some vegetables. Mustard is a must for
corned beef (it goes pretty darn well with cabbage, too).
Butter and more pepper help out those potatoes, but
you probably won't need salt (corned beef is very salty).

Slow Cooker Kielbasa Barbecue

Prep time: 8 minutes   •   Cook time: 6 to 8 hours on low or 3 to 4 hours on high   •   Serves:
4 guys or 6 regular people

2 lb. kielbasa (beef or your favorite), cut into
½-inch slices

1 (16-oz.) pkg. frozen corn

1 cup barbecue sauce

½ cup ketchup

¼ cup honey

1 TB. ground cumin

Dash hot pepper sauce

Add kielbasa, corn, barbecue sauce, ketchup, honey, cumin, and hot pepper sauce to the slow
cooker and stir to thoroughly mix. Cook on low for 6 to 8 hours. Serve in big bowls or on top
of cooked rice.

Creamy Chicken-Spinach Stew

Prep time: 10 minutes   •   Cook time: 8 to 10 hours on low or 4 to 5 hours on high hours   •
Serves: 4 guys or 6 regular people

2 lb. boneless, skinless chicken breasts, rinsed and cut into 1-inch chunks

1 large onion (baseball size), peeled and chopped into 1-inch pieces

1 (14.5-oz.) can chicken broth

1 (15-oz.) can sliced new white potatoes, drained

1 (10-oz.) pkg. frozen chopped spinach, thawed enough in the microwave to break it into chunks

1 (11-oz.) can condensed cream of mushroom soup

3 TB. sweet *paprika*

1 tsp. salt

½ tsp. ground black pepper

1 cup light sour cream

Put chicken chunks, onion, broth, potatoes, spinach, cream of mushroom soup (don't use any extra water), paprika, salt, and pepper in the slow cooker. Mix and cook on low for 8 to 10 hours or on high for 4 to 5 hours. Stir in sour cream 10 minutes before serving, then serve in big bowls.

Variation: Serve over rice or egg noodles.

Menu Manual

Paprika is a rich, red, warm, earthy-tasting spice that also lends a rich red color to many dishes. Sweet paprika is the most common type, but others are hotter.

Brewpub Beef Stew

Prep time: 8 minutes • Cook time: 8 to 10 hours on low or 4 to 5 hours on high •
Serves: 6 guys or 8 regular people

3 TB. olive or canola oil

2 lb. beef stew meat, cut into 1-inch chunks

1 (14.5-oz.) can beef broth

1 (12-oz.) bottle or can beer (your choice)

1 (10-oz.) can beef gravy

1 (1.4-oz.) pkg. vegetable soup mix

1 (10-oz.) box frozen peas

½ (1-lb.) bag (about 8 oz.) baby carrots, cut in half lengthwise

1 (8-oz.) pkg. sliced white mushrooms

1 (15-oz.) can sliced white potatoes, drained

End Run

These are just a few slow cooker recipes. For much more on this savory topic, check out Ellen Brown's terrific *The Complete Idiot's Guide to Slow Cooker Cooking.*

Heat oil in a large skillet over medium-high heat and cook beef for 4 minutes, turning, until beef is browned.

Pour beef broth, beer, and gravy into the slow cooker and stir in soup mix. Add stew beef, peas, carrots, and mushrooms and stir to thoroughly mix. Cook on low for 8 to 10 hours on low or on high for 4 to 5 hours. Stir in sliced potatoes 15 minutes before serving. Serve in big bowls.

Variation: Use onion soup mix in place of the vegetable soup mix.

The Least You Need to Know

♦ Recipes for soups, stews, chowders, and the slow cooker are often easy to assemble but reward the cook with rich flavors.

♦ You can—and should—let heat and time do the work for you. You can take all the credit for the magical results.

♦ Many recipes in this chapter take only minutes to get started, then let you go do something else.

♦ Slow cooker recipes might take all day to cook, but they are easy to prepare and, boy, are they worth the wait.

Chapter 9

Eat Your Vegetables

In This Chapter

- ◆ Salad secret ingredients add more bang for your salad buck
- ◆ Marinated vegetables: dress up those veggies!
- ◆ Fast and delicious stove top vegetables
- ◆ Weird and wonderful veggie dishes

Some guys admit that salads are their favorite meals. Yes, you read that right. Not *side dish* but *meal*. Why? Of course, some of us need to keep our girlish figures (that was a joke), but many of us are thinking about our health as well.

One of the biggest reasons, though, is that whether a side dish or a meal, salads and vegetable dishes are fast and easy. When I've got no time to cook, I tend to make one of the salads in this chapter. They're tasty, and I get extra credit from my wife for being healthy when I'm really just being lazy (that's called a win-win situation; guys are good at those).

A Salad Is a Raw Deal

Salads should be on every guy's favorites list. Since the advent of bag-o-salad at the store, salads are fast and easy and comply with our ground rules for minimum cleanup, expense, and simplicity. With a bag of salad and a bottle of dressing, you've got a vegetable side dish (there's a complicated recipe for you).

In this section we'll have a bit more fun with salad. If it's not fun, what's the point? Here you'll find salads that range from out-of-the-bag to those that include everything but the kitchen sink. A friend of mine jokes about "bachelor salad"—half a head of lettuce with a bottle of Thousand Island dressing dumped on it. We'll do better than that in this chapter. We'll add normal items you might already have in the fridge, or other secret ingredients, and we've got a salad—or a meal—assembled in 4 minutes flat that's sure to impress your guests.

> **End Run** _____
>
> One of the best inventions since sliced bread is the creation of the "bagged salad." We might take it for granted today, but just a few years ago, a guy would actually have to break apart his lettuce all by himself. Now it comes already broken apart in a bag. What's next?
>
> Bagged salads, of course, also come in many types and prices. Iceberg tends to be the cheapest, but for fun, experiment with the others. Baby spinach, for example, adds great flavor, and those dark green leaves might actually make someone think you made the salad yourself.
>
> Be sure to still rinse your salad and then drain it dry or spin it to remove water. It's a high-tech world that makes bagged salad, but low-tech bugs still occasionally make it into fresh vegetables and threaten to give us a bad stomachache—or worse.

Top Veggie Suspects for Salad

You can make salads with a lot of different ingredients depending on your taste (and what you have in the fridge). These common ones will serve as a good starting point for your salad masterpiece:

- Avocado chunks
- *Baby spinach*
- Carrots
- Celery
- Cucumbers
- *Grape tomatoes*
- Lettuce
- *Sweet onion*

Menu Manual

Baby spinach leaves are smooth and 1 to 2 inches long. They are tender and crispy, unlike older spinach, which can be too chewy for a good salad. Baby spinach is often sold alongside bags of prepared salad.

Outside of summer tomato season, stick to **grape tomatoes,** those 1-inch–long, grape- or egg-shape tomatoes that usually come in pint containers. They have the best flavor. Rinse them and chop them in half before you toss 'em in.

Sweet onions, in your grocery store produce section, will cost a little more than regular onions. They are, however, milder and sweeter. To avoid gastric distress, not to mention onion breath, be a big spender and use sweet onions—*especially* if it's date night.

Now, with these basic ingredients, let's move on to some of my favorite salad combinations.

Salad Dressings

From light vinaigrette to blue cheese, there's a dressing for every salad. You have your favorite, but keep in mind that some types of dressing go better with a salad alongside your fish while others pair better with a salad next to a T-bone (a blue cheese dressing on a side salad might make you wonder why you can't taste your bass). Here's some help:

- **Oil dressings,** such as vinegar and oil and Italian, go well with almost anything from fish to beef stew. They are a really good idea, though, for lighter foods such as chicken and fish. For many of the recipes in this chapter, start with Italian to taste the vegetables, then move on to one of the heavier types.
- **Rich dressings,** such as blue cheese, Parmesan, French, ranch, Thousand Island, and Russian, are great with salads alongside burgers, steaks, or stews.

Consider the context of your main dish when choosing your dressing. You might be surprised what a difference a dressing can make.

BYO(S)B (Beyond Your Old Salad Basics)

Veggies are the starting point for salads, but don't stop there. You can add as many tasty morsels to a salad as you can add to soup, only here you crunch instead of slurp. How about …

End Run

Minimum work and maximum taste are the priorities, but don't forget that lettuce doesn't naturally come in a bag. A head of lettuce (romaine, iceberg, Boston, and others), shredded or cut into bite-size pieces, makes the original salad foundation.

◆ **Cheeses** such as shredded or cubed mozzarella, cheddar, blue cheese, feta, cottage cheese, or Parmesan—all good atop salad greens.

◆ **Fruits** such as chopped apples, pears, cherries, mandarin oranges, grapefruit chunks, and grapes all work well in salads.

◆ **Meats,** from ham (all kinds) to cooked chicken or pork. Tiny shrimp works well, too.

◆ **Nuts**—sliced almonds, peanuts, chopped walnuts, and pine nuts—for a little salad crunch.

These are the starting point, but the sky is the limit. Hard-boiled egg is a classic in chef's salad. Don't forget croutons. A friend of mine puts Chex Mix in his salad (and it's actually pretty good). Use your imagination.

Standby Salad

Prep time: 5 minutes • Serves: 4 guys or 6 regular people as a generous side salad

1 (1-lb.) bag iceberg salad, rinsed and dried

2 cups baby spinach leaves, rinsed and dried

1 cup grape tomatoes, rinsed and sliced in half

2 carrots, scraped, sliced lengthwise, and cut into ¼-inch slices

¼ cup sweet onion slices, about 1 by ¼ inch (about ¼ medium-size sweet onion)

Italian or oil dressing to taste

Menu Manual

Toss means using salad tongs or serving spoons to gently mix the dressing into the salad so it coats all the ingredients.

Pour salad and spinach in a big serving bowl. Top with grape tomato halves, carrot chunks, and onion. Drizzle to taste with salad dressing, *toss*, and serve.

Chef Salad with Ham

Prep time: 5 minutes • Serves: 4 guys or 6 regular people as a generous side salad

1 (1-lb.) bag iceberg salad, rinsed and dried

1 to 2 cups ham, cut into ½-inch chunks

½ cup shredded cheddar cheese

Italian or other oil-based dressing

Pour salad in a big serving bowl. Top with ham, cheese, and dressing and toss.

Nut 'n' Honey Salad

Prep time: 5 minutes • Serves: 4 guys or 6 regular people as a generous side salad

1 (1-lb.) bag iceberg salad, rinsed and dried

2 TB. honey

2 TB. balsamic vinegar

2 TB. olive oil

½ cup sliced almonds

½ cup chopped walnuts

½ cup shredded cheddar cheese

Pour salad in a bowl. Put honey in a microwave-safe measuring cup and heat for 15 seconds, then stir in balsamic vinegar and olive oil. Pour this mixture over salad, top with almonds, walnuts, and cheese, and toss to mix.

Variation: For a bit more zing, add salt and ground black pepper to the dressing as you mix it.

 End Run

Check out the little packets of nuts in the salad section. They're seasoned and ready to sprinkle right into your salad bowl. The only problem is that they taste really, really good, so be careful not to eat more than half of them while you're making the salad.

Fruit and Cheese Chef Salad

Prep time: 5 minutes • Serves: 4 guys or 6 regular people as a generous side salad

1 (1-lb.) bag iceberg salad, rinsed and dried

⅔ cup crumbled blue cheese (available "pre-crumbled" at your grocery store in the refrigerated section)

2 Granny Smith apples (or other tart, crisp apple), cut in quarters lengthwise, cored, and cut into ½-inch pieces

½ cup sliced almonds

Blue cheese dressing (or your favorite; Italian also works)

Pour salad in a big serving bowl. Top with blue cheese, apples, almonds, and dressing and toss.

Variations: Chunks of pear work really well in this salad. Substitute feta cheese for the blue for another taste treat.

 End Run

Do you peel the apples or not? It's up to you. I wash my salad apples and toss in the chunks, skin and all. I like the texture and flavor, and it saves the work of peeling them. I've even heard that there are a lot of vitamins and fiber in apple peels.

If you're making a salad in advance, toss these apple chunks first with a little lemon juice. The acid in the juice delays that unappetizing browning of fruit. (And if you want to dazzle someone with your vocabulary, when you toss your apples with lemon juice, you are actually *acidulating* those apples.)

Hail Caesar Salad

Prep time: 5 minutes • Serves: 4 guys or 6 regular people as a generous side salad

1 lb. romaine lettuce, rinsed, dried, and shredded, or 1 (1-lb.) bag prepared romaine lettuce

Caesar dressing

2 cups seasoned croutons (available at your grocery store)

½ cup shredded Parmesan cheese

 End Run

Caesar dressing gets its distinctive flavor from anchovies.

Distribute shredded romaine to serving plates. Drizzle with Caesar dressing (doing this first helps croutons and Parmesan stick). Spread around croutons and cheese and serve.

One More Raw Deal

Crunchy vegetables such as carrots and celery will last a week in your fridge, so you can pull them out when you need them for a meal or a snack. Mushrooms are better to eat right away.

Vegetable Crunch Salad

Prep time: 4 minutes • Serves: 4 guys or 6 regular people as a generous side salad

1 lb. vegetables (your favorite) or a mix pre-pared to eat (carrots scraped and cut into sticks; peppers rinsed, sliced, and seeds removed, etc.)

½ cup Italian or oil dressing

Dump veggies in a big plastic or other container with a leak-proof lid. Pour dressing over, put on the lid, and give it a shake to coat everything. Eat some right away or stick bowl in the fridge and have some later.

Cooked Veggies

For most vegetables, quick cooking and simple seasoning are the best way to frame fresh vegetable flavors. That's good news for a guy who likes simplicity.

Spinach, Rome Style

Prep time: 5 minutes • Cook time: 10 minutes • Serves: 4 guys or 6 regular people as a side dish

1 lb. fresh spinach, rinsed, with stems discarded

1 TB. olive oil

1 tsp. garlic powder

Ground black pepper, freshly ground if possible

¼ cup shredded Parmesan cheese

Pour ½ inch water in the bottom of a large saucepan, set a steamer inside the pan over water, put spinach in steamer, and cover. Turn the stove to high and cook for 5 minutes or until spinach has wilted (spinach shrinks a lot as it cooks). Scoop spinach into a large bowl and pour olive oil and garlic powder over it. With a knife and fork, cut spinach into pieces (this also mixes in oil and garlic). Divide among serving plates and top with pepper and Parmesan cheese.

End Run

Freshly ground pepper adds great flavor to any food, and it's more fun than off-the-shelf ground black pepper. A pepper grinder is inexpensive, too.

Variations: You can also prepare this recipe in a large skillet. Heat 3 tablespoons olive oil over medium heat in the skillet and cook spinach, stirring, for about 5 minutes or until it's wilted. Then proceed as directed.

If you've got nutmeg, sprinkle a little on cooked spinach. Unlikely as it might sound, spinach and nutmeg make a great combination.

Baked Cauliflower

Prep time: 2 minutes • Cook time: 30 minutes • Serves: 4 guys or 6 regular people as a side dish

1 (1½-lb.) head cauliflower	1 tsp. ground cumin
3 TB. olive oil	Butter, salt, and ground black pepper to taste

Preheat the oven to 350°F. Pour ½ inch water in the bottom of a baking dish. Rinse cauliflower and cut the head in half lengthwise from stem to top. Place the two halves flat side down in the baking dish. Drizzle cauliflower with olive oil, covering as much of the top as you can, then sprinkle on cumin. Slide into the oven on the middle shelf and bake for 30 minutes or until cauliflower softens to your taste. Remove the tray from the oven, slice each piece in half again, and distribute the pieces to serving plates. Dress to taste with butter, salt, and pepper.

Broiled Green Beans

Prep time: 4 minutes • Cook time: 8 minutes • Serves: 2 guys or 3 regular people as a side dish

1 lb. fresh green beans, unappetizing stem ends removed, rinsed under cold water	¼ cup shredded Parmesan cheese
3 TB. olive oil	Salt and ground black pepper to taste

Preheat the broiler. Place green beans in a big zipper-type plastic bag or a container with a tight lid, pour in olive oil, and shake to coat all sides. Pour beans onto a baking tray and spread so they are in a single layer. Broil on the next-to-highest rack for 8 minutes, turning them once as best you can with a spatula. Remove from the oven to serving plates, sprinkle with Parmesan, salt, and pepper, and serve.

Variations: Try broiling with other crisp vegetables, such as bell peppers or asparagus. For a change in texture, you can also substitute cooking methods by baking these vegetables at 400°F for 15 minutes or until done.

Sautéed Vegetable Medley

Prep time: 2 minutes • Cook time: 8 minutes • Serves: 4 guys or 6 regular people as a side dish

2 TB. olive oil

1 TB. chopped garlic

1 (15-oz.) can mixed vegetables, drained

1 (15-oz.) can whole kernel corn, drained

Dash hot pepper sauce

Salt and ground black pepper

End Run

You can use this method for frozen vegetables as well, but double the cooking time. Fresh vegetables will cook in about the same time as canned vegetables.

Heat oil in a skillet over medium heat and cook garlic, stirring, for 2 minutes. Add vegetables and corn and heat, stirring, for 5 minutes or until heated through. Add hot pepper sauce, stir, and distribute to serving plates, seasoning to taste with salt and pepper.

Variation: Use extra corn in place of mixed vegetables.

Fried Zucchini

Prep time: 5 minutes • Cook time: 10 minutes • Serves: 4 guys or 6 regular people as a side dish

¼ cup olive oil

6 small (10-inch) fresh zucchini, washed, ends cut off, and quartered lengthwise

Salt and ground black pepper

Hot pepper sauce (optional)

¼ cup shredded Parmesan cheese

Heat oil in a large skillet over medium heat. Lay zucchini spears in the skillet in a single layer and cook for 3 minutes per side or until softened. Unless you have a really large skillet, this might need to be done in batches, half the zucchini at a time. Use a splatter screen, if you have one, to minimize cleanup of the surrounding countertop. Remove skillet from heat and, with tongs or a fork, remove zucchini to serving plates. Season to taste with salt, pepper, hot sauce (if using), and Parmesan.

Succotash

Prep time: 4 minutes • Cook time: 4 minutes • Serves: 4 guys or 6 regular people as a side dish

1 TB. butter or margarine

1 (15-oz.) can whole kernel corn, drained

2 (8.5-oz.) cans lima beans, drained

2 TB. heavy cream

Salt and ground black pepper

Melt butter in a saucepan over medium heat. Add corn, lima beans, and cream and heat, stirring, for 4 minutes or until heated through. Distribute to serving plates, seasoning to taste with salt and pepper.

Food Fumble

Cook vegetables too long, and they lose their flavor and texture. Most of us don't like *mush* for a side dish.

Sautéed Mushrooms and Bacon

Prep time: 5 minutes • Cook time: 11 minutes • Serves: 4 guys or 6 regular people as a side dish

4 strips bacon

1 lb. sliced white mushrooms

1 TB. chopped garlic

¼ cup shredded Parmesan cheese

Ground black pepper, freshly ground if possible

Cook bacon in a large skillet over medium heat for 3 to 4 minutes per side or until crispy. Remove bacon to paper towels and pour off most of the fat (leave 1 or 2 tablespoons in the skillet). Add mushrooms and garlic to the skillet and cook, stirring, for 5 minutes. Distribute mushrooms to serving plates. Crumble bacon over mushrooms, sprinkle with Parmesan cheese and pepper, and serve.

End Run

This is a great dish with some debate behind it—on whether or not a mushroom is a vegetable. Because it's regularly found in the veggie section of grocery stores and is often prepared and eaten as a vegetable, I've included it here.

Sautéed Sweet Peppers with Hot Sauce

Prep time: 5 minutes • Cook time: 5 minutes • Serves: 4 guys or 6 regular people as a
side dish

3 TB. olive oil

1 small onion (golf-ball size), peeled and cut
into ½-inch pieces

3 large green peppers (or red, yellow, or a mix),
seeds and stems removed and cut into ½-inch
pieces

Hot pepper sauce

Salt and ground black pepper

 End Run

Green bell peppers are usually cheaper than the red or
yellow varieties. The reds and
yellows have a sweeter, richer
flavor than the green varieties.

Heat olive oil in a large skillet over medium heat and
cook onion and peppers, stirring, for 6 minutes or until
peppers begin to soften but retain a crisp bite. Distribute
to serving plates and season to taste with hot pepper
sauce, salt, and pepper.

The Least You Need to Know

- A simple salad is one of the easiest side dishes to prepare.
- Salads offer a foundation for many ingredients, including fruits, cheeses, meats,
  and nuts. Add enough, and that salad's not only delicious, but it's a meal as
  well—all without any cooking.
- Quick cooking preserves natural flavors, especially when you're using fresh
  vegetables.
- Canned vegetables provide a fast option for cooked vegetable dishes.

Chapter 10

Desserts Even a Guy Can Make

In This Chapter

- ◆ Bake a dessert—yes, guys can do this!
- ◆ Make magic with store-bought desserts
- ◆ Ice cream like you've never seen it before
- ◆ Fruit: the secret dessert weapon

Sometimes even a guy has to make dessert, but it's a scary thought. Desserts have a reputation for being complicated and time-consuming, and for a number of recipes, that's true. But don't worry, we'll avoid those kinds of desserts.

In this chapter, you'll find tried-and-true desserts that are delicious, fast, and easy. You may pretend, of course, that you spent all day with the apron on.

Fast and Easy

Many of these desserts take advantage of a store-bought foundation, and all are quick to prepare.

Do take advantage of ready-to-use pie shells, especially the cookie-crumb and graham-cracker shells you can find in your grocery store. You can still take credit for having made a pie.

Chocolate-Chip Pie

Prep time: 2 minutes • Cook time: 35 minutes • Serves: 4 guys or 6 regular people

1 (20-oz.) pkg. chocolate-chip cookie dough, set out to soften for 10 to 15 minutes

1 graham-cracker–crust pie shell

½ cup chopped walnuts

½ cup chocolate chips

Vanilla or coffee ice cream

Food Fumble

Bulletin from the Guy Administration of Stomachaches (Another "G.A.S."): Serve rich desserts like Chocolate-Chip Pie in thin slices, and try to limit yourself to one slice. All right, two. This is really rich stuff. We like to remember a good meal, but not the wrong way.

Preheat the oven to 375°F. Carefully press cookie dough into pie shell (you don't want to break the shell), spreading it so it is equal in thickness across the bottom of shell. The dough will not come up to the top of shell, but that's okay (what we lack in mass we make up for in density—trust me). Spread walnuts in an even layer across top of dough and spread chocolate chips over walnuts. Press nuts and chips into dough with the back of a spoon and bake pie for 35 minutes or until dough is cooked to your liking (the more you cook it, the firmer it will get).

Top with a scoop of ice cream.

Turbo-Chocolate Ice-Cream Pie

Prep time: 10 minutes • Freeze time: 1 hour • Serves: 4 guys or 6 regular people

2 cups chocolate ice cream, softened

2 cups heavenly hash ice cream, Mississippi Mud, or other decadent chunky ice cream, softened

1 cup hot fudge sauce

½ cup chopped walnuts

½ cup chocolate chips

1 store-bought chocolate-cookie–crumb crust (graham-cracker works, too)

Mix chocolate and heavenly hash ice cream, fudge sauce, walnuts, and chocolate chips in a large bowl. Scrape gooey mixture into crust and smooth it with the back of a large spoon. (Only one taste allowed.) Put pie in the freezer for 30 minutes to 1 hour to firm. Serve sliced in wedges.

Instant Chocolate Mousse

Prep time: 10 minutes   •   Serves: 4 guys or 6 regular people

1 pint whipping cream, whipped, or 1 (16-oz.) tub light whipped topping

4 TB. instant hot chocolate powder

½ cup sugar (use only with the whipping cream)

2 tsp. vanilla

Whip cream, adding hot chocolate powder, sugar, and vanilla as you go. When your mousse doubles in size, with soft waves standing, you're ready to serve. If you're using whipped topping, simply stir in chocolate powder and vanilla but omit sugar.

End Run

Whipping cream might sound like work, but it's not too bad. All you need is an electric or hand beater and a big bowl (if you've got time, chill the bowl in the fridge for a few minutes to speed up whipping). Pour the whipping cream in the bowl and beat it until it expands and starts to form waves that stand up on their own, usually about 4 minutes. The flavor is great.

Turbo-Chocolate Brownies

Prep time: 5 minutes   •   Cook time: 35 minutes   •   Serves: 8 guys or 10 to 12 regular people

1 (19- to 21-oz.) pkg. fudge brownie mix

½ cup bittersweet chocolate chips

½ cup milk chocolate chips

¼ cup sour cream (in addition to the liquid ingredients specified for the brownies)

½ tsp. vanilla

Prepare brownies according to package directions, mixing in bittersweet and milk chocolate chips, sour cream, and vanilla. Bake according to package directions and prepare yourself for an explosion of chocolate flavor.

Variations: White chocolate works in place of chocolate chips. M&M's are a nice substitution, too. Crumbled toffee is also delicious.

Pumpkin Mousse

Prep time: 5 minutes • Serves: 4 guys or 6 regular people

2 cups milk

1 cup solid-packed canned pumpkin—not pumpkin pie filling

2 (3.4-oz.) boxes instant vanilla pudding mix

1 tsp. pumpkin or apple pie spice (or ½ tsp. cinnamon)

1 cup whipped topping

Combine milk, pumpkin, pudding mix, and pumpkin spice. Stir in whipped topping and serve.

Variation: Put one of these "mousse" recipes in a pie shell, chill for a while, and you've got pie.

Menu Manual

This simple, rich *mousse* is adapted from my book *The Complete Idiot's Guide to 20-Minute Meals.*

A **mousse** is not something to put in your hair, although the concept behind it is the same—food (or hair) that is light and fluffy. A dessert mousse often gets its lightness from egg whites or whipped cream.

Fruit Frenzy

Fruit-based dishes are among the easiest and most reliable desserts, for the simple reason that you're not creating flavor, you're simply figuring out the best way to highlight those great flavors already there.

Pear Sundae

Prep time: 5 minutes   •   Serves: 2 guys or 3 regular people

1 (15-oz.) can Bartlett pear halves (or slices) in pear juice, juice poured into a cup for later

Vanilla ice cream

Chocolate sauce

Whipped cream

Scoop a pear half or a few slices into a tall glass, top with a scoop of ice cream, then more pear, then another scoop of ice cream. Drizzle with chocolate sauce and some pear juice, top with whipped cream, and serve.

Variation: Peeled fresh pear slices are terrific as a base for this sundae.

Dizzy Fruit

Prep time: 5 minutes   •   Serves: 4 guys or 6 regular people

1 (20-oz.) can pineapple chunks in water, drained, or 2 cups fresh

½ pint fresh blueberries, rinsed

2 cups grapes, rinsed

½ cantaloupe, balled with a *melon-baller*

2 to 3 TB. *amaretto*

Whipped cream

Put pineapple, blueberries, grapes, and cantaloupe in a large bowl, pour amaretto over, gently stir, and serve in small bowls (or huge martini glasses), topping with whipped cream.

Menu Manual

A **melon-baller** resembles a small ice-cream scoop. You use it for much the same action, although you're scooping melon rather than ice cream. Using the small round scoops and making balls tends to be more attractive than using a knife and cutting melon bricks.

Amaretto is a popular almond liqueur. A small drizzle works flavor-enhancing magic on fruit.

Baked Blueberry Crumble

Prep time: 10 minutes • Cook time: 10 minutes • Serves: 4 guys or 6 regular people

1 cup sugar

3 TB. all-purpose flour

½ tsp. salt

1 (16-oz.) pkg. frozen blueberries, thawed

4 TB. (½ stick) butter

¼ cup firmly packed dark brown sugar

½ cup quick oatmeal (not old-fashioned or instant)

½ tsp. ground cinnamon

Vanilla ice cream

Preheat the broiler and set the top rack at the next-to-highest level. Mix sugar, flour, and salt in a small bowl. Place blueberries in a large bowl, pour sugar mixture over berries, and mix. Pour berries into a pie plate.

In a 2-cup measuring cup, melt butter in the microwave for 30 seconds. Add brown sugar, oatmeal, and cinnamon to butter in the measuring cup and mix with a spoon. Spread this mixture over blueberries. Place the pie plate in the microwave and cook for 6 minutes. If your microwave does not have a turntable, turn the dish a couple times to ensure even cooking. Remove the pie plate from the microwave and slide it under the broiler for 4 minutes or until top begins to brown and crisp. Serve topped with scoops of vanilla ice cream.

Variation: Don't stop with blueberries. Strawberries are a natural in this dish, as are raspberries and pitted cherries. Mixed frozen fruits add some fun, too.

Baked Apples

Prep time: 10 minutes   •   Cook time: 35 minutes   •   Serves: 4 guys or 8 regular people

3 TB. butter

¼ cup firmly packed dark brown sugar

½ cup raisins

½ tsp. ground cinnamon

4 Granny Smith apples (or other tart baking apple), cut in half lengthwise and core scooped out with a paring knife or melon baller so there's a slight bowl in each apple half

Vanilla ice cream

Preheat the oven to 350°F. In a 2-cup measuring cup, melt butter in the microwave for 30 seconds. Add brown sugar, raisins, and cinnamon to butter in the measuring cup and mix with a spoon. Place apples, cut side up, in a baking pan with a lid. Distribute butter-sugar-raisin mixture among apple halves. Pour ¼ inch water in the base of the baking pan, put on the lid, and slide it into the oven. Cook for 35 minutes or until apples are soft. Carefully distribute apple halves to serving plates, top with a scoop of vanilla ice cream, and serve.

Fruit and Cream

Prep time: 5 minutes   •   Serves: 4 guys or 6 regular people

1 qt. fresh blueberries, rinsed

1 cup sour cream

½ cup light cream

¼ cup sugar

Distribute blueberries among serving bowls. Mix sour cream, light cream, and sugar in a small bowl and spoon on top of blueberries.

Variation: This works just as well with raspberries, strawberries, and even grapes.

Pears in Wine Sauce

Prep time: 5 minutes • Cook time: 15 minutes • Serves: 4 guys or 6 regular people

½ cup cooking sherry or cooking wine

½ cup water

½ cup firmly packed dark brown sugar

1 tsp. apple pie spice, or 1 tsp. ground cinnamon

1 tsp. lemon juice

4 ripe pears, peeled, sliced in half lengthwise, and cored

Heat sherry, water, brown sugar, apple pie spice, and lemon juice in a small saucepan or skillet over medium heat until liquid begins to bubble. Place pear halves, cut side down, in the skillet, turn the heat to low, and simmer for 12 minutes or until fruit is tender. Remove fruit with a slotted spoon to serving plates. Turn the heat to high and cook the remaining sauce, stirring, for 2 to 3 minutes until it thickens and becomes a syrup. Drizzle this syrup over each serving of pears and serve. People will taste it and say "Wow!"

Honeyed Fruit and Nuts

Prep time: 5 minutes • Cook time: 5 minutes • Serves: 4 guys or 6 regular people

3 TB. butter or margarine

¼ cup dried cherries, cranberries, or raisins

4 ripe pears, peeled, cored, and sliced

¼ cup honey

½ cup chopped walnuts

½ tsp. ground cinnamon

Whipped cream

Melt butter in a large skillet over medium heat. Add dried fruit and sauté for 2 minutes. Add pears and sauté for 2 more minutes. Add honey, walnuts, and cinnamon and cook, stirring, for 2 final minutes. Distribute to serving plates, topping with whipped cream.

Variation: Who could object to vanilla ice cream in place of the whipped cream? Or maybe in *addition* to whipped cream …

Cakes—at Least in Name

What favorite dessert is light and fluffy and has a reputation for being hard to make? That would be cake, and this section will show a few methods a guy can cheat (um, "work smart") his way into cake for dessert.

Cherry-Chocolate Shortcake

Prep time: 10 minutes • Cook time: 15 minutes • Serves: 4 guys or 6 regular people

2¼ cups baking mix such as Bisquick (if you're making shortcake)

¾ cup whole milk (if you're making shortcake)

1 (21-oz.) can cherry pie filling

Whipped cream

Chocolate sauce

Preheat oven to 400°F. Pour baking mix into a big bowl. Thoroughly mix in milk with a fork to make dough. Sprinkle some flour on the counter and dump dough on floured counter. Flatten it with your hands or a rolling pin to about ¾ inch thick and use the rim of a juice glass (or a cookie cutter) to cut circles ideally about 3 inches across. Place dough circles on a baking tray, slide the tray in the oven, and bake for 10 to 12 minutes or until nicely browned.

Pull the tray out of the oven, cool for a minute, and slice each biscuit, uh, "shortcake," in half horizontally so you have two pancake-shape halves. Put the bottom halves on serving plates and scoop a spoonful of cherry pie filling onto each shortcake. Top with shortcake tops, scoop on some more filling, top with whipped cream, drizzle with chocolate sauce, and serve.

Variations: Use store-bought shortcake.

Also, use strawberries for the classic version of this dish. Other berries, such as blueberries or raspberries, also work. Whenever you're using fresh fruit, put the rinsed fruit in a bowl (cut in the case of strawberries or whole for smaller berries) and sprinkle them with sugar. Let them sit for 20 minutes so the natural juices can come out.

Food Fumble

To avoid dessert mush, don't put juicy fruit on top of short-cake until just before you want to serve it.

Cheater's Chocolate Cheesecake

Prep time: 5 minutes plus chilling time   •   Serves: 4 guys or 6 regular people

2 (8-oz.) pkg. whipped cream cheese

1 cup sour cream

1 (3.9-oz.) pkg. instant chocolate pudding mix

1 chocolate-cookie–crumb-crust pie shell (or graham-cracker-crust; available at your grocery store)

In a large bowl, mix cream cheese, sour cream, and chocolate pudding mix. You will need a strong spoon. Scrape filling into pie shell, smooth out with the spoon, and chill for an hour or two while you watch *Doctor No* for the twenty-fifth time.

End Run

The shelves at your grocery store are full of mixes designed for one purpose that can be used for another (somebody had to invent onion dip made with soup mix). That idea goes double for desserts. That pudding mix is not just for pudding, the cake mix is not just for plain old cake, and the baking mix is not just for pancakes. You might call this "thinking outside the box"—literally.

For more on mix magic, check out *The Complete Idiot's Guide to Cooking with Mixes*, by Ellen Brown.

Blueberry-Peach Dump Cake

Prep time: 5 minutes   •   Cook time: 50 minutes   •   Serves: 6 guys or 8 to 10 regular people

1 (15-oz.) can blueberries in syrup, syrup poured off into a separate cup

1 (8.5-oz.) can sliced peaches in syrup, syrup poured off into the cup with the blueberry syrup

1 (16-oz.) box yellow cake mix

8 TB. (1 stick) butter, melted

Preheat oven to 350°F. Grease a 9×13-inch cake or baking pan. Pour, uh, I mean *dump*, blueberries and peaches into the pan and smooth them out to be roughly level. (One test spoonful of fruit is allowed.) Pour cake mix on top of fruit and use the back of a large spoon to even things out. Mix about ½ fruit syrup with melted butter and pour it over the cake mix. (Use the rest of the syrup for something else.) Bake for 50 minutes or until cake is firm. Scoop into messy blocks with a big spoon and serve. Whipped cream or ice cream make delicious toppings.

Variations: There are as many variations for this cake as there are fruits in cans. Cherry pie filling combined with crushed pineapple was one of the originals. Apple pie filling also works. If you're using fruits without syrup (as in fresh fruits), mix ½ cup sugar with the fruit.

Food Fumble

When you're melting butter in the microwave, put a lid or some plastic wrap over the bowl or cup you're using. Butter has a tendency to splatter all over, and that goes against one of our ground rules, "Cleanup should be minimal." Using low or medium power for longer also minimizes butter explosions.

The Least You Need to Know

- Fruit-based desserts are a good bet because they are simple and tasty. As they cook, all you have to do is focus on the flavor that's already there.
- Delicious desserts can be made quickly from store-bought ingredients—from cake mixes and pie shells to ice cream.
- Creamy textures and flavors have universal appeal and make many recipes sure winners.
- Don't hesitate to use quick stove top, broiling, and baking recipes. You'll impress whoever tries the results, even if it's just you.

Part **3**

Survival Rations

In this practical part, we'll focus on tasty, efficient, and simple meals. During the week, for example, there's no time to hang out in the kitchen between work and sleep, so you need something good and fast.

On a similar theme, we'll make big batches of hearty dishes that will keep you in meals not just tonight, but tomorrow, too (and maybe the day after that).

You'll find a chapter on those rare meals that kids will eat (and that taste good to adults, too). One topic that's both practical *and fun* is food the ladies will like and then those they won't. (Hint: Serve those when you're on your own.) We'll close by tipping our sombrero to south-of-the-border cuisine.

Chapter 11

Weeknight Food: Jump-Start the Meal

In This Chapter

- Why did the chicken make such a good meal?
- Magic with ground beef
- Fast rice and pasta meals
- Forget side dishes—veggie dishes great all by themselves

During the week, people (and not just guys) need something tasty, yet quick and convenient. This chapter will survey both quick-and-homemade dishes and meals put together from purchased and ready-to-go ingredients, including a visit to the deli, the freezer section, and, of course, the canned food aisle.

Also, many of the meals in this chapter (or in this book for that matter) make great use of leftover pasta and rice. The next time you make some, double the batch and keep the rest in the fridge. Those leftovers will jump-start a meal like nothing else.

That's today's lesson, grasshopper.

Shake Your Tail Feathers

This set of poultry-based recipes will have you—and your fellow diners—clucking with delight.

Curried Chicken and Rice

Prep time: 5 minutes • Cook time: 8 minutes • Serves: 4 guys or 6 regular people

3 TB. olive oil

2 boneless, skinless chicken breasts (about 1 lb. total) cut into ½-inch chunks

1 medium onion (pool-ball size), peeled and chopped into ½-inch pieces

1 TB. curry powder

1 tsp. ground cumin

1 cup chicken broth

1 cup plain yogurt or light sour cream

½ cup raisins

1 crisp apple, cored and cut into ¼-inch pieces

4 cups cooked rice

Salt and ground black pepper

End Run

Skinless chicken—whether we're talking about boneless breasts or canned—is generally considered a very healthy meat, low in fat, low in carbohydrates, and high in protein.

Heat oil in a large skillet over medium heat. Add chicken, onion, curry powder, and cumin and cook, stirring, for 6 minutes or until chicken is cooked through and is no longer pink in the center. Add chicken broth, yogurt, raisins, and apple and heat, stirring, for 1 minute longer. Distribute rice among bowls (or plates) and spoon a big helping of curried chicken on top of rice. Serve, passing salt and pepper along with it.

Chicken Zucchini

Prep time: 10 minutes   •   Cook time: 55 minutes   •   Serves: 6 guys or 8 regular people

3 TB. olive oil

2 boneless, skinless chicken breasts (about 1 lb. total) rinsed, patted dry on paper towels, and cut into ½-inch chunks

1 medium onion (pool-ball size), peeled and chopped into ½-inch chunks

4 zucchini squash (about 2 lb.), ends cut off, chopped into ½-inch chunks

2 cups stuffing mix (available in grocery stores)

1 (10.75-oz.) can condensed cream of chicken soup

1 cup sour cream

¼ cup margarine or butter, cut into 1 tsp.-size pieces

Preheat the oven to 350°F. Heat oil in a large skillet and cook chicken, stirring, for 5 minutes or until chicken is cooked through and no longer pink in the center; turn off heat. Meanwhile, put onion and zucchini in a saucepan and add enough water to just cover vegetables. Put the saucepan on the stove over high heat and bring to a boil. Cook for 3 minutes, then dump vegetables into a colander in the sink. Grease a large baking dish. Spread ½ stuffing mix in an even layer on the bottom of the pan, then spread, in layers, cooked chicken, condensed chicken soup, onion-zucchini mix, sour cream, and remaining stuffing mix. Dot top of stuffing mix with pieces of margarine. Bake for 45 minutes, uncovered, in the oven on the middle rack. Serve with pieces of crusty bread and you've got a meal. Actually, for a family, you've got more than one meal.

Variation: You can use canned chicken to save the step of cooking the chicken breasts. Or leave the chicken out for a vegetarian dish.

End Run

Walter Horning, retired from the Natick, Massachusetts Police Department, has a reputation at the station for being a great cook. He suggested Chicken Zucchini, but he's modest about it. "Everything I make is really simple and easy," he explains, "but the guys like it." I don't know about you, but that sounds like an endorsement to me.

Chicken Pot Pie

Prep time: 5 minutes • Cook time: 45 minutes • Serves: 4 guys or 6 regular people

3 TB. olive oil

2 boneless, skinless chicken breasts (about 1 lb. total) cut into ½-inch chunks

2 (15-oz.) cans mixed vegetables, drained

1 (10.75-oz.) can condensed cream of chicken soup

1 cup sour cream

2 tsp. Italian seasoning

Dash hot pepper sauce (optional)

1 (16-oz.) tube buttermilk biscuit dough

Preheat oven to 350°F. Heat oil in a large skillet over medium heat and cook chicken, stirring, for 5 minutes or until chicken is cooked through and no longer pink in the center. Put chicken, vegetables, soup (don't use any extra water), sour cream, Italian seasoning, and hot pepper sauce (if using) in a large baking dish and stir to mix. Smooth out mixture with the back of a large spoon. Open biscuit dough and stretch dough circles to about double their original size. Arrange dough over top of pot pie filling so it covers most of filling and dough is still in a single layer (don't worry about covering everything). Slide into the oven on the middle rack and bake for 45 minutes or until crust is nicely browned.

Variation: If you're short on time, use canned chicken and skip the cooking-chicken step.

Steak Yum: Beef-Based Dinner Recipes

Beef is a flexible, easy-to-cook foundation for a meal. Keep a pound of ground beef (or other ground meat) in the freezer for emergencies. When the cupboard is bare, thaw that ground beef in the microwave and you're minutes from a meal.

Here are some of my favorite beef dishes.

Skillet Ground Beef Dinner

Prep time: 4 minutes • Cook time: 10 minutes • Serves: 4 guys or 6 regular people

1 lb. lean ground beef

1 medium onion (pool-ball size), peeled and chopped into ½-inch chunks

½ (8-oz.) pkg. fresh sliced white mushrooms or 1 (4-oz.) can sliced mushrooms, drained

2 (15-oz.) cans mixed vegetables, drained

3 TB. Italian dressing

2 TB. Worcestershire sauce

Hot pepper sauce (optional)

½ cup shredded Parmesan cheese

Cook ground beef and onion in a large skillet over medium heat, stirring, for 4 minutes. Add mushrooms and continue cooking for 4 minutes or until meat is cooked through and no red remains. Drain excess fat; add vegetables, Italian dressing, Worcestershire sauce, and hot pepper sauce; and heat, stirring, for 2 minutes. Serve in bowls or on plates (or over rice), topping each serving with Parmesan cheese.

Variation: Make this with ground poultry, pork, or even lamb.

> **End Run**
>
> Go to town with this recipe. Almost any vegetable will work in place of the mixed vegetables (I've made a version with frozen artichoke hearts and garlic that had friends asking for the recipe). If you've got leftover pasta or rice, stir it in to make a one-pot meal.

Vegetable, Beef, and Rice Stew

Prep time: 5 minutes • Cook time: 15 minutes • Serves: 6 guys or 8 regular people

3 TB. olive oil

1 large onion, peeled and chopped into ½-inch pieces

1 TB. chopped garlic

2 tsp. ground cumin

2 tsp. Italian seasoning

½ tsp. ground mustard seed (optional)

2 (15-oz.) cans beef broth

1 lb. cooked ground beef or cooked steak, cut into ½-inch pieces

1 (10-oz.) pkg. frozen spinach, thawed, or 4 cups chopped fresh Swiss chard, rinsed and dried

2 small yellow squash or zucchini, ends cut off, rinsed, and cut into ½-inch pieces

8 cups cooked white rice

Salt and ground black pepper

Heat oil in a large skillet over medium heat and cook onion for 5 minutes or until onion is translucent and soft. Add garlic, cumin, Italian seasoning, and mustard seed (if using) and cook, stirring, for 1 minute. Add beef broth and bring to a boil. Add cooked ground beef, spinach, and squash. Reduce heat to a simmer, cover, and cook for 5 minutes or until vegetables have softened to the desired texture. Remove from heat. Serve in large bowls over cooked rice, seasoning to taste with salt and pepper.

Variation: This recipe will also work with leftover cooked steak, cut into strips, or with ground pork, poultry, or lamb. If you want to use raw ground beef, simply add it with the onions, cook for 8 minutes or until done, drain the fat, and continue with the rest of the recipe.

Marinated Steak Tips

Prep time: 5 minutes plus marinating time   •   Cook time: 8 minutes   •   Serves: 2 guys or 3 regular people

1 lb. steak tips, sliced ½-inch thick

½ cup Eric's Spicy Italian Marinade and Sauce (recipe in Chapter 2)

Place steak tips in a bowl, pour marinade over, and stir around with a fork to coat all sides. Put the bowl, covered, in the fridge for several hours. When you're ready to cook, preheat the grill and cook for 4 minutes per side or until cooked to your liking (rare, medium, or well done).

If you're in a rush, you can cook these right away, but there's a great flavor benefit from letting them marinate for a while in the fridge. You'll have time to watch the extended version of *The Return of the King* (or even do a day's work), come back, and those flavorful treasures will be ready to cook.

Variation: Don't have 30 seconds to make the marinade? Use Worcestershire sauce instead.

> **End Run**
>
> If you end up with leftover steak from this recipe, use it in Vegetable, Beef, and Rice Stew (recipe earlier in this chapter). For more leftover wisdom, see Chapter 12.

Other Easy Meat and Seafood Recipes

Here are several fun weeknight recipes that emphasize speed of preparation and interesting flavors.

Microwave Broccoli and Ham

Prep time: 4 minutes   •   Cook time: 5 minutes   •   Serves: 4 guys or 6 regular people

1 (1-lb.) head broccoli, stems peeled and broken into 1-inch florets

⅔ cup Italian dressing

2 (¾-lb.) ham steaks, cut into ½-inch cubes

4 cups cooked rice

½ cup shredded Parmesan cheese

Put broccoli and dressing in a microwave-safe bowl and microwave for 4 minutes, covered with plastic wrap. Then stir in ham steak and heat for another minute until broccoli is crisp-tender. Distribute rice to serving plates, top with ham-broccoli mixture, and sprinkle generously with Parmesan cheese.

Shrimp and Rice Stew

Prep time: 2 minutes • Cook time: 5 minutes • Serves: 4 guys or 6 regular people

3 TB. olive oil

2 TB. chopped garlic

1½ cups dry white wine

1 (15-oz.) can chicken stock

1 lb. (70 to 110 count) cooked shrimp, tails off

2 bunches scallions, roots and dark green tops removed, rinsed, and chopped into ¼-inch pieces

3 cups cooked white rice

3 TB. teriyaki sauce

Salt and ground black pepper (optional)

Heat olive oil in a large skillet over medium heat and cook garlic for 3 minutes. Add wine and stock and bring the liquid to a low boil. Add shrimp (frozen is fine) and scallions, return to simmer, and cook for 4 minutes or until heated through.

Meanwhile, set out four bowls. Place ⅔ cup hot rice in each bowl. When shrimp broth is done, pour an equal amount into each bowl, drizzle each bowl with teriyaki sauce, season to taste with salt and pepper if desired, and serve.

Far East Sausage and Rice

Prep time: 5 minutes • Cook time: 15 minutes • Serves: 4 guys or 6 regular people

1 lb. sweet Italian sausage meat or whole sausages cut into ½-inch slices

1 medium onion (pool-ball size), peeled and chopped into ½-inch chunks

2 large sweet peppers (red or green), seeds and stems removed and chopped into ½-inch chunks

2 (4-oz.) cans sliced mushrooms, drained, or 1 (8-oz.) pkg. sliced white mushrooms

4 cups cooked rice

3 TB. soy sauce

3 eggs, beaten

Cook sausage in a large skillet over medium heat, stirring, for 8 minutes or until cooked through and no longer pink. Remove sausage with a slotted spoon to a plate with paper towels. Drain most of the fat, leaving 1 or 2 tablespoons in the skillet (enough to coat the bottom), and add onion and peppers. Cook vegetables for 5 minutes or until softened. Add mushrooms, cooked sausage, rice, and soy sauce and cook, stirring, for 2 minutes. Then turn the heat to high, pour in beaten eggs, and cook, stirring, for 4 minutes or until eggs are cooked.

Serve with a side salad and you've got a great meal.

Variation: Use teriyaki sauce instead of soy sauce.

End Run

According to family cook Roger Bridgeman, "For about 15 minutes' work, this meal makes you look like a hero and fools the neighbors and in-laws into thinking you're a good guy and a nice family man. Not a bad deal for rice and sausage."

Instant Pizza

Prep time: 4 minutes • Cook time: 10 minutes • Serves: 4 guys or 6 regular people

2 (14-oz.) pre-cooked pizza crusts

1 cup pizza sauce or plain pasta sauce

2 (8-oz.) pkg. shredded mozzarella cheese

⅔ cup thinly sliced pepperoni (about ⅓ [6-oz.] pkg.)

Preheat the oven to 400°F. Set out pizza crusts on the counter. Pour about ½ cup sauce on each and spread it around with the back of a spoon for a thin, even layer. Sprinkle cheese over both crusts and arrange pepperoni in a single layer over cheese. Bake for 10 minutes or until cheese has melted. Place pizza on a cutting board and slice into wedges with a sharp knife.

Food Fumble

Pizza cooks quickly, so don't let yourself get distracted by the Victoria's Secret ad. An extra couple minutes might burn the crust.

End Run

Pizza can be the platform for a huge variety of ingredients. Some of my favorites:

- ◆ Sliced white mushrooms
- ◆ Sautéed onions
- ◆ Feta cheese
- ◆ Sliced black olives
- ◆ Sliced grape tomatoes
- ◆ Sliced artichoke hearts
- ◆ Cooked chicken pieces
- ◆ Cooked ground hamburger, sausage, or poultry

And these are just for starters. What's your favorite?

Ham Stir-Fry

Prep time: 4 minutes • Cook time: 6 minutes • Serves: 4 guys or 6 regular people

3 TB. canola oil

½ lb. snow pea pods

2 (¾-lb.) ham steaks, cut into ½-inch chunks

1 (11-oz.) can mandarin orange segments, drained

1 (8-oz.) can sliced water chestnuts, drained

3 TB. teriyaki sauce

2 TB. sesame seeds

Heat oil in a large skillet or *wok*, add pea pods, and cook for 3 minutes. Add ham, orange, and water chestnuts. Cook, stirring, for 3 minutes or until heated through. Drizzle with teriyaki sauce, stir to mix, and serve in bowls on its own—or even better, over rice. Sprinkle each serving with sesame seeds.

Variation: Use broccoli florets, green beans, or even peas in place of the pea pods. Broccoli will need to be cooked a little longer; green beans and peas will take about the same time as the snow peas.

Menu Manual

To **stir-fry** is to cook food in a wok or skillet over high heat, moving and turning the food quickly to cook all sides. A **wok** is a large, metal bowl-shape device used across Asia for cooking. It is used much as a skillet is in other parts of the world. Unfortunately, it is generally only suitable for use on a gas cooktop. If you're cooking with gas, consider getting one. They're inexpensive, large enough to hold an entire meal, and different enough to inspire interest and fun.

Dinner with Vegetables

Sometimes a vegetable-based meal is just what the doctor ordered (sometimes literally, but that's another story). These hearty meals send you away happy, without meat. These will also work as hearty side dishes.

Broccoli Garlic Pasta

Prep time: 5 minutes • Cook time: 15 minutes • Serves: 4 guys or 6 regular people (with pasta leftovers)

1 lb. penne or other chunky pasta	¼ cup water
3 TB. olive oil	½ cup Italian dressing
2 TB. chopped garlic	Dash hot pepper sauce
1 (1-lb.) head broccoli, stems peeled and broken into 1-inch florets	1 (8-oz.) pkg. shredded mozzarella cheese

Cook pasta. While pasta is cooking, heat oil in a large skillet over medium heat and cook garlic for 3 minutes, stirring. Add broccoli, water, Italian dressing, and hot pepper sauce. Cook, covered, for 8 minutes or until broccoli is crisp-tender. Pasta should be done by now; drain it and distribute to serving plates. Sprinkle a generous layer of mozzarella on each plate of pasta and spoon broccoli mixture on top of cheese, making sure to spoon up some of the savory liquid, too.

Red Beans and Rice

Prep time: 5 minutes • Cook time: 15 minutes • Serves: 4 guys or 6 regular people (with pasta leftovers)

3 TB. olive oil

1 medium onion (pool-ball size), peeled and chopped into ½-inch pieces

2 tsp. Cajun seasoning

2 TB. chopped garlic

1 cup chicken broth

1 (15-oz.) can red kidney beans, drained and rinsed

½ tsp. ground black pepper

4 cups cooked rice

1 TB. lime juice

Salt to taste

Heat oil in a large skillet over medium heat and sauté onion and Cajun seasoning for 5 minutes, stirring. Add garlic and cook for another minute. Turn the burner to high and add broth, kidney beans, and pepper. Cook, stirring, for 8 minutes. Distribute hot rice to serving bowls or plates. Spoon red bean mixture over rice on serving plates, drizzle with a little lime juice, and season to taste with salt.

The Least You Need to Know

- Keep chicken on hand as a building block for fast, tasty meals.
- Ground meats, including beef, poultry, pork, and even lamb, provide great flavor, are convenient and fast to prepare, and can even be frozen for emergencies.
- Incorporate pasta or rice into a recipe to create a hearty, one-pot meal.
- A good vegetable dish can be a meal all by itself.

Chapter 12

Leftover Living

In This Chapter

- Magic with pasta, rice, and meat dishes
- Take a few extra minutes to save an hour tomorrow
- Dinner jump-starts from fridge leftovers
- Meals that taste even better the second time around

Ah, leftovers. You get home, you're tired and grumpy, and the last thing you want to do is cook. You open the fridge, and there in front of you is a pan of leftover casserole. *Saved!* You don't have to cook tonight. Heck, there's enough here that you don't have to cook tomorrow night, either.

Many guys harbor a not-so-secret habit of buying in bulk to avoid a trip later. The same approach applies to cooking. You can prepare a range of tasty dishes once in a large batch and enjoy them later with no prep time and practically no cleanup.

This chapter serves up some of my favorite leftover-oriented meals. They'll keep in the fridge for days, and you can even freeze most of them in small packages just right for another night. Keep a hunk of lasagna in the freezer, for example, and you're prepared for any food-deficit emergency.

Pasta

Pasta dishes, as we've already seen, are popular for many great reasons. They are quick to prepare and work with many other ingredients. For our purposes here, many pasta dishes also make terrific leftovers.

American Chop Suey

Prep time: 10 minutes • Cook time: 20 minutes • Serves: 6 guys or 8 regular people

1 (16-oz.) pkg. macaroni or other shaped pasta	2 TB. chopped garlic
1 lb. lean ground beef	1 (14.5-oz.) can tomato sauce
1 medium onion (pool-ball size), peeled and chopped into ½-inch pieces	Double dash hot pepper sauce (optional)
2 large green peppers, stems and seeds removed and chopped into ½-inch pieces	Salt and ground black pepper
	Grated Parmesan cheese

Cook pasta. While pasta is cooking, cook ground beef in a large skillet along with onion, green peppers, and garlic until beef is cooked, about 7 minutes. Pour off fat. Add tomato sauce and hot pepper sauce (if using) and cook, stirring, for another 2 minutes.

When pasta is done, drain water and return pasta to the pot. Scrape ground beef–tomato mixture into the pot on top of pasta and stir to mix. Serve with a big spoon, seasoning to taste with salt and pepper and topping with Parmesan cheese. Stick the rest in a big, covered container in the fridge.

Parmesan-Herb Pasta

Prep time: 5 minutes • Cook time: 15 minutes • Serves: 6 guys or 8 regular people

1 lb. spaghetti	2 TB. Italian seasoning
½ cup olive oil	¾ cup shredded Parmesan cheese
2 TB. chopped garlic	Salt and ground black pepper

Cook spaghetti. While spaghetti is cooking, heat oil in a small saucepan or skillet over medium heat. Add garlic and Italian seasoning and cook, stirring, for 3 minutes. Turn off heat under the saucepan. When spaghetti is done, drain and return to cooking pot. Pour oil, garlic, and herbs over pasta and toss to coat. Distribute to serving plates; top with a generous layer of Parmesan cheese and season with salt and pepper.

Lasagna

Prep time: 15 minutes • Cook time: 55 minutes • Serves: 6 guys or 8 regular people

1 lb. lasagna noodles

3 TB. olive oil

2 medium onions (pool-ball size), peeled and chopped into ½-inch pieces

1 lb. bulk sweet Italian sausage meat or link sausage cut into ½-inch pieces

1 tsp. salt

2 tsp. Italian seasoning

½ tsp. crushed red pepper

2 (14.5-oz.) cans tomato sauce

1 (2-lb.) tub ricotta cheese, part skim

2 (8-oz.) pkg. shredded part-skim mozzarella

½ cup shredded Parmesan cheese

Cook lasagna noodles until *al dente*. Drain and run some cold water over them so they don't get any softer.

Heat olive oil in a large skillet over medium heat and cook onions, sausage, salt, Italian seasoning, and red pepper, stirring, for about 8 minutes, until sausage meat is cooked through. Drain fat.

Now, let's make layers. Start with a large casserole or baking dish and layer:

♦ Enough tomato sauce to cover the bottom of the dish

♦ A single layer of lasagna noodles to cover sauce

♦ ½ ricotta (spread it with the back of a big spoon)

♦ ½ cooked sausage-onion mixture

♦ ½ shredded mozzarella

♦ ½ tomato sauce

Repeat, starting with lasagna noodles and reserving ½ cup mozzarella to put on top. Top with Parmesan cheese and remaining mozzarella.

Slide lasagna into the oven and bake for 45 minutes to 1 hour or until cheese has melted and top is nice and bubbly. Take it out of the oven and set it on a heatproof surface to cool for 10 minutes. Cut with a sharp knife and serve with a spatula.

Lasagna makes some of the best leftovers ever.

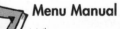

Menu Manual

When pasta is **al dente,** which is Italian for "against the teeth," it is neither soft nor hard, but just slightly firm against the teeth. This, according to many pasta aficionados, is the perfect way to cook pasta.

Outside-the-Box Mac and Cheese

Prep time: 5 minutes • Cook time: 10 minutes • Serves: 4 guys or 6 regular people

1 (14.5-oz.) pkg. macaroni and cheese mix

2 (10-oz.) cans chunk water-packed white chicken meat, drained

1 (14.5-oz.) can diced tomatoes, drained

1 TB. Worcestershire sauce

Dash hot pepper sauce

1 cup shredded mozzarella, cheddar, or Monterey Jack cheese

Food Fumble

You can easily heat pasta dishes in the microwave, just don't overdo it or you'll reinvent tough leather shoelaces. Heat leftover plain pasta by submerging it for a minute in boiling water or even by heating it in a skillet with olive oil.

Prepare mac and cheese according to the package directions. Pour completed macaroni in a microwave-safe baking dish and stir in chicken, tomatoes, Worcestershire sauce, and hot pepper sauce. Sprinkle shredded cheese over the top and heat in the microwave for 4 minutes or until cheese on top melts. Serve, scooping helpings with a big spoon.

Variations: Skillet-cooked ground chicken, turkey, pork, or beef can be used in place of the canned chicken.

Rice

Much of the world survives on rice dishes of various kinds. And as with pasta, there are great ease-of-prep and flexibility reasons.

Salsa, Chicken, and Rice

Prep time: 5 minutes • Cook time: 20 minutes • Serves: 4 guys or 6 regular people

2 cups uncooked long-grain white rice

3 TB. olive oil

2 medium onions (pool-ball size), peeled and chopped into ½-inch pieces

1 (15-oz.) can chunk water-packed white chicken meat, drained

1 (16-oz.) jar chunky medium salsa (or your favorite)

2 (2.25-oz.) cans sliced black olives, drained

½ (16-oz.) tub (1 cup) sour cream

Salt and ground black pepper

Cook rice. While rice is cooking, heat oil in a large skillet over medium heat and cook onion for 5 minutes. Mix in chicken, salsa, and olives and heat through. When rice is done, add chicken mixture to rice and mix thoroughly. Distribute to serving plates, topping each serving with 1 spoonful sour cream. Season to taste with salt and pepper.

Variation: Brown rice is a delicious substitute for the white rice. It has more flavor and is better for you, but it does take longer to cook.

Food Fumble

When it comes to leftovers in the fridge, use a FIFO (first in, first out) approach. Finish what you put in 3 days ago (first in) before you get to the dish you made last night. That way, you avoid refrigerator compost experiments.

Ellen Brown, illustrious technical editor for this book, has a guideline that's worth a grin: "Leftovers are like house guests. Get rid of them after four days."

Rice with Mushrooms and Bacon

Prep time: 5 minutes • Cook time: 20 minutes • Serves: 4 guys or 6 regular people

2 cups uncooked white rice

8 strips bacon

1 medium onion (pool-ball size), peeled and chopped into ½-inch pieces

1 (8-oz.) pkg. sliced white mushrooms

¼ tsp. hot pepper sauce

1 (8-oz.) pkg. shredded mozzarella cheese

Salt and ground black pepper

Cook rice. While rice is cooking, fry bacon in a large skillet over medium heat, about 4 minutes per side or until crisp. Remove bacon to a plate covered with paper towels. Pour off most of bacon fat, leaving 1 or 2 tablespoons to cover the bottom of the skillet. Cook onion in the skillet for 5 minutes. Add sliced mushrooms and hot sauce and cook, stirring, for 4 minutes. Mix mushroom-onion mixture and mozzarella into rice and distribute to serving plates. Crumble bacon on top of each serving and season to taste with salt and pepper.

Chicken, Tomato, and Rice

Prep time: 2 minutes • Cook time: 45 minutes • Serves: 4 guys or 6 regular people

3 TB. olive oil

1 medium onion (pool-ball size), peeled and chopped into ½-inch pieces

1 TB. Italian seasoning

1 (15-oz.) can water-packed chunk white chicken meat, drained

1 cup pasta sauce

4 cups hot cooked rice

Salt and ground black pepper

⅓ cup shredded Parmesan cheese

Heat oil in a large skillet over medium heat and cook onion and Italian seasoning, stirring, for 5 minutes. Add chicken, cook for 2 minutes; then add pasta sauce and cook for 3 minutes more. Finally, stir in rice and heat through, about 2 minutes.

Season with salt and pepper and sprinkle with Parmesan cheese.

Meats

In this section, you'll find a shortlist of meat dishes that will be delicious tonight—and be a life-saver when you have no time to cook dinner tomorrow.

Chili-Baked Chicken

Prep time: 5 minutes   •   Cook time: 45 minutes   •   Serves: 4 guys or 6 regular people

1 egg

2 TB. olive oil

1 cup breadcrumbs

1 TB. chili powder

4 chicken leg quarters (about 3 lb.) or other chicken parts

Preheat the oven to 375°F. Crack egg in a bowl and mix in olive oil with a fork. Place breadcrumbs on a plate next to the bowl and mix in chili powder. Set a baking tray next to the plate with breadcrumbs. Take each piece of chicken, turn it in egg so all sides are coated, roll it in breadcrumbs, and set it on the baking tray. Slide the tray into the oven and cook for 45 minutes or until chicken is cooked through and the juices run clear.

Roast Turkey

Prep time: 10 minutes   •   Cook time: 2½ to 3 hours   •   Serves: 8 guys or 14 regular people (plus leftovers)

1 (10- to 13-lb.) hen turkey

½ cup olive oil

2 TB. chopped garlic

2 TB. Italian seasoning

Salt and ground black pepper

Preheat the oven to 325°F. Rinse turkey under cold running water and pat it dry with paper towels. In a bowl, mix olive oil and garlic. Place turkey in a large roasting pan without the grill or a large casserole dish. Drizzle turkey inside and out with garlic olive oil. Then sprinkle turkey inside and out with Italian seasoning, salt, and pepper. Cook for 2½ to 3 hours. Spoon juices over the top of the turkey every 20 or 30 minutes (this is called *basting*). If there are no juices at first, use a little more olive oil. Turkey is done when an instant-read meat thermometer registers 180°F when inserted into the thickest part of the thigh and the juices run clear when you do a test cut in the thickest parts.

Cover turkey lightly with aluminum foil and cool turkey for 15 minutes, then slice. Serve with cooked vegetables alongside or simply bread and salad.

Turkey Gravy

Prep time: 5 minutes • Cook time: 5 minutes • Serves: 6 guys or 8 regular people

Pan *drippings*

1 TB. soy sauce

¼ cup all-purpose flour

1 (15-oz.) can low-salt chicken broth

Salt and ground black pepper

Menu Manual

Drippings are the juices and fat that flow from meat—turkey in this case—as it cooks. Pan drippings offer a flavorful base for gravy.

Scrape drippings from your roasting pan into a small saucepan over medium heat and stir in soy sauce. Slowly stir in flour and cook, stirring, for 5 minutes and then slowly stir in chicken broth. Season to taste with pepper and, if necessary, salt.

Spoon gravy over slices of turkey on serving plates for a savory, creamy treat.

Beer, Beef, and BBQ Casserole

Prep time: 10 minutes • Cook time: 45 minutes • Serves: 6 guys or 8 regular people

3 TB. olive oil

1 medium onion (pool-ball size), peeled and chopped into ½-inch pieces

1 TB. Italian seasoning

2 lb. sirloin tips, cut into ½-inch chunks

½ (12-oz.) can beer (What you do with the other half is up to you ...)

½ cup barbecue sauce

2 TB. Worcestershire sauce

1 (14.5-oz.) can diced tomatoes, drained

1 (8-oz.) pkg. sliced white mushrooms

½ cup Italian-style breadcrumbs

½ cup shredded cheddar cheese

Preheat the oven to 400°F. Heat oil in a large oven-safe skillet over medium heat and cook onion and Italian seasoning, stirring, for 5 minutes. Add sirloin tips and cook for 6 minutes, stirring, or until steak is cooked. Stir in beer, barbecue sauce, Worcestershire sauce, diced tomatoes, and mushrooms. Sprinkle breadcrumbs and cheese over the top and slide the skillet into the oven for 25 minutes or until casserole is bubbling. Serve in bowls. Crusty warm bread alongside is a natural.

Magic Teriyaki Stir-Fry

Prep time: 2 minutes • Cook time: 10 minutes • Serves: 2 guys or 3 regular people

3 TB. olive oil

1 medium onion (pool-ball size), peeled and chopped into ½-inch pieces

1 (9-oz.) box frozen snow peas or sugar snap peas, thawed, or 2 cups fresh

1 cup cooked steak, cut into ¼-inch strips

3 TB. teriyaki sauce

4 cups hot cooked rice

Heat oil in a wok or large skillet over medium heat and cook onion, stirring, for 3 minutes. Add snow peas and cook for 4 minutes. Add cooked steak pieces and heat for 3 minutes or until heated through. Add teriyaki sauce and toss to coat.

Distribute rice to serving plates and top with teriyaki mixture.

Variation: Leftover steak goes beautifully in this dish, but you can also use raw beef. Add it when you're cooking the onion. To continue the turkey theme in this section, use leftover cooked turkey instead of steak.

 End Run

The most remarkable thing about my mother is that for thirty years she served the family nothing but leftovers. The original meal has never been found.

—Calvin Trillin, food writer (and guy)

Chicken and Spinach Casserole

Prep time: 2 minutes • Cook time: 45 minutes • Serves: 6 guys or 8 regular people

1 (16-oz.) pkg. egg noodles

1 (10.75-oz.) can condensed cream of mushroom soup

1 (10-oz.) can water-packed chunk white chicken, drained

1 (10-oz.) pkg. frozen spinach, thawed and drained

1 (15-oz.) can corn kernels, drained

1 cup milk

½ cup light sour cream

Double dash hot pepper sauce

1 (8-oz.) pkg. shredded cheddar cheese

End Run

Have a cat or dog? They will love that chicken water you drain from the can.

Preheat the oven to 350°F. Prepare noodles according to package directions, drain, and return to the pasta pot. Add soup (don't use any extra water), chicken, spinach, corn, milk, sour cream, and hot pepper sauce to pasta and stir to mix. Pour mixture into a large baking dish, spread cheese over top, and bake for 30 minutes or until casserole begins to bubble and cheese is melted.

The Least You Need to Know

◆ Make dinner once with extra ingredients, and the effort pays dividends of instant, heat-and-serve meals for days afterward.

◆ Leftovers often taste better the second time around when the flavors have had time to mix.

◆ Make extra pasta or rice when you cook and give your next meal a leftover jump-start.

◆ Leftovers are easy to prepare and require little or no cleanup.

Chapter 13

Food Your Kids Will Eat

In This Chapter

- ◆ Tricks to get kids to eat—and love—their dinner
- ◆ A few healthful ingredients that can work wonders
- ◆ Fast kid favorites
- ◆ Kid-approved dinner-table classics Dad will love, too

Finding recipes that most kids will like—and that parents can agree with—is something like the quest for the Holy Grail. All kids will like ice cream for dinner, I suppose, but even a guy knows that that's not a balanced meal.

Anyone who tries to get his kids to eat a balanced meal knows how hard it can be. Every kid is different, but most have picky preferences Dad must deal with, either by accommodating or overriding.

These recipes will show just how far some of us are willing to go to get the kids to eat. The little secret is that the adults often end up having more fun than the kids …

Fast but Good

In this section, we shamelessly serve up fast favorites, regardless of whether they're easy (homemade), or *super easy* (based on canned foods). Either way, these are all taste treats.

Peanut Butter Piggies

Prep time: 5 minutes • Cook time: 6 minutes • Serves: 4 guys or 6 kids, can easily be doubled

8 strips bacon

8 hot dog rolls or 8 pieces of bread

Peanut butter

Food Fumble

When toasting hot dog rolls or other white bread products, keep a close eye on them to prevent burning. Most have sugar in the mix, which browns very quickly. Some stores are starting to sell whole-wheat hot dog and hamburger buns, which provide a chance to sneak healthful food into kid diets.

Cook bacon in a skillet for 3 to 4 minutes on a side or until crisp. When crisp, remove to paper towels. Toast hot dog rolls (if you have a wide-slot toaster or in a toaster oven). If you're using hot dog rolls, spread peanut butter inside roll, insert a piece of bacon, and serve. If you're using bread, spread peanut butter on one slice, lay two pieces of cooked bacon on peanut butter, and cover with other slice.

Rover in a Down Jacket

Prep time: 5 minutes • Cook time: 12 minutes • Serves: 4 guys or 6 regular people as a side dish

1 (16-oz.) pkg. buttermilk biscuit dough

8 cooked hot dogs (most come cooked)

Ketchup

Mustard

Preheat the oven to 375°F. Open biscuit dough package and, one by one, stretch biscuits to about double their size. Wrap 1 stretched biscuit around 1 hot dog and squeeze dough on the other side so it encases dog, but with a little bit of dog sticking out each end. Set on a baking tray. Bake for 12 minutes or until biscuit dough is crisp and golden on the outside.

Serve with ketchup and, if your kids tolerate it, mustard.

Presto Pizza

Prep time: 5 minutes   •   Cook time: 12 minutes   •   Serves: 4 guys or 6 regular people as a side dish

1 (16-oz.) pkg. buttermilk biscuit dough

1 cup pasta sauce, tomato sauce, or pizza sauce

1 (8-oz.) pkg. shredded mozzarella or other cheese

Preheat the oven to 375°F. Open biscuit dough package and, one by one, stretch biscuits to at least twice their size. Lay stretched dough on a baking tray (or a couple trays), spread 1 spoonful sauce on dough, and sprinkle with shredded cheese. Bake for 12 minutes or until cheese is melted and dough is crisp and golden on the outside.

"Murder" Burgers

Prep time: 5 minutes   •   Cook time: 10 minutes   •   Serves: 4 kids, can easily be doubled

8 strips bacon

1 lb. lean ground beef, made into 4 large hamburgers

4 thick slices cheddar cheese

4 hamburger buns

Lettuce and tomato slices (optional)

Ketchup

Mayonnaise

Cook bacon and burgers in a large skillet over medium heat, about 4 minutes per side. About 2 minutes after you flip burgers, remove crisp bacon to paper towels and top burgers with cheddar cheese. Slide hamburger buns into the toaster or under the broiler. When burgers are done, arrange buns on plates and distribute burgers.

Top each with 2 pieces bacon, lettuce, and slices of tomato (if using) and serve with ketchup and mayonnaise.

Food Fumble

Benson's, a tiny lunch place on Route 20 in Wayland, Massachusetts, is a popular stop for everyone from the dentist across the street to truckers on the way through town. Benson's bacon cheeseburger is legendary, although you don't want to eat too many of them (keep the name in mind).

TuniOs

Prep time: 4 minutes   •   Cook time: 4 minutes   •   Serves: 2 kids (can be doubled)

1 (15-oz.) can SpaghettiOs

1 (6-oz.) can water-packed chunk white tuna, drained

1 cup shredded part-skim mozzarella cheese

Mix SpaghettiOs and tuna in a small microwave-safe baking dish. Spread shredded mozzarella over the top and microwave for 4 minutes or until cheese begins to melt.

 End Run

Canned pasta products, such as SpaghettiOs, taste different from freshly cooked pasta. Some people love 'em, others don't. Because they're ready to go, however, they enable you to turn out an incredibly quick meal.

Gimmick Pizza

Prep time: 5 minutes   •   Cook time: 10 minutes   •   Serves: 4 kids

1 (23- to 24-oz.) store-bought cheese pizza

¼ lb. sliced pepperoni

Other edible decorations, such as sliced ham, thinly sliced onion, olives, mushrooms, or whatever your kids will eat

Decorate pizza with fun in mind. The starting point might be a smiley face (pepperoni eyes, sliced onion eyebrows). You could make pizzas vampires (a slice of pepperoni cut in half makes good sharp fangs), a monster (sliced onion ears), and just about any shape you want using a slice of ham etched on a cutting board (a car, a rocket, etc.).

Variation: Prepare using the Instant Pizza recipe in Chapter 11 as a base.

Loony Tuna

Prep time: 10 minutes • Cooking time: 6 minutes • Serves: 4 kids (one melt each, double recipe for more)

1 (6-oz.) can water-packed chunk white tuna, drained

¼ cup mayonnaise

½ cup chopped celery

Butter or margarine

8 slices white or whole-wheat bread

4 slices American cheese (or your favorite)

4 slices black olive

In a bowl, mix tuna, mayo, and celery. Butter 1 side of each piece of bread. Heat a large skillet over medium heat. Set 1 piece bread, butter side down, in skillet. Scoop an equal amount of tuna mixture on each piece in the skillet, spreading with the spoon (careful not to burn yourself). Top with 1 piece cheese and 1 piece bread, this time butter side up. Cook for 3 minutes per side or until cheese is melted and the outside of the sandwiches are browned and crisp.

Remove cooked sandwich and cut in half diagonally. Set one triangle in the center of a plate. Cut the other half in half again, so you have two smaller triangles. One triangle is the "tail" (set it right-angle-in against the long end of the big half); the other triangle is a "fin" (set it against the bottom of the big half). Place an olive-slice eye on the big half on the side away from the tail and serve.

Grilled Cheese

Prep time: 6 minutes • Cooking time: 6 minutes • Serves: 4 kids (one each, double recipe for more)

Butter or margarine

8 slices white or whole-wheat bread

4 slices cheddar cheese (or your favorite)

Butter 1 side of each piece of bread. Heat a large skillet over medium heat. Set 1 piece bread, butter side down, in skillet, top with 1 piece cheese and 1 piece bread, this time butter side up. Cook for 3 minutes per side or until cheese is melted and the outsides of the sandwiches are browned and crisp.

Variation: Grilled cheese sandwiches are a natural vehicle for tasty fillings, from cooked chicken and crisp bacon to tuna (see Loony Tuna; recipe follows). Sliced mushrooms are also great (although probably not for kids).

End Run

Health experts recommend whole-wheat bread, but sometimes kids object. Grilled cheese sandwiches, however, are a good place to sneak in whole wheat.

Tomato soup is a time-honored classic combo with grilled cheese. Other soups work well, too, making this meal the kid comfort-food antidote for any cold weather.

Classic Kid Favorites

These recipes bring uncomplicated flavors and probably warm memories. They also are an invitation to play with your food—in a good way.

Monster Meat Loaf

Prep and cook time: About 1 hour • Serves: 2 to 4 kids (plus plenty of leftovers for later)

Meat Loaf (recipe in Chapter 3), carefully loosened from its pan and planted on a platter

2 green olives (The kind stuffed with pimiento peppers are perfect.)

8 potato sticks

1 large carrot, scraped and sliced on the diagonal, resulting in oval ⅛-inch slices about 1 inch wide and 2 inches long

Cut a 2-inch slice off one end of meat loaf (do this really carefully to avoid having it break apart). Slice this piece on the diagonal, so you have two triangular pieces. Put one triangle on each end of meat loaf, wide side against the loaf, so the slice slopes to the ground on each end. On one end (the "front"), use toothpicks to fix 2 olives (these are eyes). On the other end (the "tail"), arrange potato sticks as spikes at the end of the tail. Stick carrot slices, long end in, from front to back to create stegosaurus ridges.

Invite your carnivores to the table. A salad can be "palm trees."

Variation: You can use toothpicks in place of potato sticks, but this is only appropriate if your kids are old enough to know not to eat the toothpicks.

End Run

My kids were suspicious of this big lump with spikes down the middle until I told them it was really a stegosaurus. Then they were both meat-eating dinosaurs. They had thirds, with extra dino blood, uh, ketchup. I'm not sure who has more fun, the kids or me. All right, so our dinner table is a strange place ...

Ultimate Steak Fries

Prep time: 10 minutes • Cook time: 20 minutes • Serves: 4 kids (plus leftovers as a side dish)

5 large Yukon Gold or Russet Burbank potatoes, scrubbed and sliced lengthwise into wedges or spears about ½ inch thick

3 TB. canola oil

Salt

Ketchup

Menu Manual

Most so-called "french fries" are deep-fried in oil. These steak fries are baked, a process that uses a lot less oil and, therefore, a lot less fat.

Preheat the oven to 400°F. Place potato wedges in a large bowl and pour canola oil over them. Stir with a big spoon to coat and sprinkle with salt. Arrange wedges on a baking tray, skin side down where possible, in a single layer with the pieces not touching each other. Bake for 20 minutes or until fries are crisp and golden on the outside and soft on the inside.

Serve with additional salt, if desired, and ketchup.

Macaroni and Cheese with a Secret

Prep time: 5 minutes • Cook time: 10 minutes • Serves: 4 kids (plus leftovers)

1 (14.5-oz.) pkg. macaroni and cheese mix

1 lb. sweet Italian sausage links

End Run

Get your kids to "help" you cook. When they watch dinner in progress and see something they helped make, they're a lot more likely to eat it.

Prepare mac and cheese according to package directions. Meanwhile, cook sausage in a large skillet over medium heat for 8 minutes or until done and no pink remains. Cut sausage into ½-inch chunks in the skillet. With a slotted spoon to leave the melted fat in the skillet, scoop sausage into macaroni and mix. Serve, scooping helpings with a big spoon.

Chicken Tortellini Soup

Prep time: 10 minutes • Cook time: 20 minutes • Serves: 4 kids (plus leftovers as a side dish)

2 TB. olive oil

1 medium onion (pool-ball size), peeled and chopped into ¼-inch pieces

2 large carrots, scraped, ends removed, cut into ¼-inch pieces

2 stalks celery, ends removed, cut into ¼-inch pieces

3 (15-oz.) cans chicken broth

2 tsp. Italian seasoning

½ lb. dry tortellini

1 (15-oz.) can water-packed chunk white chicken meat, drained

Salt and ground black pepper

Heat oil in a large saucepan over medium heat and cook onion, carrots, and celery, stirring, for 5 minutes. Add chicken broth and Italian seasoning and bring soup to a boil. Add tortellini and cook for 15 minutes or until pasta is done to your liking. Add chicken meat and season to taste with salt and pepper. Heat for 2 minutes and serve soup in bowls.

And Don't Forget ...

Guys often like what kids like (and vice versa), so many of the recipes in other parts of this book are also likely to be kid-friendly (omit the spicy recipes). A few kid candidates include the following:

- Can-Do Beef Stew, Pork Chops and Spicy Applesauce Cream, and Roast Chicken Dinner (recipes in Chapter 3)
- Pasta with Italian Chicken Pasta Sauce, Homemade Tomato Sauce, Chicken Marsala Pasta, and Spaghetti with Meatballs (recipes in Chapter 4)
- Marinated Ham Steaks, Barbecued Chicken, Perfect Steak, and Grilled Southwest Salmon (recipes in Chapter 5)
- Skillet Ham and Egg Dinner and Beergoggle Fried Fish (recipes in Chapter 6)
- Scalloped Potatoes with Ham, Tuna on the Waves, Beak in a Blanket, and Roast Beef (recipes in Chapter 7)
- Broiled Green Beans and Succotash (recipes in Chapter 9)
- Skillet Ground Beef Dinner (recipe in Chapter 11)

End Run

For kid favorites, I could list every dessert in Chapter 10, but you already know that they will eat those. The challenge is to get them to eat the real meal first.

♦ Chili-Baked Chicken, American Chop Suey, and Roast Turkey (recipe in Chapter 12)

♦ "Breakfast for Dinner" (Recipes in Chapter 20; I don't know what the psychology is here, but kids seem to consider a breakfast dish at dinnertime a real treat.)

♦ And more!

The Least You Need to Know

♦ Foods kids love can also be adult favorites.

♦ One key to success with kids at the dinner table is to have fun. Play a little by decorating the plate, and the kids (and you!) will look at dinner as a game (but in a good way).

♦ It's possible to work healthful ingredients into a meal and still get kid approval. (They don't have to know you used whole-wheat bread.)

♦ This chapter focuses on kid favorites, but don't forget to use many of the other kid-tested favorites in other parts of this book.

Chapter **14**

Food the Ladies Will Love ... and Hate!

In This Chapter

- ◆ Savory, creamy dishes that will appeal to both of you
- ◆ Simple recipes that could even be called elegant
- ◆ Heat up things with hot peppers and other spirited ingredients
- ◆ The first annual musical fruit festival

This chapter plays with two ends of the dinner spectrum. There are times when a guy should think about his significant other and prepare a meal that appeals to both of them. (Sort of like when a guy would really rather watch *Men in Black* one more time, but to be considerate he goes and gets *On Golden Pond*. ... *Well, maybe not that bad.*)

Then there are times when a guy is on his own, and he gets to bring out food that the ladies might not want to eat. That's the second part of this chapter.

Food the Ladies Will Love

A guy can win a lot of points by preparing a meal that appeals to his significant other. Those warm feelings can also help you get out of the doghouse and back into the house (by way of the stove top).

Lemon-Sautéed Chicken

Prep time: 5 minutes • Cook time: 8 minutes • Serves: 1 guy and 1 significant other

3 TB. olive oil

1 TB. chopped garlic

½ tsp. dried rosemary

1 lb. boneless, skinless chicken breasts, separated into serving-size pieces (about 4 by 2 inches), rinsed and patted dry on paper towels

2 TB. lemon juice

Salt and ground black pepper

Heat oil in a large skillet over medium heat and cook garlic and rosemary for 1 minute, stirring. Add chicken breast pieces in a single layer and cook for 4 minutes per side or until fully cooked, no longer pink, and the juices run clear. Remove chicken to serving plates, squeeze lemon juice into the skillet, and cook, stirring, for 30 seconds. Drizzle skillet juice over chicken on the plates and serve, seasoning to taste with salt and pepper.

Variation: Use lime juice—but less, ¼ lime—in place of lemon juice.

 Menu Manual

Kitchen stores and catalogs sell a nifty device usually called a *lime squeezer.* It looks sort of like a garlic press except it's big enough to squeeze half a lemon or lime. This is a fun thing to have for recipes like Lemon-Sautéed Chicken, but it's essential for making a true margarita with fresh-squeezed lime juice—like they make in Acapulco.

Frozen Margarita

Prep time: 10 minutes • Serves: 2 adults 2 margaritas each

2 TB. kosher salt

6 limes, cut in half

4 oz. tequila

½ cup sugar

Ice

Pour salt on a plate, rub the rims of 2 glasses with the cut side of 1 lime, and dip the glass into salt so it rims the glass.

Squeeze lime juice into a blender, add tequila and sugar, and add a handful ice. Process until mixture reaches a slushy consistency. To thicken, add more ice. Pour into salt-rimmed glasses and serve.

Variation: These can be made "virgin" (without alcohol).

Shrimp and Prosciutto Soup

Prep time: 4 minutes • Cook time: 5 minutes • Serves: 4 plus leftovers

2 TB. olive oil

1 large onion (baseball size), peeled and chopped into ½-inch pieces

1 TB. chopped garlic

4 (15-oz.) cans chicken broth

2 large, red-skinned potatoes, scrubbed and cut into ½-inch cubes

1 tsp. salt

¼ tsp. ground black pepper

1 tsp. dried oregano

½ tsp. crushed red pepper (optional)

1 (10-oz.) pkg. frozen spinach, thawed with the water squeezed out

1 (14.5-oz.) can diced tomatoes with juice

1 (16-oz.) pkg. frozen cooked shrimp, peeled with tail off (51 to 70 count)

½ cup diced prosciutto

2 TB. fresh-squeezed lemon juice

Heat oil in a saucepan or large skillet over medium heat. Cook onion for 6 minutes, stirring. Add garlic and cook for 2 additional minutes. Add chicken broth and cubed potatoes and bring to a boil. Reduce heat, stir in salt, black pepper, oregano, and red pepper (if using), and simmer for 10 minutes. Stir in spinach, tomatoes, shrimp, and prosciutto. Return to a simmer and cook until potatoes are soft. Turn off heat, stir in lemon juice, and serve, seasoning if desired with additional salt and pepper.

Cream Sole

Prep time: 5 minutes • Cook time: 10 minutes • Serves: 1 guy and 1 significant other

1 lb. white fish fillets such as sole, cod, or haddock

Pinch salt

Pinch ground black pepper

2 TB. fresh-squeezed lemon juice

¼ cup heavy or whipping cream

2 TB. grated Parmesan cheese

End Run

You have to make a choice when it comes to lemon juice: Use the bottled stuff or squeeze it yourself. For flavor, there's just no comparison—go for the fresh. Keep a couple lemons in the fridge, and squeezing fresh juice will be as easy as unscrewing a bottle.

Preheat the oven to 350°F. Thoroughly rinse fillets in cold water, pat dry, and put into a greased baking dish. Sprinkle with salt and pepper and drizzle with lemon juice. Top fillets with whipping cream (spread over the whole piece) and Parmesan cheese. Bake for 10 to 15 minutes, depending on thickness, or until fish is cooked and opaque in the center. Divide between serving plates with a spatula (careful, the fish will want to break apart).

Serve with fresh bread and a salad and you'll be out of the doghouse.

Shrimp Scampi

Prep time: 10 minutes • Cook time: 6 minutes • Serves: 1 guy and 1 significant other, plus leftovers to toss with pasta tomorrow

1 lb. fresh raw shrimp (medium size, or 31 to 35 count), peeled and deveined

1 TB. chopped garlic

¼ cup olive oil

¼ cup chopped fresh parsley

Salt and ground black pepper

Kebab skewers (available in grocery stores), soaked in water to cover for 15 minutes

Lemon wedges

Preheat the grill. Put shrimp in a bowl. In a separate bowl or cup, mix garlic, olive oil, and parsley. Pour olive oil mixture over shrimp and stir to coat. Season with a few shakes each of salt and pepper and thread shrimp onto bamboo skewers, maybe 5 to a skewer. Grill for 3 minutes per side and serve with lemon wedges.

Sesame Broccoli

Prep time: 4 minutes　•　Cook time: 5 minutes　•　Serves: 1 guy and 1 significant other

½ (10-oz.) head broccoli, broken into florets about 1 inch across, stems discarded

1 TB. fresh-squeezed lemon juice

2 TB. olive oil

2 tsp. fresh-grated *ginger* or ½ tsp. powdered ginger

Sesame seeds

Salt

Using a stove top steamer or a saucepan with a lid, heat ½ inch water to boiling, add broccoli florets, and steam for 4 minutes. Scoop broccoli into a bowl. Mix lemon juice, olive oil, and ginger in a small dish and pour over broccoli. Toss to coat, sprinkle with sesame seeds, and serve, seasoning to taste with salt.

Variation: Sesame Broccoli can be prepared in the microwave. Place broccoli and water in a microwave-safe bowl with a lid and microwave for 3 minutes or until crisp-tender. Remove and prepare per conventional directions.

Menu Manual

Available in fresh root or powdered form, **ginger** adds a pungent, sweet, and spicy quality to a dish. It is a very popular element of many Asian and Indian dishes.

Originally from Asia, **sesame seeds** are shaped like watermelon seeds but are much smaller (about ⅕ the size). The most common form in our stores is a sort of tan color. The nutty flavor and crunchy texture are popular in Asian dishes and baked goods.

Skillet Chicken and Apples

Prep time: 10 minutes   •   Cook time: 10 to 15 minutes   •   Serves: 1 guy and 1 significant other, with leftovers

3 TB. olive oil

1 medium onion (pool-ball size), peeled and chopped into ½-inch pieces

2 tsp. chopped garlic

1 lb. boneless, skinless chicken breast, cut into ½-inch pieces, rinsed and patted dry on paper towels

½ tsp. ground ginger

1 tsp. Italian seasoning

1 (10-oz.) pkg. frozen spinach, thawed with water squeezed out of it

¼ cup raisins

1 Granny Smith apple, cored and cut into ½-inch pieces

Salt and ground black pepper

End Run

I adapted this unusual, tasty dish from my book, *The Complete Idiot's Guide to 20-Minute Meals* at the suggestion of several readers who thought this might be just the thing for the category of "foods the ladies will love."

In a large skillet, heat oil, then cook onion and garlic for 5 minutes. Add chicken pieces, ginger, and Italian seasoning and cook, stirring and turning the pieces, for 6 to 8 minutes or until chicken is cooked through, no longer pink, and the juices run clear. Add spinach, raisins, and apple and cook for 3 to 4 minutes until greens are wilted.

Serve immediately with salt and pepper. Verdict from wife and houseguests will be, "Delicious." Aw, shucks.

Variation: Fresh kale, cabbage, chard, or fresh spinach are great substitutes for spinach.

Crisp Haddock

Prep time: 8 minutes • Cook time: 8 minutes • Serves: 1 guy and 1 significant other

1 lb. haddock or other white fish fillets

⅓ cup yellow or white cornmeal

⅓ cup whole-wheat flour

1 tsp. kosher salt

1 tsp. Italian seasoning

½ cup milk

¼ cup olive oil

Lemon wedges

Rinse fillets in cold water and pat dry with paper towels. Mix cornmeal, flour, salt, and Italian seasoning in a bowl and dump the mixture onto a plate. Pour milk in the bowl you just used to mix flour mixture (this saves cleaning multiple bowls). Dip fillets in milk, then in flour mixture, turning to coat both sides. Place coated fillets on a sheet of plastic wrap. Heat oil in a large skillet over medium heat. Set fillets in the skillet and cook for about 3 minutes per side or until cooked through, turning them gently with a slotted spatula. Move sizzling, crispy fish to serving plates and serve immediately with lemon wedges.

End Run

One of the stereotypes about men and women is that women are interested in low-fat foods and guys aren't. Of course, this isn't true (at least not universally), but there is some truth to the fact that a lot of guys are suspicious of anything that makes a low-fat or "healthful" claim. We think *the stuff must taste like cardboard*. But nothing is farther from the truth. Healthful food relies on fresh texture, flavor, and seasoning for its appeal, and how can we object to that? Keep an eye on health, and you'll live long enough to see the fiftieth anniversary of *The Matrix*. Now that's something that can give a guy a purpose.

Chicken with Pepper Cream

It's easy to fall in love with this dish. Hmm. It's easy, fast, and has a spicy-creamy sauce. I wonder what the appeal is?

Prep time: 8 minutes • Cook time: 10 minutes • Serves: 1 guy and 1 significant other

1 lb. boneless, skinless chicken breasts, separated into serving-size pieces (about 4 by 2 inches), rinsed and patted dry on paper towels

Salt and ground black pepper

3 TB. olive oil

½ (15-oz.) can (about 1 cup) chicken broth

1 tsp. paprika

⅔ cup low-fat sour cream

Menu Manual

To **reduce** is to heat a broth or sauce to remove some of the water content, resulting in more concentrated flavor and color.

Sprinkle chicken with salt and pepper. Heat oil in a large skillet over medium heat and cook chicken for 4 minutes per side or until cooked, no longer pink, and juices run clear. Remove to serving plates (keep in the oven on warm or cover with foil so they stay warm), turn up the heat to high, and add broth, paprika, salt, and pepper (to taste). Cook, stirring, for 5 minutes or until broth *reduces* by about half.

Turn off the heat, stir in sour cream, and spoon this savory sauce over chicken breasts on the serving plates.

Food the Ladies Will Hate

Guys dream about these foods—perfect for when you have the house to yourself and no one will criticize the indoor air quality.

Pasta Tossed with Hot Peppers and Oil

Prep time: 5 minutes • Cook time: 15 minutes • Serves: 4 guys or 6 regular people, plus leftovers

1 lb. spaghetti or your favorite pasta

¼ cup olive oil

1 medium onion (pool-ball size), peeled and chopped into ½-inch chunks

1 TB. chopped garlic

1 tsp. crushed red pepper flakes

½ cup sour cream

Shredded Parmesan cheese

Salt and ground black pepper

Cook pasta. While water heats, catch a few minutes of *Starship Troopers*, then heat oil in a large skillet over low to medium heat and sauté onion, garlic, and red pepper flakes for 5 minutes. When pasta is done, drain it and return it to the pasta pot. Scrape oil-pepper-onion mixture on top of pasta, add sour cream, and stir to mix. Serve immediately, topping with Parmesan, salt, and pepper.

Variations: Adding green to this dish is visually appealing, and you also get credit for adding a vegetable. A handful of chopped fresh parsley, added at the end, looks and tastes great. Or you can add spinach (fresh or the frozen stuff that has been thawed and drained) during the last couple minutes of onion-cooking.

Food Fumble

You know your own tolerance for highly seasoned or gas-inducing foods. Don't harm yourself.

Onion Rings

Prep time: 5 minutes • Cook time: 15 minutes • Serves: 2 guys or 3 regular people

1 large sweet onion (such as Vidalia), peeled and sliced crosswise into ¼-inch–thick slices

1 egg

¼ cup milk

1 cup all-purpose or whole-wheat flour

½ tsp. garlic salt or regular salt

½ cup canola oil

Separate onion slices into rings. In a big bowl (a cereal bowl works great), whisk egg and milk with a whisk or a fork. In another bowl, mix flour and garlic salt. Heat oil in a medium-size skillet over high heat. Drop 1 onion ring into egg mixture, turn it in flour, and place it in the skillet. Repeat the procedure with the other rings, until you've got a single layer of rings in the skillet. Cook for about 2 minutes per side, then remove to a plate covered with paper towels while you cook the rest. You'll end up with a plate mounded with crispy onion rings (unless you eat them all in the process). Eat them while they're hot.

Food Fumble _____

A splatter screen is a good idea with onion rings. (Remember our ground rule: "Cleanup should be minimal.")

Easy Hot Pepper Pizza

Prep time: 5 minutes • Cook time: 10 minutes • Serves: 2 guys or 3 regular people
(easily doubled)

1 (14-oz.) pkg. prepared pizza crust (available in grocery stores)

Double dash hot pepper sauce

½ cup pasta or pizza sauce

1 cup shredded mozzarella cheese

1 (4.5-oz.) can chopped green chilies, drained, or sliced fresh jalapeño peppers, seeds removed

Preheat oven to 450°F. Set pizza crust on a baking tray. Add hot sauce to pasta sauce and stir. Pour sauce on crust and spread into a uniform layer with the back of a spoon. Sprinkle cheese over sauce and spread around chilies. Bake pizza for about 10 minutes or until crust is crispy and cheese is melted. Slice into wedges on a cutting board and serve.

Variation: Add other toppings along with chilies. Chopped cooked chicken and pepperoni work well, as do mushrooms and sliced black olives.

Chili Pasta

Prep time: 5 minutes • Cook time: 20 minutes • Serves: 4 guys or 6 regular people as part of a pasta and sauce meal (There will be some pasta left over.)

1 lb. uncooked penne (or your favorite pasta)

1 (26-oz.) jar plain pasta sauce

1 TB. chili powder

1 tsp. ground cumin

1 lb. cooked *chorizo* sausage (available in many grocery stores), cut into ½-inch chunks

½ cup sour cream

Cook pasta. While water is heating, pour pasta sauce in a saucepan and stir in chili powder, cumin, and cooked chorizo. Turn the heat to between low and medium and simmer sauce, stirring once in a while, while pasta cooks. Serve over pasta.

A spoonful sour cream on top completes the picture.

Variation: Use cooked hot Italian sausage in place of the chorizo or omit sausage altogether.

Menu Manual

Chorizo is a delicious spicy pork sausage, popular in Mexico. Its seasonings include (of course) chili.

A Symphony with Musical Fruit

Beans are rich, hearty, and loaded with nutrition. They come in fun varieties and colors, and they're easy to use, straight from the can. Lately they've become even more popular because of their role in "good-carb" diets. Everything is good, except the minor issue of natural gas. That's why Beano is so popular.

Baked Beans with Ham

Prep time: 10 minutes • Cook time: 6 to 8 hours on low or 3 to 4 hours on high (overnight, or enough time for a James Bond multi-movie extravaganza) • Serves: 4 guys or 6 regular people

1 (15.5-oz.) can red kidney beans, drained and rinsed

1 (15.5-oz.) can cannellini beans, drained and rinsed

1 (15.5-oz.) can small white beans, drained and rinsed

1 (¾-lb.) smoked ham steak, chopped into ½-inch pieces

1 medium onion (pool-ball size), peeled and chopped into ½-inch chunks

½ cup maple syrup

½ cup molasses

2 TB. prepared mustard

½ cup ketchup

½ cup water

Pour kidney, cannelli, and white beans into a slow cooker and stir in ham, onion, maple syrup, molasses, mustard, ketchup, and water. Turn heat to low, put on the cover, and cook for 6 to 8 hours on low or 3 to 4 hours on high. Stir in a little more water if beans seem too dry.

Variations: Use brown sugar instead of maple syrup. A meaty ham bone left over from a ham dinner is perfect in place of ham steak. Different kinds of beans (pink or even garbanzo) are great in this dish, too.

End Run

The traditional method of making baked beans calls for *dried* navy beans (rather than canned). It's easy, but be sure to allow the time. Put 1 pound navy beans in a saucepan and pour enough cold water over them to leave 3 inches over the top. Heat to boiling, reduce heat to low, and go do something else for half an hour. Come back, turn off the heat, put the lid on the beans and water, and go away again, this time for an hour and a half or until those beans are soft. (Test one by chewing on it. It doesn't have to be mushy because it will have more time to soften in the slow cooker.) Drain beans and use in the Baked Beans with Ham recipe.

Windy City Chili

Prep time: 5 minutes   •   Cook time: 20 minutes   •   Serves: 4 guys or 6 regular people

1 lb. lean ground beef

1 (16-oz.) can refried beans

1 (15-oz.) can crushed tomatoes with juice

1 (15.5-oz.) can red kidney beans, drained and rinsed

1 (15.5-oz.) can black beans, drained and rinsed

1 (15.5-oz.) can pinto beans, drained and rinsed

1 (16-oz.) jar hot salsa

3 TB. chili powder

1 TB. ground cumin

1 cup shredded Monterey Jack or other cheese

1 cup sour cream

Cook ground beef in a skillet over medium heat, stirring, until meat is cooked. Drain fat. Stir in refried beans; tomatoes; kidney, black, and pinto beans; salsa; chili powder; and the cumin. Cook, stirring, over low heat for 10 minutes or until heated through. Distribute to serving bowls, top with cheese and sour cream, and serve.

Variation: After cooking ground beef, add all ingredients to a slow cooker and cook for 6 to 8 hours on low or 3 to 4 hours on high. This takes more time than stove top cooking, but the flavors blend and become even richer.

⚍

The Least You Need to Know

- Flavor, texture, and how a dish looks—its "visual appeal"—all affect how much you'll both like a dish.
- Fresh, healthy ingredients appeal to everyone.
- Rich but highly spiced dishes are good to indulge in when you're on your own.
- Don't overdo a good thing by eating an entire batch of baked beans. I need you to live to try the recipes in the next chapter.

Chapter 15

Mexican-Inspired Dishes

In This Chapter

- ◆ Delicious, fast, and convenient south-of-the-border dishes
- ◆ The secrets of a quick in-case-of-emergency tortilla-based meal
- ◆ Tortilla chips: not just a snack!
- ◆ Your meal gets a free ride when your beans are refried (and other bad rhymes about good food)

In this chapter, we'll check out our old friends, Mr. and Mrs. (or should I say Señor and Señorita) *Quesadilla* and their cousins, the tostadas, enchiladas, tacos, and nachos. The tortilla is the common instrument for recipes in this chapter—but we'll play a lot of different tunes with it. The variety comes in large part from the universe of fillings, including the following:

- ◆ Bacon
- ◆ Bean sprouts
- ◆ Beef (cooked ground beef, steak strips, etc.)
- ◆ Cheese surprises (feta, mozzarella, and Swiss—not authentic at all, but they work great)
- ◆ Chicken
- ◆ Chili (the cooked kind)

Menu Manual

A **quesadilla** is, at its most basic, two tortillas with something in between (sort of like a grilled cheese sandwich). The "in between" is what makes all the difference. Cheese is a natural. Start with Monterey Jack or cheddar; Swiss might not be what you would use first in Mexico, but it's still delicious. You'll also use meats, vegetables, and of course, southwestern-style seasonings.

- Corn
- Garlic
- Guacamole
- Ham
- Lettuce
- Limes
- Olives
- Onions
- Refried beans
- Salsa
- Scallions
- Shrimp
- Tomatoes
- Tuna
- Turkey

And we'll also use a whole range of seasonings, including basil, chili powder, cilantro, cumin, oregano, paprika, crushed red pepper, and more.

Tortilla 101

Until I visited my brother Andrew at the University of Arizona in Tucson years ago, I had no idea how many things could be done with a tortilla. Here are just a few possibilities:

- **Soft tortillas:** These soft wheat tortillas are sold in grocery stores in 8- and 12-inch sizes (I'll call them "small" and "large," respectively). They're great for wrapping, rolling, grilling, broiling, and just about any other cooking method you can think of.

- **Taco shells:** You know these, they're crispy, usually made from corn, and conveniently pocket-shape for all that filling.

- **Chips:** You know all about these, too—they take up half the store these days. Choices include flavored (with brands such as Doritos), plain, blue corn, white corn, yellow corn, organic, and more. Name your favorite.

With these tortilla building blocks in mind, here are some recipes to get us started. Some use classic combinations of ingredients, others take some poetic (uh, culinary) license.

End Run _____

I've focused mostly on meal-type foods in this chapter. There are, of course, many appetizer-type foods that make good use of traditional Mexican seasonings (think: dip). Several of these bad boys are in the next chapter because they're traditional for The Big Game.

Chicken Quesadillas

Prep time: 5 minutes　•　Cook time: 8 minutes　•　Serves: 2 guys or 3 regular people

1 (10-oz.) can or 2 (5-oz.) cans water-packed chunk white chicken meat, drained

2 TB. dried onion flakes (optional)

½ tsp. chili powder

3 TB. olive oil

6 (8-inch) flour tortillas

1 (8-oz.) pkg. shredded Mexican-style or cheddar cheese

½ cup sour cream or light sour cream

Salsa

Mix chicken and onion flakes (if using) with chili powder in a bowl. Heat oil in a large skillet over medium heat. Place 1 tortilla in the skillet and spread a layer of cheese, then chicken meat, then another layer of cheese. Top with another tortilla. Heat for about 1 minute, then carefully flip quesadilla with a spatula and cook for another minute (just until cheese melts). Move crisp quesadilla to a serving plate and cook the next one. To serve, cut into wedges and top with a spoonful of sour cream and maybe some salsa.

Variation: Got a few more minutes and want even more flavor? Sauté 1 medium onion (cut into ½-inch pieces) in the skillet first. Scoop onion out to a plate and follow the recipe from the point of adding a tortilla (add onion along with chicken).

 End Run _____

Lower-oil options for cooking quesadillas include broiling and baking. For broiling, simply assemble your dish on a baking tray and broil for a couple minutes per side until tortillas are toasted and cheese is melted. For baking, spray your quesadilla with a bit of vegetable oil spray and bake in a preheated 450°F oven for about 4 minutes per side.

Bacon-Cheddar Quesadillas

Prep time: 5 minutes • Cook time: 8 minutes • Serves: 2 guys or 3 regular people

½ lb. bacon

3 TB. bacon fat or olive oil

6 (8-inch) flour tortillas

1 (8-oz.) pkg. shredded cheddar cheese

2 scallions, roots and dark green parts removed, rinsed, and cut into ⅛-inch pieces (optional)

½ cup sour cream or light sour cream

Cook bacon in a large skillet over medium heat until crispy. Remove bacon to a plate with paper towels and pour off most fat, leaving just enough to coat the skillet. Place 1 tortilla in the skillet and spread a layer of shredded cheese, then bacon, scallion (if using), then another layer of cheese. Top with another tortilla. Heat for about 1 minute, then carefully flip quesadilla with a spatula and cook for another minute until cheese melts. Move quesadilla to a serving plate and cook the next one. To serve, cut into wedges and top each piece with a spoonful of sour cream and a sprinkling of chopped scallions.

Food Fumble

One cooking option for your Bacon-Cheddar Quesadillas is to cook it right in the bacon fat. The result is delicious, but keep health in mind. Your doctor will be happier if you pour off that (saturated) fat and use mostly canola or olive oil instead. Enjoy saturated fat in moderation.

While we've got fat on our thoughts, try "light" sour cream instead of the high-octane full-fat stuff. The taste is pretty good. I don't like the flavor of fat-free sour cream very much, but if you do, go for it.

Quesadillas with Tuna and Sliced Black Olives

Prep time: 5 minutes • Cook time: 8 minutes • Serves: 2 guys or 3 regular people

1 (10-oz.) can or 2 (6-oz.) cans water-packed chunk white tuna, drained

1 (2.25-oz.) can sliced black olives, drained

1 celery stalk, rinsed, trimmed, and cut into thin, ⅛-inch slices

½ tsp. chili powder

3 TB. olive oil

6 (8-inch) flour tortillas

1 (8-oz.) pkg. shredded Mexican-style or cheddar cheese

½ cup sour cream or light sour cream

Salsa

Mix tuna, olives, and celery with chili powder in a bowl, mashing tuna with a spoon to break down any big chunks. Heat oil in a large skillet over medium heat. Place 1 tortilla in the skillet and spread a layer of shredded cheese, then ⅓ tuna mixture, then another layer of cheese. Top with another tortilla. Heat for 2 minutes, then carefully flip quesadilla with a spatula and cook for another minute until cheese melts. Move quesadilla to a serving plate and cook the next one. To serve, cut into wedges and top with a spoonful of sour cream and salsa.

Pepperoni Tostada-Pizza

Prep time: 5 minutes • Cook time: 4 minutes • Serves: 2 guys or 4 regular people

2 (12-inch) flour tortillas

1 (8-oz.) pkg. shredded Mexican-style cheese

½ cup sliced pepperoni

1 cup sour cream

Preheat the broiler. Arrange tortillas on a baking tray. Slide under the broiler on the top rack for 1 minute until tortillas begin to crisp. Remove tray from broiler, divide cheese among tortillas, spreading to an even layer, and then top with pepperoni. Slide your pizzas—I mean tostadas— back under the broiler and broil for 3 minutes, watching carefully to prevent burning. Pull them out when cheese melts, slice, and serve with sour cream.

End Run

Soft tortillas will last for several weeks in the freezer, earning them a spot in the "emergency food" category. Pull them out, thaw for 1 minute in the microwave wrapped in plastic wrap, and you're ready to go. Soft tortillas are also available these days made with white and wheat flour as well as in variations such as spinach.

Turkey Tostada

Prep time: 6 minutes • Cook time: 4 minutes • Serves: 2 guys or 4 regular people

6 (8-inch) flour tortillas

1 (8-oz.) pkg. shredded Mexican-style or cheddar cheese

1 cup salsa (your favorite), drained of excess liquid in a colander if very juicy

2 (5-oz.) cans water-packed chunk white turkey meat, drained

½ cup sour cream or light sour cream

Preheat the broiler. Arrange tortillas on a baking tray (or two, depending on the size of the tray). Slide under the broiler on the top rack for 1 minute until tortillas begin to crisp. Flip and toast for another minute (or less), just until turning crisp. Remove tray from broiler, divide cheese among tortillas, and then add salsa, spreading to an even layer. Top with turkey and broil for 3 minutes. Watch this carefully to prevent burning. Pull out *tostadas* when cheese melts, slice, and serve with sour cream.

Variation: Used canned chicken, tuna, or even ham in place of the turkey.

Menu Manual

The **tostada** is sort of a south-of-the-border cross between a pizza and an open-face sandwich made with a tortilla instead of bread. (Before my Mexican friends start getting cranky with me, let me admit that's a *very* general description!) The filling options are the same as for quesadillas. Cooking is quicker because our package is thinner and they're cooked all at once under the broiler.

Shrimp Tostadas

Prep time: 6 minutes   •   Cook time: 4 minutes   •   Serves: 2 guys or 4 regular people

4 (8-inch) flour tortillas

1 (8-oz.) pkg. shredded Mexican-style or cheddar cheese

½ tsp. chili powder

2 (4-oz.) cans tiny cocktail shrimp, drained

1 TB. fresh-squeezed lime juice

Sour cream (optional)

Preheat the broiler. Arrange tortillas on a baking tray (or two, depending on the size of the tray). Slide under the broiler on the top rack for 1 minute until tortillas begin to crisp. Remove tray from broiler and divide cheese among tortillas, spreading to an even layer. Carefully *dust* each tortilla with chili powder, spread on shrimp, and *drizzle* with lime juice. Slide these beauties back under the broiler for 3 minutes, watching carefully to prevent burning. Pull them out when cheese melts, slice, and serve with sour cream (if using).

Food Fumble

Don't add excess wet ingredients (such as salsa) to dishes you want to be crispy (such as tostadas). *Limp Tostada* might be an interesting name for a band, but it's not a good food description.

Menu Manual

To **dust** is to evenly spread a dry ingredient (in this case, seasoning) across the surface of a dish. Dust, using your fingers, from at least 6 inches above the dish to avoid unappetizing flavor clumping. To **drizzle** is to lightly sprinkle drops of a liquid over food. Drizzling is often the finishing touch to a dish.

Steak and Cheese Burritos

Prep time: 8 minutes • Cook time: 8 minutes • Serves: 4 guys or 6 regular people

1 lb. sirloin steak (or your favorite), cut into ¼-inch-wide strips

2 TB. olive oil

Juice of ½ lime

1 TB. chili powder

1 (16-oz.) can fat-free refried beans

4 (12-inch) flour tortillas

1 (8-oz.) pkg. shredded Mexican-style cheese

Sour cream and salsa

Preheat the grill. Put steak strips in a bowl and pour olive oil and lime juice over them, turning to coat. Sprinkle strips with chili powder and grill for about 3 minutes per side or until cooked.

Food Fumble

For convenience and the least amount of hassle, I prefer indoor grilling for steak strips. If you're using an outdoor grill, be sure to lay the strips across the grill so you minimize risk of sacrificing your food to the coals below. That could be another commandment: "Thou shalt minimize risk of sacrificing your food to the fire."

While steak is cooking, scrape refried beans into a microwave-safe bowl and heat for 2 minutes to loosen them. Turn off the heat under steak when done. Set out tortillas and in the middle of each, set a line of steak strips lengthwise, topped by cheese and hot refried beans. Fold one tortilla end over each end of line of steak strips, then wrap the sides around the filling. Serve, one per plate, along with sour cream and salsa for topping. You can pick up burritos or eat them with a knife and fork if you've added a lot of topping.

Variation: Wrap sour cream and/or salsa *inside* your burrito, especially if you like to wave your food around while you eat it. Skillet cooking works for the steak if grilling is not an option.

Quick Nachos

Prep time: 5 minutes • Cook time: 6 minutes • Serves: 2 guys or 4 regular people

1 (16-oz.) bag salted white corn tortilla chips (not flavored)

1 cup salsa (your favorite)

2 (8-oz.) pkg. shredded Mexican-style cheese

Pinch chili powder

Sour cream

Spread chips on 2 plates in a couple layers (there will be chips left over). Spoon salsa over chips, top with shredded cheese, sprinkle with chili powder, and microwave each plate for 2 to 3 minutes or until cheese melts. Top each plate with a spoonful of sour cream and serve.

Veggie Burrito

Prep time: 10 minutes   •   Cook time: 2 minutes   •   Serves: 2 guys or 4 regular people

1 (16-oz.) can fat-free refried beans

1 large tomato, rinsed, cored, seeded, and chopped into ¼-inch pieces

1 (4.5-oz.) can chopped green chilies, drained

4 (12-inch) flour tortillas

1 (8-oz.) pkg. shredded Mexican-style cheese

Sour cream and salsa

Scrape refried beans into a microwave-safe bowl and heat for 2 minutes to loosen them. Mix tomato and chilies into refried beans. Set out tortillas, and in the middle of each, set a line of hot refried beans topped with shredded cheese. Fold one *burrito* end over each end of line of filling, then wrap the sides. Serve, one per plate, along with sour cream and salsa for topping (these can also be wrapped inside).

Menu Manual

A **burrito** is a dish made by wrapping a tortilla around a savory filling, often served with a sauce or topping.

Loaded Dinner Nachos

Prep time: 5 minutes   •   Cook time: 15 minutes   •   Serves: 4 guys or 6 regular people

½ lb. lean ground beef

1 cup salsa (your favorite)

½ (16-oz.) can fat-free refried beans

1 TB. chili powder

1 (16-oz.) bag salted white corn tortilla chips (not flavored)

2 (8-oz.) pkg. shredded Mexican-style cheese

Sour cream

Cook ground beef in a skillet over medium heat for 8 minutes or until cooked. Drain fat, turn heat to low, and stir in salsa, refried beans, and chili powder. Cook for 4 minutes or until heated through. Meanwhile, spread chips on 4 plates in a couple layers. Spoon ground beef mixture over chips, top with shredded cheese (cheese will begin to melt over ground beef, but you can also help it along by heating each plate for 1 minute in the microwave), and serve with a spoonful of sour cream on top.

A La Carte Tacos

Prep time: 10 minutes • Cook time: 8 minutes • Serves: 4 guys or 6 regular people

1 lb. lean ground beef

½ cup salsa

1 TB. chili powder

½ tsp. salt

10 taco shells

1 (8-oz.) pkg. shredded Mexican-style cheese

1 large tomato, rinsed, cored, seeded, and chopped into ¼-inch chunks

Stir ground beef in a large skillet over medium heat for 8 minutes or until cooked. Drain fat, stir in salsa, chili powder, and salt, and heat for another 3 minutes.

Spoon some ground beef mixture into each taco shell and top with cheese and chopped tomato.

Variations: Add just about any ingredient listed at the beginning of this chapter. Tuna tacos are a good thing (really). Chicken, turkey, and bacon are also great. Add guacamole and olives, lettuce, and chopped sweet onion. You *can* do this at home.

Other Must-Try Dishes from the Southwest Trail

And finally, a few recipes too good not to include in this chapter …

Guacamole

Prep time: 10 minutes • Serves: 4 guys or 6 regular people (as an appetizer)

2 ripe avocados, pits removed, flesh scooped out

½ cup sour cream

½ (4.5-oz.) can chopped green chilies, drained

3 TB. fresh-squeezed lemon juice

1 tsp. chopped garlic

½ tsp. salt

Dash hot pepper sauce

½ (14.5-oz.) can diced tomatoes, drained

Place avocado, sour cream, chilies, lemon juice, garlic, salt, and hot pepper sauce in a food processor and whirl it for 10 seconds or until everything is combined but dip is not totally smooth, or mash it well with a fork or potato masher. Scrape guacamole into a serving bowl, stir in diced tomatoes, and serve with tortilla chips.

The Least You Need to Know

◆ Tortilla-based recipes are quick and easy to prepare, perfect "survival rations."

◆ Soft tortillas are also extremely flexible in form, from quesadillas to tostadas to enchiladas (and more). Fillings start with cheese, but the sky is the limit.

◆ These recipes make the most of quick-cooking methods, including stove top cooking, broiling, and microwave cooking.

◆ You might have met some of these dishes, like nachos, as a snack, but they work equally well as a fun meal. There's nothing wrong with fun at dinner.

Part 4

Big Games and Big Themes

In Part 4, we take our inspiration from events (or themes) that call for a certain type of food. Take game day: We have a long tradition of savory appetizers and comfort-type meals to chow on during the game.

In another chapter, I've included recipes from one of my favorite sources of inspiration—the fire station. You'll find "outdoor food"— recipes perfect for the campground but just as good at home.

And, of course, there's date night. Here we serve up recipes do-able for the average guy, but with enough class to make you look good at that romantic meal. Of course we then address the "How do you like your eggs?" question with a chapter on not only eggs, but also terrific breakfasts of all kinds.

Then we'll set out a holiday meal a guy can be proud of (but won't take all week to prepare). And you'll find practical, specific wine advice, including a checklist of great wines and producers you can use whether you're buying wine at home or at a restaurant.

Chapter **16**

The Big Game

In This Chapter

- Invite a dip to the game
- Favorite the-guys-are-over-watching-the-game appetizers
- Spuds for the couch potato
- Game-day classics

Don't starve during the long game ... but don't rely on just chips, either. This chapter includes foods perfect to accompany a game and a group of friends. We'll look at dips that are easy, fast, and different from the same old, same old. We'll meet a hot potato or two, and be glad we did. We'll find out that veggies can be a man's best friend. Finally, we'll look at some hearty meal dishes that will make you wish every day was game day.

Appetizers I: Watch the Game Sitting Next to a Dip

These dips are all hearty, flavorful, and fast. Bring one with you to the game, and your best friend will be a dip.

Fast Pass Fiesta Dip

Prep time: 5 minutes   •   Serves: 4 guys or 6 regular people as an appetizer (can be doubled)

1 (16-oz.) can fat-free refried beans

1 (8-oz.) tub whipped chive-flavored cream cheese

1 cup hot or medium salsa (your favorite)

1 cup shredded Mexican-style cheese

1 (1¼-oz.) can sliced black olives

End Run

If you've got stubborn refried beans that don't want to spread, microwave them in your serving dish for 1 or 2 minutes, then spread them, while telling them in a thick accent, "Ve haf vays of making you spread …"

Spread refried beans over the bottom of a small (8×8) serving dish. Spread cream cheese across beans, then spread salsa over that. Spread shredded cheese over salsa and top with black olives. Serve with tortilla chips.

Variation: This dip can be served as is, or you can microwave it on high for 2 minutes or until cheese is melted. (Be sure you're using a microwave-safe dish.)

Layered Dip

Prep time: 5 minutes   •   Serves: 8 guys or 10 to 12 regular people as an appetizer

1 (15-oz.) can fat-free refried beans

2 (5-oz.) cans water-packed chunk white chicken meat, drained

1 (16-oz.) tub sour cream or light sour cream

1 (1.25-oz.) pkg. taco seasoning mix, or 1 TB. chili powder

1 (16-oz.) pkg. guacamole

1 (8-oz.) pkg. shredded Mexican-style or cheddar cheese

1 cup salsa (your favorite)

Spread refried beans on the bottom of a large serving or baking dish with straight sides. Thoroughly mix chicken, sour cream, and taco seasoning in a bowl and spread mixture over refried beans. Spread guacamole over chicken layer. Mix shredded cheese and salsa and spread over guacamole. If possible, make this 1 or 2 hours before serving and let it hang out in the fridge, where the flavors will blend. Serve with tortilla chips.

Variation: For added zing, mix 1 (4.5-oz.) can chopped green chilies, drained, with salsa and cheese layer. You could also substitute cooked ground beef for chicken. This dish is also great heated.

Easy Chili Dip

Prep time: 5 minutes   •   Serves: 4 guys or 6 regular people as an appetizer

1 cup hot salsa (your favorite)

1 cup (8 oz.) sour cream or light sour cream

½ (8-oz.) pkg. shredded Mexican-style or Monterey Jack cheese

1 TB. fresh-squeezed lime juice

1 TB. chili powder

1 tsp. salt

Dash hot pepper sauce

Mix together salsa, sour cream, cheese, lime juice, chili powder, salt, and hot pepper sauce in a serving bowl and give it some time in the fridge for the flavors to spread. Serve with tortilla chips.

Variation: You can also heat this in the microwave for about 2 minutes. Stir after heating, then serve.

End Run

Why stick things in the fridge? When dry seasonings are mixed into wet ones (like chili powder into a dip), it takes time for the flavors to spread evenly. Time in the fridge spreads that rich flavor and makes a dip great. Of course, half the time I make a dip and can't wait to eat it myself. It will taste fine as prepared, but it will taste *better* if you wait.

Cheesy Tuna Spread

Prep time: 5 minutes   •   Serves: 4 guys as an appetizer

1 (12-oz.) can or 2 (6-oz.) cans water-packed white tuna, drained

1 (8-oz.) tub whipped chive-flavored cream cheese

½ cup sour cream or light sour cream

½ cup shredded Parmesan cheese

Dash hot pepper sauce

Pinch salt

Mix together tuna, cream cheese, sour cream, Parmesan, hot pepper sauce, and salt in a serving bowl. Serve with wheat crackers and a spreading knife.

Musical Fruit Bean Dip with Roasted Peppers

Prep time: 5 minutes • Serves: 6 to 8

1 (16-oz.) can cannellini beans, drained and rinsed

½ cup roasted red peppers

½ brick (4 oz.) cream cheese, softened

Juice of ½ lemon

1 TB. chopped garlic

½ tsp. salt

Pinch freshly ground black pepper

Dash hot pepper sauce, such as Tabasco (optional)

Olive oil for processing if necessary (1 or 2 TB.)

In a food processor, process beans, red peppers, cream cheese, lemon juice, garlic, salt, black pepper, and hot sauce (if using) to a creamy, smooth texture similar to dips made with sour cream. If the dip is too thick, add a little olive oil while processing. Serve with crunchy bread sticks or tortilla chips.

Variation: Substitute nonfat cottage cheese for the cream cheese for a lower-fat recipe. Bottled lemon juice can be used in place of fresh lemon juice.

Buffalo Chicken Dip

Prep time: 5 minutes • Serves: 4 guys or 6 regular people as an appetizer

2 (5-oz.) cans water-packed chunk white chicken meat, drained

1 cup chunky blue cheese salad dressing

1 cup wing hot sauce

Food Fumble

The hot sauce in this recipe is *not* the fiery hot pepper sauce that comes in tiny bottles. You can use that hot pepper sauce, but start with ¼ teaspoon and see how you like it.

Combine chicken, dressing, and hot sauce in a serving bowl, breaking the larger chunks of chicken. Serve with a sturdy grain-based dipper like bagel or pita crisps.

Variation: Heat in the microwave for 4 to 5 minutes.

End Run

My friends insisted that I just had to include this dip, adapted from my book *The Complete Idiot's Guide to 5-Minute Appetizers,* in this chapter. Okay, okay, so this tastes like the chicken wings you had in college. That's the point.

Appetizers II: Other Game-Day Starters

These classics are probably those favorites you never thought you could make at home. But you can, grasshopper, yes, you can.

Potato Skins

Prep time: 5 minutes • Cook time: 1 hour, 15 minutes (1 hour of that unattended) • Serves: 4 guys or 6 regular people as a hearty appetizer

6 large baking potatoes	1 (8-oz.) pkg. shredded cheddar cheese
6 strips bacon	1 cup (8 oz.) sour cream or light sour cream
½ stick (4 TB.) butter or margarine	Salt and ground black pepper

Preheat oven to 400°F. Jab each potato several times with a fork. Place potatoes on a baking tray and bake for about 1 hour while you watch the pre-game show. When potatoes are done, you should be able to pierce each with a fork easily. Remove potatoes from the oven to cool for a few minutes so you can handle them. Turn the oven to the broiler setting.

While potatoes are cooling, cook bacon in a large skillet over medium-high heat for 4 minutes per side or until crispy. Remove bacon to a plate covered with paper towels.

Cut each potato in half lengthwise and using a spoon, carefully scrape out some flesh from each half, leaving a layer about ¼ inch thick. Save scraped-out potato in a bowl for another use such as Cream of Potato Soup (recipe later in this chapter). Set skins on a baking tray, cut side up.

Melt butter in a microwave-safe container and brush or drizzle on the cut side of skins. Broil on the next-to-highest rack for 5 minutes or until skins are sizzling and beginning to brown. Slide the baking tray out and top each potato with shredded cheese and ½ piece crisp bacon along the middle. Slide potatoes back under the broiler and broil for 2 minutes or until cheese melts. Arrange skins on a platter surrounding a bowl with sour cream for dipping or spreading. Season skins, if desired, with salt and pepper.

Food Fumble

As potatoes (or "taters") cook, steam builds up inside those skins, sometimes causing an explosion. Prevent a potato grenade by pricking potato skins with a fork. That allows the steam to escape, and you don't have to clean the inside of your oven (or microwave) later.

Buffalo Wings

Prep time: 5 minutes • Cook time: 20 minutes • Serves: 6 guys or 9 regular people

4 lb. chicken wings	¼ to ½ cup wing hot sauce
Salt and ground black pepper	1 cup chilled blue cheese dressing
1 stick butter or margarine	Celery sticks (optional)

Preheat oven to 425°F. Snip and discard wing tips. Cut each wing in half at the joint. Rinse under cold water and pat dry with paper towels. Sprinkle with salt and pepper. Arrange wings in a single layer on two baking trays and bake for 25 to 30 minutes (the pre-game show is calling again) or until done. Melt butter in a microwave-safe bowl and mix in hot sauce. Arrange wings on a big platter and drizzle with sauce (save any extra sauce in a bowl alongside for dipping). Serve with a bowl of blue cheese for cool-off dipping and celery sticks (if using) as a hot sauce antidote. Lean over the coffee table as you eat these so you don't wreck the sofa.

Variation: For faster (but messier) cooking, use a deep skillet with 4 cups cooking oil. Heat oil and cook wings in batches over medium heat for 10 minutes. Be sure to use a splatter screen.

Artichoke Fritters

Prep time: 5 minutes • Cook time: 10 minutes • Serves: 4 guys or 6 regular people as an appetizer

2 (9-oz.) pkg. frozen artichoke hearts	1 cup Italian-style breadcrumbs
2 eggs	⅓ cup olive oil
¼ cup milk	

Pour artichoke hearts into a microwave-safe bowl and thaw them in the microwave (about 5 minutes on defrost). Mix eggs and milk in another bowl with a whisk or a fork and pour the mixture over artichoke hearts, stirring to coat. Pour breadcrumbs on a plate and, using a knife and fork, lift hearts from the bowl, roll in breadcrumbs, and set aside. Heat oil in a large skillet over medium-high heat. Add artichokes to skillet in a single layer. Cook for 3 minutes per side or until coating is crispy. Move cooked artichoke hearts to a serving plate. If you want to get fancy, stick a toothpick in each.

Where's the Beef? (and Other Main Courses)

You need more than just snacks for a long game. You need a meal. Here are some of my favorite meals that will add something to the game.

DogHouse Dogs

Prep time: 5 minutes • Cook time: 10 minutes • Serves: 4 guys or 6 regular people

8 hot dogs (your favorite)

2 cups hot chili or 1 (15-oz.) can no-bean chili

8 hoagie rolls, long rolls, or sub rolls

½ sweet onion (about 1 cup) peeled and chopped into ¼-inch pieces

Mustard

Cheddar cheese, sliced into about 1- by 5-inch pieces

Boil enough water to cover hot dogs in a saucepan. When water reaches boiling, lower dogs into water and cook over low heat for 5 minutes. Drain water. Heat chili for 3 minutes in the microwave or until hot.

Preheat the broiler. Split open each roll and arrange them side by side on a baking tray. Put 1 dog in each roll, top with chili, chopped onion, and mustard. Lay 1 piece cheese over each dog, slide the tray under the broiler, and broil for 2 minutes or until cheese melts and tops of buns brown. Serve to comments like "Wow!"

Popcorn Shrimp

Prep time: 5 minutes • Cook time: 5 minutes • Serves: 4 guys or 6 regular people

1 lb. (36 to 45 count) raw shelled small shrimp, tail off

2 cups Italian-style breadcrumbs

2 eggs

½ cup canola oil

Hot pepper sauce

Salt and ground black pepper

Set up ingredients as close to the stove top as possible to minimize mess. Put shrimp in a large bowl and breadcrumbs in a smaller bowl. In a third bowl or measuring cup, whisk eggs and pour over shrimp. Toss shrimp and coat in egg mixture. Heat oil in a large skillet over medium heat. Using a slotted spoon, lift a spoonful of shrimp into crumbs, turn to coat, and move shrimp to the skillet. Cook shrimp for about 4 minutes or until golden and crisp. Move to a serving plate and serve with hot pepper sauce, salt, and pepper. Then watch 'em vanish.

Chicken Spuds

Prep time: 5 minutes • Cook time: 17 minutes • Serves: 4 guys or 6 regular people

4 large baking potatoes	1 tsp. Italian seasoning
½ (14-oz.) can (about 1 cup) diced tomatoes, drained	1 (8-oz.) pkg. shredded Mexican-style or cheddar cheese
1 (5-oz.) can water-packed chunk white chicken meat, drained	Sour cream or light sour cream
	Salt and ground black pepper

Jab each potato several times with a fork. Place potatoes on a microwave-safe plate or baking dish and microwave on high for about 12 minutes or until potato is cooked (microwaves vary in power). When potatoes are done, you should be able to pierce each with a fork easily.

While potatoes are cooking, mix tomatoes, chicken, and Italian seasoning in a bowl. Remove potatoes when done, stick chicken mixture into the microwave, and cook it for 3 minutes or until the mixture is hot.

Slice each potato lengthwise from the top almost to the bottom and split it open so you get a nice big V-shape space. Divide chicken-tomato mixture among potatoes, then top each potato with shredded cheese. Heat in the microwave one more time until cheese melts, about 2 minutes. Serve, topping with sour cream and seasoning to taste with salt and pepper.

Molten Lava Chili

Prep time: 5 minutes • Cook time: 30 minutes • Serves: 4 guys or 6 regular people

1 lb. lean ground pork or beef	3 TB. chili powder
1 (15-oz.) can fat-free refried beans	1 TB. ground cumin
1 (15-oz.) can red kidney beans, drained and rinsed	1 tsp. hot pepper sauce or to taste
1 (16-oz.) jar hot salsa	1 cup (4 oz.) shredded Monterey Jack or other cheese
1 (4.5-oz.) can chopped green chilies, drained	1 cup (8 oz.) sour cream or light sour cream

Cook ground pork in a large skillet over medium heat, stirring, for 8 minutes or until meat is cooked and no longer pink. Drain fat. Stir in refried beans, kidney beans, salsa, chilies, chili powder, cumin, and hot pepper sauce. Cook, stirring occasionally, over low heat for 20 to 30 minutes. Distribute to serving bowls, top with shredded cheese and sour cream, and serve. Keep plenty of fire-extinguishing cold beverages and bread handy.

Game-Day Kebabs

Prep time: 10 minutes • Cook time: 10 minutes • Serves: 4 guys or 6 regular people

1½ lb. sirloin tips, cut into 1-inch pieces

½ cup your favorite marinade from Chapter 2 or the store or plain ol' Italian dressing.

1 (8-oz.) pkg. white button mushrooms, cut in half lengthwise if large

½ large sweet onion (such as Vidalia), peeled and cut into 1-inch pieces

3 green, yellow, or red bell peppers, stems and seeds removed and cut into 1-inch pieces

If you have time, put steak tips in a bowl a couple hours in advance (or even that morning), pour ½ marinade over, stir to coat, and store, covered, in the fridge until cooking time. This will give you the best flavor, but it doesn't kill the recipe if you don't get to it.

Preheat the grill. While the grill is heating, assemble kebabs on your *skewers*, alternating ingredients: 1 piece of steak, then 1 mushroom, 1 onion, 1 pepper, another piece of steak, and so on. Arrange your kebabs on a platter and drizzle remaining marinade over all. Grill for 5 minutes per side or until steak is done to your liking.

Menu Manual

Skewers are thin wooden or metal sticks, usually about 8 inches long, that are perfect for assembling kebabs, dipping food pieces into hot sauces, or serving single-bite food items. They're in your grocery store, usually in the kitchen tools section. Wooden skewers should be soaked for 10 minutes before using to minimize the chance of burning them.

Homemade Sausage Pizza

Prep time: 5 minutes • Cook time: 10 minutes • Serves: 2 guys or 4 regular people
(easily doubled)

1 (14-oz.) pkg. prepared pizza crust (available in grocery stores)

½ cup (4 oz.) pasta or pizza sauce

1 cup shredded mozzarella cheese

2 cooked sausage links, cut into ½-inch slices

Preheat the oven to 450°F. Set pizza crust on a baking tray. Pour pasta sauce on crust, spread it around with the back of the spoon, and sprinkle cheese over sauce. Spread your sausage around and bake pizza in the oven for about 10 minutes or until crust is crispy and cheese is melted. Slice into wedges on a cutting board and serve.

End Run

Don't know what to put on a pizza? There are so many choices, your question becomes "Where to begin?" Here are some ideas:

- ◆ **Meats:** Pepperoni, ham, bacon, cooked ground beef, canned chicken—you name it.
- ◆ **Veggies:** Sweet onion, garlic, sliced peppers, sliced olives, sliced mushrooms, sliced tomatoes, etc.
- ◆ **Cheese:** Pizza doesn't just mean mozzarella. Try feta, goat's milk cheese, cheddar, Swiss, and others.
- ◆ **Fruit:** Pineapple.

And this is just for starters.

The Least You Need to Know

- ◆ Appetizers can be fast and easy to make, perfect when you need to spend more time watching the cheerleaders.
- ◆ Potato skins are not just for restaurants. You can make them to eat right on your very own sofa.
- ◆ Game-day meal recipes provide flavor for a crowd but won't keep you in the kitchen too long.
- ◆ From kebabs to pizza and chili, these favorite recipes will add fun to game day.

Firefighter Food

In This Chapter

- ◆ Recipes with proven station appeal
- ◆ Quick, tasty meals plus a few more time-involved dishes that are worth the wait
- ◆ More delicious stove top and grill meals good for the firehouse or your house
- ◆ A wide range of dishes with a common base: ground beef

Many firefighters are passionate cooks. At fire stations in large towns, shifts (or groups) are on duty 24 hours a day for several days at a time. These guys need to eat (I use the term *guy* here in the general sense, acknowledging women firefighters). On each shift, the same person often has the job of station cook. Meals are large, satisfying, and economical—naturals to fit in this book.

I want to give special thanks to the cooks at the Fire Department in Natick, Massachusetts, for their time and patience. I have included a number of their suggestions (with some adaptation).

Firehouse Basics

One cook in Natick, Captain Mike Lentini, echoes one of the themes of this book. "I love to cook," he says, "but I hate cleaning." Anything he can do to speed up cleanup is good in his book. One- or two-pot meals are the way to go.

Culture has a lot to do with favorites, says Lentini. Alluding to his Italian heritage, he admits that he's most at home with seafood and pasta. For others at the station, chicken, roasts, burgers, and steaks top the favorites list.

Twice-Baked Potatoes

Prep time: 10 minutes • Cook time: 1 hour, 15 minutes • Serves: 4 guys

4 large baking potatoes, scrubbed

1 (8-oz.) pkg. cream cheese, softened

1 stick (4 oz.) butter or margarine, cut into small pieces and softened

Salt and ground black pepper

½ cup shredded cheddar cheese

Preheat the oven to 400°F. Stab potatoes a few times with a fork (no potato grenade weapons of mass destruction in this kitchen), and bake potatoes for 1 hour on a baking tray while you work on your Cub Scout's Pinewood Derby car. (Guess what my family task was while I was trying out these potatoes. Try attaching wheels to a raw baking potato instead. A potato is much easier to whittle.) Potatoes are done when you can easily pierce each with a fork.

Bring spuds out of the oven (leave the oven on) and slice them in half lengthwise. Cool for a few minutes if necessary so you can handle them. Use a spoon to scoop potato out of skin (be careful not to damage skins). Put potato in a bowl. Add cream cheese, butter, and a sprinkling of salt and pepper; mash with your fork or masher until you get to the consistency you like (you can beat them with an electric mixer if you like fluffy potatoes). Spoon mashed potato mixture back into potato skins on the baking tray, top with shredded cheese, and bake for 15 minutes or until golden.

End Run

Thanks to Tom Topham, cook for Shift 3 at the Natick Fire Department, for this recipe.

To soften cream cheese, either leave it out for 30 minutes to warm up or take it out of its foil wrapper and microwave it (in a bowl) for 20 seconds. You can also buy whipped cream cheese that is soft already.

Crunchy-Sweet Chili Chicken

Prep time: 5 minutes   •   Cook time: 25 minutes   •   Serves: 4 guys or 6 regular people

1 cup Italian-style breadcrumbs

2 TB. chili powder

3 TB. honey

2 TB. canola oil

4 large boneless, skinless chicken breasts (about 2 lb.), rinsed and patted dry on paper towels

Preheat the oven to 350°F. Mix breadcrumbs and chili powder in a large bowl. Combine honey and oil in a cup and drizzle over chicken breasts, turning to coat. Dredge breasts through breadcrumbs and place them on a baking tray. Bake for 25 minutes or until cooked through, no longer pink, and juices run clear.

End Run

To make the honey easier to mix, heat it for 30 seconds in the microwave, then stir in the oil.

Hamburg Fricassee

Prep time: 5 minutes   •   Cook time: 15 minutes   •   Serves: 4 guys or 6 regular people

1 lb. lean ground beef

3 stalks celery, washed, trimmed, and cut into ¼-inch slices

1 medium onion (pool-ball size), peeled and chopped into ½-inch pieces

1 TB. chopped garlic

4 cups hot mashed potatoes

1 (14.75-oz.) can beef gravy

1 tsp. Italian seasoning

Salt and ground black pepper

Cook ground beef, celery, onion, and garlic in a large skillet over medium heat, stirring, for 8 minutes or until beef is cooked. Now is also the time to cook mashed potatoes (recipe later in this chapter) if you didn't buy them. Drain fat from the skillet and mix in gravy and Italian seasoning. Add salt and pepper to taste. Cook for another 2 minutes. Distribute mashed potatoes among serving plates (make a crater in each helping), ladle meat over, and serve.

Menu Manual

To **fricassee** is to cook something in a buttery, flavorful broth, from poultry to seafood and meats, and then make a creamy sauce from the liquid. Although this recipe is not traditional, it captures some of that rich flavor.

Station Favorite Meat Loaf

Prep time: 10 minutes   •   Cook time: 1½ hours   •   Serves: 6 guys or 8 regular people

2 lb. lean ground beef

¾ cup tomato juice

¾ cup Italian-style breadcrumbs

2 eggs, lightly beaten

¼ cup chopped fresh parsley

2 TB. chopped garlic

1 tsp. dried oregano, or 1 TB. fresh

1 tsp. salt

½ tsp. ground black pepper

10 slices imported boiled ham (about ½ lb.)

¾ (8-oz.) pkg. (1½ cups) shredded mozzarella cheese

4 sprigs parsley

Preheat the oven to 350°F. In a big bowl, mix ground beef, tomato juice, breadcrumbs, eggs, chopped parsley, garlic, oregano, salt, and pepper. Scoop loaf mixture onto a piece of wax paper on the counter and mush mixture into a rough rectangle shape, about 8 by 12 inches. (The wax paper is handy for keeping the loaf from sticking to the counter, but this can be done carefully without it.) Lay ham slices over the top of meat loaf mixture, then spread ¾ cup shredded cheese over ham. Carefully roll the loaf over itself lengthwise, using the wax paper to help you get started. Pinch the edges to keep cheese from falling out. Place the rolled meat loaf in an oiled loaf or baking pan, slide meat loaf into the oven, and cook uncovered for 1½ hours or until done. A meat thermometer is really handy—when the loaf hits 160°F, you're done. Remove, sprinkle with remaining ¼ cup cheese, slide back into the oven, turn off the oven, and get the rest of the dinner ready. By the time you're ready to serve, cheese will be melted. Decorate with parsley sprigs (presentation is everything) and serve.

End Run

Thanks to Barry Forrest, cook for Shift 1 at the Natick Fire Department, for this recipe.

Rosy the Pork

Prep time: 10 minutes　•　Cook time: about 2 hours　•　Serves: 6 guys or 10 regular people, with high leftover probability

1 (4-lb.) boneless pork loin roast	½ tsp. salt
1 tsp. dried rosemary	¼ tsp. ground black pepper
½ tsp. dried thyme	

Preheat the oven to 350°F. Place roast on a roasting pan (a pan with a rack insert that allows fat to drip away from the meat) or in a casserole or baking pan. Sprinkle roast on all sides with rosemary, thyme, salt, and pepper, and rub seasonings into meat with the back of a spoon. Some roasts have a fat side; if your does, put the fat side up (this adds flavor as the fat melts while it cooks and runs down and through the roast).

Slide roast into the oven on the center rack and cook for 1 hour or until done. (Roast is done when the temperature, using a meat thermometer, reaches 160 to 170°F or juices run clear when roast is cut with a knife.) Remove from the oven and let roast hang out for 10 to 15 minutes (it's called "resting") before carving.

Serve with baked potatoes, green beans, and the traditional pork partner—applesauce.

Food Fumble

Keep a close eye on your roast as you approach the "done" stage. A roast cooked just right is juicy and delicious. An overcooked roast will start to dry out and be much less appealing.

 End Run

This delicious and easy roast will serve a lot of people. The decision you'll need to make is on the size of the roast. (A pork loin roast runs from 2 to 4 pounds. A shoulder roast runs 5 to 7 pounds and is usually cheaper per pound. These directions assume the smaller roast; add an additional 30 minutes per pound for the larger version.)

Chicken-Broccoli Pasta

Prep time: 10 minutes • Cook time: 10 to 15 minutes • Serves: 4 guys or 6 regular people

½ lb. uncooked penne pasta

3 TB. olive oil

1 medium onion (pool-ball size), peeled and chopped into ½-inch pieces

1 tsp. Italian seasoning

1 lb. boneless, skinless chicken breasts, cut into 1-inch pieces, rinsed and patted dry on paper towels

1 TB. chopped garlic

½ cup dry white wine, or water

1 head broccoli, washed and cut into 1-inch florets (It's up to you whether you want to use the stems or not.)

½ tsp. salt

Pinch ground black pepper

Grated Parmesan cheese

Cook pasta. While pasta is cooking, heat oil in a large skillet and cook onion and Italian seasoning for 3 minutes, stirring. Add chicken and garlic and cook for another 2 minutes. Add wine (or water) and broccoli and cook, stirring and turning chicken, for 8 minutes or until chicken is cooked through and no longer pink. Sprinkle salt and pepper on chicken pieces as you cook. Drain cooked pasta, distribute it to serving plates, and top with big spoonfuls of chicken and broccoli mixture.

Serve, passing Parmesan cheese.

Skillet Beef and Potato Dinner

Prep time: 5 minutes • Cook time: 15 minutes • Serves: 4 guys or 6 regular people

1 medium onion (pool-ball size), peeled and chopped into ½-inch pieces

1 lb. lean ground beef

1 (15-oz.) can sliced white potatoes, drained

1 (9-oz.) pkg. frozen peas and pearl onions

1 tsp. Italian seasoning

½ tsp. hot pepper sauce

½ tsp. salt

Pinch ground black pepper

Cook onion and ground beef in a large skillet over medium heat, stirring, for 8 minutes or until beef is cooked. Drain fat from the skillet and mix in potatoes, peas and pearl onions, Italian seasoning, hot pepper sauce, salt, and pepper. Cook for another 5 minutes, stirring occasionally, and serve.

Variation: Substitute other vegetables for peas and pearl onions. Ground sausage also works well in place of ground beef. Canned vegetables, drained, will also work fine, and the dish will be ready even faster.

Tuna-Choke Casserole

Prep time: 20 minutes • Cook time: 45 minutes (unattended) • Serves: 6 guys or 8 regular people

½ lb. penne pasta

1 (16-oz.) can artichoke hearts, drained

1 cup light sour cream

2 (10.75-oz.) cans condensed cream of mushroom soup

1 (12-oz.) can water-packed chunk white tuna, drained

3 TB. minced dried onion

1 tsp. Italian seasoning

½ cup breadcrumbs

½ cup shredded Parmesan cheese (plain or Italian style)

2 TB. olive oil

Cook pasta. Preheat the oven to 375°F. When pasta is done, drain and return it to its cooking pot. Add artichokes, sour cream, soup (don't use extra water), tuna, onion, and Italian seasoning. Mix and scrape mixture into a big, greased baking dish. Mix breadcrumbs and Parmesan cheese in a bowl and sprinkle mixture over top of casserole. Drizzle olive oil over top of breadcrumbs and bake casserole for 45 minutes.

Variation: For a really big batch, double this recipe. Use frozen peas or peas-and-pearl-onions combo (thawed) in place (or in addition to) artichokes.

Mashed Potatoes

Prep time: 10 minutes • Cook time: 15 minutes • Serves: 6 guys or 8 regular people

6 large potatoes, peeled and chopped into 1-inch pieces

½ tsp. salt

Pinch ground black pepper

¾ cup milk

6 TB. (¾ stick) butter or margarine

Put potato chunks in a big microwave-safe container with a lid. Add about ½ cup water, sprinkle potatoes with salt and pepper, cover, and cook on high heat for 15 minutes or until potatoes are soft. Measure milk into a big microwave-safe measuring cup and add butter in two pieces (so it sinks into milk and doesn't splatter inside the microwave). Microwave milk and butter for 1 minute to warm it, pour it over potatoes, and mash away with your fork or masher until you get the consistency you like. Don't worry about a few lumps; those make it look homemade (that's a good thing).

If you want to go further, you can take your mashed product and use a whisk or hand blender to make them even more fluffy.

End Run

If you become a fan of homemade mashed potatoes—there is that risk after seeing how easy they are—pick up one of those handy potato-mashing tools. They're cheap and do a better job than a fork.

End Run

Mashed potatoes are another one of those favorites a guy might think is hard to make. (That belief is why they sell mashed potatoes in the deli and those big boxes of "instant mashed potatoes.") Mashed potatoes, however, are easy and quick to make. Give 'em a try. You'll see what I mean.

By the way, did you know potato flakes are what film makers use as "snow"? It gives a whole new meaning to catching snowflakes on your tongue …

Hungarian Goulash

Prep time: 10 minutes • Cook time: 1 hour, 15 minutes (including an hour of cooking time while you watch *The X-Files*—first season only please, guys have *some* taste) • Serves: 4 guys or 6 regular people

3 TB. olive oil

1 large onion (baseball size), peeled and chopped into ½-inch pieces

2 lb. beef stew meat, cut into 1-inch pieces

2 stalks celery, washed, trimmed, and cut into ½-inch pieces

1 (14.5-oz.) can tomato sauce

1 (15-oz.) can beef broth

1 (15-oz.) can mixed vegetables, drained, or 2 cups chopped fresh vegetables

½ cup ketchup

3 TB. sweet paprika

1 TB. prepared mustard (your favorite)

1 tsp. salt

¼ tsp. ground black pepper

Heat oil in a large stockpot over medium heat and cook onion, stew meat, and celery, stirring, for 10 minutes or until beef is cooked. Add tomato sauce, beef broth, mixed vegetables, ketchup, paprika, mustard, salt, and pepper. Turn the heat to between medium and low and cook for 1 hour, stirring during the commercial breaks. To serve, ladle into big bowls. Put a salad and some crusty bread with this and you've got a great meal.

Variation: Add 1 (8-oz.) package sliced white mushrooms along with vegetables. After beef is browned, cook the rest in a slow cooker for 8 to 10 hours on low heat or 4 to 5 hours on high heat. That will allow enough time for some serious couch aerobics.

Sausage-Stuffed Peppers

Prep time: 10 minutes   •   Cook time: 35 minutes   •   Serves: 4 guys or 6 regular people

1 lb. bulk sweet Italian sausage or ground pork

1 medium onion (pool ball size), peeled and chopped into ½-inch pieces

1 TB. chopped garlic

1 (14.5-oz.) can diced tomatoes with juice

1 (15.5-oz.) can black beans, drained and rinsed

1 cup Italian-style breadcrumbs (plain will work, too)

2 TB. Worcestershire sauce

1 tsp. Italian seasoning

1 tsp. salt

¼ tsp. ground black pepper

4 large bell peppers, sliced in half lengthwise, stems and seeds removed

½ (4-oz.) pkg. shredded cheddar cheese

Preheat the oven to 375°F. Cook sausage, onion, and garlic in a large skillet over medium heat, stirring, for 8 minutes or until sausage is cooked. Drain fat from the skillet and mix in tomatoes, beans, breadcrumbs, Worcestershire sauce, Italian seasoning, salt, and pepper. Cook and stir for 4 minutes.

End Run

According to the guys at the firehouse, a good meal should include a main course, bread, a vegetable (and maybe a potato of some kind), and still not cost more than $5 per person.

While sausage is cooking, put pepper halves, cut side up, in a microwave- and oven-safe baking dish (you'll use this in the oven, too) and add ¼ inch water to the dish. Microwave peppers for 5 minutes or until they have softened. Distribute sausage filling among peppers in the baking dish (keep a little water in the bottom). Bake for 10 minutes. Then, during the next commercial break, distribute shredded cheese and bake for another 10 minutes or until cheese is melted. Place two stuffed pepper halves on each plate and serve.

Playing with Fire: Grill Recipes

Firefighters aren't afraid of fire when it comes to cooking, either. They grill all year.

Monster Burgers

Prep time: 8 minutes   •   Cook time: 8 to 10 minutes   •   Serves: 4 guys or 6 regular people

1½ lb. lean ground beef

2 tsp. Worcestershire sauce

¼ tsp. ground black pepper

4 to 6 ripe tomato slices (¼ inch or thinner)

4 to 6 sweet onion slices (¼ inch or thinner)

Toasted hamburger buns

Preheat the grill. In a bowl, mix ground beef, Worcestershire sauce, and pepper. Divide ground beef into 8 to 12 equal-size patties and flatten each to be very wide and thin (wide enough to overlap tomato and onion slices all around). Set onion and tomato on 4 patties, lay the other 4 patties on top, and pinch the sides to close, forming 4 large burgers "with a secret." Grill directly over the coals for 4 to 5 minutes per side or until cooked through. Place each burger on a toasted bun and serve. Blue cheese dressing is great on these burgers.

 End Run

To make these burgers taste even better, cook the onions for 5 minutes in olive oil.

Hawaiian Steak Strips

Prep time: 10 minutes • Cook time: 8 minutes • Serves: 4 guys or 6 regular people

1½ lb. sirloin (or your favorite cut) sliced *across the grain* into ½-inch strips

¼ cup teriyaki sauce

3 TB. olive oil

1 medium onion (pool-ball size), peeled and cut into ¼-inch pieces

1 tsp. chopped garlic

1 (8-oz.) can crushed pineapple with juice

1 (4.5-oz.) can sliced mushrooms, drained

Menu Manual

Steak, as you probably know, is muscle. Muscle fibers tend to run parallel to each other. To cut a steak **across the grain** is to make a cut across those fibers. The resulting strips are much more tender and easier to cut than a strip cut with the grain.

Preheat the grill. Place steak strips in a bowl and pour teriyaki sauce over. When grill is ready, grill steak strips for 3 minutes per side directly over the coals or until cooked. Save teriyaki sauce. While steak is cooking, heat oil in a skillet over medium heat and cook onion and garlic for 3 minutes, stirring. Add teriyaki sauce and cook another 3 minutes; then add pineapple with juice and mushrooms and heat for 1 minute.

Distribute grilled steak to serving plates and spoon pineapple sauce across each serving.

Grilled Chicken and Vegetables

Prep time: 5 minutes • Cook time: 10 minutes • Serves: 4 guys or 6 regular people

1 large sweet onion (such as Vidalia), peeled and sliced into ½-inch slices

3 (8-inch) zucchini squash, ends removed, each sliced lengthwise into 4 spears

1½ lb. boneless, skinless chicken breasts, breast halves separated and sliced lengthwise into long pieces, each about 1½ by 5 inches

Juice of ½ lime, or 2 TB. lime juice

¼ cup olive oil

2 tsp. Italian seasoning

Salt and ground black pepper

Put onion and zucchini in a large bowl. Rinse chicken pieces under cold water, pat dry with paper towels, and place chicken breasts in another bowl. Pour lime juice and then olive oil over vegetables, turning to coat. Holding back vegetables, pour lime juice/olive oil mixture over chicken in the other bowl. Turn pieces to coat. Sprinkle vegetables with 1 teaspoon Italian seasoning and a pinch of salt and pepper. Sprinkle breasts with remaining 1 teaspoon Italian seasoning and another pinch salt and pepper. Put chicken on the center of the grill and arrange vegetables around, being careful to keep zucchini spears across the grill to avoid losing them into the fire. Cook for 4 minutes per side or until done. When you turn chicken, drizzle chicken with remaining olive oil/lime juice from chicken bowl. When you turn vegetables, drizzle with liquid from the veggie bowl.

Distribute chicken and vegetables to serving plates. Add a big piece of fresh bread and you've got a great summer meal.

The Least You Need to Know

♦ If you're looking for inspiration for guy-tested, comfort-food meals, head for the firehouse.

♦ Firehouse-style recipes tend to be quick to prepare, use inexpensive ingredients, and can be served in large quantities.

♦ Quick-cooking ingredients, such as chicken breasts, steaks, pasta, and ground beef, are staples at the fire fighters' dinner table.

♦ These recipes also use practical, simple cooking methods, including stove top, grill, and microwave cooking.

Chapter 18

Let's Take It Outside: Campground and Picnic Food

In This Chapter

- ◆ Fast and tasty fireside meals
- ◆ A recommended campground kitchen kit
- ◆ Hearty, one-pot meals easy to fix in the great outdoors
- ◆ Making camping and picnic life easier by preparing ahead

Even more than at home, a camping meal has to be quick, convenient, and easy to clean up—and use a minimum of tools that you have to carry, or worse, that can be forgotten.

This chapter is divided into three sections focused on dishes with some advance prep, meals done ahead of time, and meals where everything is done on-site.

The little secret of these recipes is that they are really fast and easy. So don't feel like you have to save this good stuff just for camping. Try it tonight and pretend you're out under the stars.

Note: This food is not for survival camping, but rather for recreational, usually "drive-in" camping, the kind you do for a weekend with a bunch of friends or with the family. We're not going to be hiking into the wilderness with this food.

Your Handy Campground Kitchen Kit

To make camping life even better, set up a bin to be your "camping kitchen." I stock mine with items I've practically worn out in the kitchen but that are perfect for camping. (Nobody's going to object if I get that old skillet black with soot from a campfire.) When it's time to camp, my camping kitchen bin always comes along, and I know I'll be all set.

Checklist items to include are:

❏ A can opener (This is a biggie!)

❏ A big skillet (Keep it stored in newspaper so the soot doesn't get everywhere.)

❏ A saucepan

❏ A couple decent, sharp knives

❏ Spoons for stirring

❏ A spatula

❏ A cutting board

❏ A plastic container or zipper bags with Italian seasoning, chili powder, salt, and ground black pepper

❏ A grill for your fire, in case one is not available (Keep it stored in newspaper so the soot doesn't get everywhere.)

❏ A plastic dishpan with a brush and soap (Much as I don't want to admit it, life would not be good without these.)

❏ A campstove (optional)

❏ A dish towel

❏ An oven mitt

❏ Instant coffee

❏ Trash bags

❏ Matches!

Assemble at the Picnic Table (with Some Advance Prep)

When it's getting dark and the tent is still in its bag, there's no time to waste. For that reason, it's a great idea to have done some advance prep to speed dinner on its way and to use some tricks to get a head start.

Remember that saying about "a watched pot never boils"? They were talking about camping. You're there, you're hungry, and the only thing you can do is watch that pot of water.

It pays to think carefully about food before you get to the campground. A little bit of prep, say boiling water and making pasta, can be done much more quickly at home than on the road.

Easy Meatball Subs

Prep time: 5 minutes • Cook time: 10 minutes • Serves: 4 guys or 8 regular people

1 lb. meatballs (about 1 inch across, from the deli, from the freezer section, or easy home-made)

1 (26-oz.) jar pasta sauce (your favorite)

½ lb. sliced provolone cheese

8 split sub rolls

Mix meatballs and pasta sauce in a saucepan or skillet over heat. Cook until hot, stirring a couple times. Keep in mind that meatballs will take longer to heat if they are frozen! Meanwhile, lay provolone slices inside sub rolls. Ladle or spoon hot meatballs and sauce over provolone in rolls. Cheese will begin to melt. Serve with salad.

You'll make a big, drippy mess with these subs, but this will be the best meal you've had in a month.

End Run

Head for your grocery store's freezer aisle, and you'll find packages of frozen meatballs. Throw them in the cooler, and they'll start to thaw on the way there while keeping the beer cold at the same time.

Lemon-Garlic Chicken Breasts

Prep time: 5 minutes • Cook time: 10 minutes • Serves: 4 guys or 6 regular people

2 TB. olive oil

1 TB. chopped garlic

1½ lb. boneless, skinless chicken breasts, cut into 1-inch-thick strips, rinsed and patted dry on paper towels

1 tsp. Italian seasoning

Salt and ground black pepper

Juice of ½ lemon, or 2 TB. lemon juice

Heat oil in a skillet, add garlic, and cook, stirring, for 1 minute. Meanwhile, turn strips of chicken in a bowl, sprinkling with Italian seasoning, salt, and pepper. Add chicken to the skillet and cook for about 4 to 5 minutes per side or until done and the juices run clear. Squeeze lemon juice over chicken and serve.

Serve with bread and a bagged salad for a civilized fireside meal. Life is good.

Variation: Cut chicken at home and mix it with Italian seasoning, salt, and pepper in a plastic container with a lid for your cooler. This will save on-site time.

End Run

Chicken breasts are great for camping and outdoor cooking because they are fast and easy to cook. Plus, messy leftovers are kept to a minimum. (Bones from drumsticks and wings are fine at home, but at a campsite they attract unwanted midnight visitors. I need all the sleep I can get when I'm camping.)

Boneless, skinless breasts are also low-fat, maybe a useful counterbalance for some of the less-healthful stuff we eat by the fire.

Spiced Corn

Prep time: 5 minutes • Cook time: 5 minutes • Serves: 4 guys or 6 regular people as a vegetable side dish

2 (15-oz.) cans whole kernel corn, drained

1 (14.5-oz.) can diced tomatoes with juice

1 (4.5-oz.) can chopped green chilies, drained

1 TB. chili powder

Salt and ground black pepper

Mix corn, tomatoes with juice, chilies, and chili powder in a skillet, and heat for about 5 minutes, stirring, or until hot. Serve, seasoning to taste with salt and pepper.

Campfire Home Fries

Prep time: 5 minutes • Cook time: 10 minutes • Serves: 4 guys or 6 regular people

¼ cup canola oil

1 small onion (golf-ball size), peeled and cut into ½-inch pieces

2 (15-oz.) cans sliced white potatoes, drained

Salt and ground black pepper

Heat oil in a skillet and cook onion, stirring, for 3 to 5 minutes or until softened. Add potatoes and cook, stirring, for another 5 minutes or until the edges of potato slices begin to brown. Sprinkle with salt and pepper while cooking.

Serve with ketchup.

Variation: Sprinkle with shredded cheese just before serving.

Make Ahead

You can make some of these dishes at the campsite if chuck-wagon cooking is your thing, but it's a lot easier to make them at home. Then all you have to do is throw them in the cooler and heat them up when you get the fire started. Plus you get more time to watch the fire when you get there. *Ahhh*. Camping.

Baked Stuffed Potatoes

Prep time: 5 minutes at home • Cook time: 1 hour (unattended) at home, 5 minutes at the campsite • Serves: 4 guys or 6 regular people

4 large baking potatoes

1½ cups ham, chopped into ¼-inch chunks (about ½ [¾-lb.] ham steak)

1 (4.5-oz.) can sliced mushrooms, drained

2 TB. butter or margarine, cut into 8 pieces

1 (8-oz.) pkg. shredded cheddar cheese

Salt and ground black pepper

Sour cream (optional)

Preheat oven to 400°F. Jab each potato several times with a fork. Place potatoes on a baking tray and bake for about 1 hour or until the fork easily pierces potato. Remove potatoes from the oven to cool for a few minutes so you can handle them.

Slice each potato lengthwise, about ¾ through, and spread the sides to create a big V-shape cavity. Distribute ham, mushrooms, 2 teaspoons butter, and cheese to each potato. Add salt and pepper to taste. Wrap each potato securely in aluminum foil with the seam on top and stick in the fridge until you pack the cooler for camping.

Food Fumble

Be careful about putting foil-wrapped potatoes (or other things) on the grill directly over the fire. They will heat fast, true, but even in the foil those spuds will burn.

On-site, put potatoes (seam side up) near the edge of the fire. Heat with one side to the fire for 15 minutes, then the other side for another 15 minutes while you get the rest of dinner ready. Put 1 potato on each plate, opening at the top, and enjoy. Add some sour cream if you like.

Pasta Stew

Prep time: 5 minutes on-site   •   Cook time: 20 minutes at home to cook the pasta, 10 minutes on-site   •   Serves: 4 guys or 6 regular people

1 lb. sweet Italian sausage links, cut into 1-inch pieces

1 medium onion (pool-ball size), peeled and chopped into ½-inch pieces

1 TB. Italian seasoning

5 cups cooked penne (or other shape) pasta (starts as about 2 cups dry)

1 (28-oz.) jar four-cheese pasta sauce (or your favorite)

1 (15-oz.) can mixed vegetables, drained

Salt and ground black pepper

Grated Parmesan cheese

Cook sausage, onion, and Italian seasoning in a large skillet over the fire or camp stove, stirring, for 8 minutes or until sausage is cooked and no longer pink. Drain fat. Stir in pasta, sauce, and vegetables and heat, continuing to stir, for another few minutes. Serve in bowls, seasoning to taste with salt and pepper and, of course, Parmesan.

 End Run

Use cooked sausage (you can cook it yourself or buy precooked chicken sausage or kielbasa) to speed up this dish even more.

 Menu Manual

I won't specify "high," "medium," or "low" for these recipes because it's just too tough to adjust how that log burns. (A camp stove is better.) Just try to find heat somewhere between "barely warm" and "inferno." The higher the heat, the faster your food will cook, but the more carefully you'll need to watch it to prevent burning.

Potato Salad

Prep time: 10 minutes • Cook time: 10 to 15 minutes • Serves: 4 guys or 6 regular people

1½ lb. *new potatoes*, between the size of golf balls and pool balls (number of potatoes will vary according to the size)

1 small onion (golf-ball size), peeled and chopped into ½-inch pieces

½ tsp. salt

3 TB. white vinegar

1 celery stalk, trimmed, rinsed, and cut into ¼-inch pieces

⅓ cup mayonnaise

3 TB. sweet hamburger relish

3 TB. prepared mustard

½ tsp. dried dill

¼ tsp. ground black pepper

Menu Manual

New potatoes are young, thin-skinned potatoes that are smaller than those big ol' baking types. They cook quickly, and you don't need to peel them. (Remember, "Keep it simple!")

Brush potatoes under running water. Put potatoes and chopped onion in a saucepan and add just enough cold water to cover. Sprinkle with salt. Heat to boiling and cook for 15 minutes or until potatoes are cooked (soft enough for a fork to easily sink into potato). Drain water and dump spuds into a big bowl. Pour vinegar over and slice them into ½-inch-thick slices. Add celery. In another bowl, mix mayo, relish, and mustard. Mix sauce with potatoes, sprinkle potatoes with dill and pepper, and you're ready to go. Or you can stick this in the fridge until you're ready to pack the cooler.

Ham and Pasta Salad

Prep time: 10 minutes   •   Cook time: 15 to 20 minutes (pasta cooking time)   •   Serves: 4 guys or 6 regular people

1 lb. penne pasta

1 (¾-lb.) ham steak, cut into ½-inch chunks

1 (10-oz.) bag fresh spinach, rinsed, stems removed, and coarsely chopped

1 sweet onion (such as Vidalia), peeled and finely chopped

½ cup bottled Italian dressing

1 (8-oz.) pkg. shredded cheddar cheese

Cook pasta and drain. Mix pasta, ham, spinach, and onion. Pour dressing over, mix again, and top with shredded cheese. It's gorgeous.

Italian Chicken

Prep time: 5 minutes   •   Cook time: 10 minutes   •   Serves: 4 guys or 6 regular people

1½ lb. boneless, skinless chicken breasts, cut into 1-inch-thick strips, rinsed and patted dry on paper towels

¼ cup olive oil

½ package Italian dressing mix

¼ cup shredded Parmesan cheese

Put chicken in a big resealable bag or plastic container with a lid. Add oil, close, and shake to coat. Open the bag, then sprinkle in Italian dressing mix and Parmesan. Close bag, shake it again, stick the bag or container in the cooler, and head to the campground.

At the campground, upend the bag into a skillet, making sure to get oil out of the bag and into the fry pan. Cook, turning the pieces, for about 8 minutes or until chicken is cooked.

Barbecued Pork Chops

Prep time: 5 minutes • Cook time: 1¾ hours (mostly unattended) • Serves: 4 guys or 6 regular people

2 TB. butter or olive oil	1 tsp. salt
8 pork chops (bone-in), about 3 lb.	1 tsp. celery seed
1 cup water	½ tsp. nutmeg
½ cup ketchup	1 bay leaf
⅓ cup cider vinegar	

Food Fumble

Bay leaf adds great flavor, but it doesn't get much softer as it cooks. Removing it after cooking is a good idea.

End Run

Fellow camper Andy Frankenfield rescues a campground meal every year with these delicious chops. Guys love them, wives love them, and kids eat 'em.

Preheat the oven to 325°F. Heat butter in a large skillet over medium-high heat and brown chops about 2 minutes per side. Meanwhile, mix water, ketchup, vinegar, salt, celery seed, nutmeg, and bay leaf in a bowl. Place chops in a big casserole dish with a lid, pour sauce over, cover, and bake for 1½ hours or until very tender, while you try to patch the holes in the tent from last year.

Remove bay leaf and put chops with their sauce in a plastic container with a lid or a resealable bag. These can be heated quickly in a skillet with the sauce or even eaten cold.

Cook the Whole Thing On-Site

If you're a little more adventurous and want to do all the work (quick work) at the campsite, here are several recipes for you. For these, all you need to do is remember to bring the ingredients and your supplies.

Honey-Beer Ham Steaks

Prep time: 5 minutes   •   Cook time: 10 minutes   •   Serves: 4 guys or 6 regular people

½ (12-oz.) can beer

½ cup firmly packed dark brown sugar

¼ cup prepared mustard

2 (¾-lb.) ham steaks

Mix beer, brown sugar, and mustard in a bowl. Pour ½ this mixture into a skillet over the fire or the camp stove, add ham steaks, and pour remaining beer mixture over the top. Cook for 4 minutes per side or until heated through and maybe even browning a little. Cut each steak in half or in thirds, put 1 piece on each plate, and top with sauce from the pan.

 End Run

Ham steaks are great served with a big can of baked beans. Add those beans to the same skillet. They'll mix with the sauce and taste even better.

Fast Dinner Hash

Prep time: 10 minutes   •   Cook time: 10 to 15 minutes   •   Serves: 4 guys or 6 regular people

2 TB. cooking oil

2 (15-oz.) cans roast beef hash

1 (14.5-oz.) can peas and pearl onions, drained

1 (8-oz.) can sliced mushrooms, drained

1 (4.5-oz.) can chopped green chilies

2 TB. Worcestershire sauce

Heat oil in a large skillet over the fire or the stove and add hash. Mix in peas and onions, mushrooms, chilies, and Worcestershire sauce. Heat, stirring, for 5 minutes or until heated through. Serve in bowls or on plates.

Variation: For the campfire version of hearty diner food, crack an egg over hot hash mixture in the skillet and stir over heat until egg is cooked.

Campground Choucroute

Prep time: 5 minutes • Cook time: 5 minutes • Serves: 4 guys or 6 regular people

2 TB. cooking oil	1 tsp. *caraway* seeds (optional)
1 lb. cooked kielbasa, cut into ½-inch slices	1 (15-oz.) can sliced white potatoes, drained
1 (14.5-oz.) can sauerkraut, drained and *rinsed*	Spicy brown mustard

Heat oil in a large skillet and cook kielbasa, stirring, for a few minutes or until it begins to brown. Add rinsed sauerkraut, caraway seeds (if using), and potatoes and heat, stirring, until the mixture is heated through. Distribute to serving plates, spread with spicy brown mustard, and enjoy.

Variation: If you have a few extra minutes, cook a chopped onion in 3 tablespoons olive oil, then add kielbasa, sauerkraut, and potatoes.

Menu Manual

Choucroute is French for "sauerkraut." But before you accuse me of getting all froufrou, it's also the name for a delicious one-pot meal from Alsace made with sauerkraut, sausage (or other meat), and potatoes.

It's up to you whether you want to **rinse** your sauerkraut. Doing so makes it more mild and, to me, appetizing. Rinsing is as simple as running water over your kraut in a colander, or squeezing the liquid out of the can, adding cold water, and squeezing it again a few times.

If you've got **caraway** seeds at home, bring them along for this dish. They add great flavor—like rye bread—and are traditionally believed to counteract some of the undesirable after-effects of eating cabbage (as in sauerkraut).

Skillet-Fried Fresh Fish

Prep time: 10 minutes   •   Cook time: 10 minutes   •   Serves: a taste for each guy (hey, this is only one fish!)

¼ cup canola or olive oil

1 (½- to 1-lb.) fresh fish

Salt and ground black pepper

½ lemon, cut into wedges

Cleaning: Clean your fish as soon as possible after you've caught it. Bring the fish, a *fish scaler*, a sharp paring knife, and a cutting board away from the campsite. (By the water is ideal.) Using the paring knife, make a 1-inch cut just behind the eyes (above the gills) and all the way through fish. This severs the backbone of fish. (It's important not to cut lower and sever the intestines—the bile, a green/black substance, can impart a bitter taste to the flesh.) Grasp fish body in one hand and the head in the other and pull off the head, bending it down and away from the body of the fish. Most of the intestines will come along with the head. Again using the knife, make a cut along the belly of the fish and clean out any remaining intestines. Discard the head. (If you have to keep it at the campsite, double-wrap it in plastic and keep it out of reach of animals.) Place fish on the cutting board and hold down the tail with your left hand (if you're right-handed). Using the scaler, scrape from the end of the fish toward where the head used to be, bearing down. Scales will begin to flake off. Scale all of this side of the fish up to the gills, turn the fish, and scale the other side. (Scales will fly around.) Rinse your scaled fish in cold water.

Cooking: Heat oil in a skillet, season fish with salt and pepper, and cook fish for about 4 minutes per side or just until flesh turns white and flakes easily. Remove fish to a serving plate, squeeze lemon juice over, and carefully remove flaky bites with a fork.

Depending on the type of fish, there will, at a minimum, be bones along the center and probably along the back. They'll be tiny bones, but still, you don't want to eat them.

Menu Manual

If you're planning to fish—and hopefully eat what you catch—add a **fish scaler** to your kitchen kit. This nifty little device is designed to flake those scales right off the fish and is much easier than attempting the task with a knife (or bad language).

Food Fumble

Cleaning a fish takes some practice, and you'll be likely to make a mess, so take your fish, your scaler or knife, and your cutting board away from the campsite. Those scales will attract animals—and they won't smell great after a while, either.

Oh, yeah, and be sure the fish you're preparing is one that's safe to eat.

Two-Minute Sour Cream Fruit Cocktail

Prep time: 5 minutes   •   Serves: 4 guys or 6 regular people

2 (15-oz.) cans chunky mixed fruit (no sugar added), juice poured off into a bowl

1 (8-oz.) can pineapple chunks in juice, drained

1 cup light sour cream (left over from your potatoes)

Mix mixed fruit, pineapple, and sour cream in a bowl. Mix in a little juice you saved if you like more liquid. Serve in bowls or cups.

The Least You Need to Know

- ◆ Cooking time is limited at the campground (especially when it's getting dark). Use fast cooking methods to make the best use of your time.
- ◆ A prepared set of campground kitchen tools will ensure you don't get stuck with a can and no can opener.
- ◆ Minimize cleanup by preparing the entire meal in one pot.
- ◆ Take the time to prepare some things in your kitchen at home and leave more time to enjoy the campfire.

Chapter 19

Food for Love (Date Night)

In This Chapter

- ◆ Setting the stage for romance with food
- ◆ Easy, classy appetizers for two
- ◆ Seductive seafood
- ◆ The magic of cream sauces

From the day Og and Ogette lovingly gnawed a mammoth leg to tonight's candlelit meal, food and romance have gone together. For a lot of us, a first date, or any night out, revolves around food. The meal we serve sends signals, starting with how much you care. Plunk down a plastic tray of take-out fish, and that says something. But serve that same fish with an easy cream sauce from your own oven, and you send a completely different message.

This chapter highlights recipes that will both impress *and* be easy to do. Then you'll be ahead of the game.

But don't forget to shower.

Romantic Food 101

Why, you ask, is food such a big part of a romantic encounter? Class is in session …

We've All Got to Eat

(Corollary: We're all interested in food.) If you're just meeting someone and you don't know her interests, you can at least assume she'll be interested in good food. The meal helps you both have fun, and fun means she might actually like being with you. Kind of makes sense, doesn't it?

Food Is Sensual

Don't worry, I'm not going to get all R-rated on you. But keep in mind that food, aside from being fuel, sets the tone. You can help set the atmosphere with what you serve. Think of slightly unusual ingredients (message: "This is a special occasion") and creamy, luxuriant textures.

Food as Aphrodisiac

Don't go too crazy here—science has yet to prove that your love life will improve if you eat oysters. Still, it's kind of fun to indulge in some of these supposed love-enhancing ingredients, especially when chocolate is on the list. Forget about the rhino horn.

Presentation Is Everything

When thinking about romance, think outside the plate to the space around it. When you're cooking at home, think about all the things that impact the meal. I might like Led Zeppelin (all right, so I'm old), but now is not the time to crank up the tunes. Those old stacks of *Sports Illustrated* on the table? They gotta go. Can't see the floor? A vacuuming would be nice.

End Run

The classic date is dinner and a movie. Especially on a first date, food is an important prop just in case you need something to talk about. Same goes for the movie, even if it's a bad one. I'm still amazed my girlfriend married me after I took her to see *Neighbors*.

Food Fumble

Be realistic about what you're trying to accomplish and go easy on yourself. Don't stress out over making a meal perfect—just make it fun and show you care. That effort will go a long way.

To help you a little, here are some secrets to a romantic meal:

- Bakery (unsliced) bread, warmed in the oven (Big, crusty chunks of bread invoke a warm, comfortable feeling.)

- Candles

- Soft music

- Special touches such as a tablecloth and flowers

- A clean dining room (If your place is usually a mess, the effort to clean says a lot about how much you care.)

End Run

Keep in mind that the most important message you send by lighting candles, setting music, etc., is to show that you care and that it's worth it to you to make an extra effort to put on a special meal. That message will be heard loud and clear.

- A fire in the fireplace (If you've got a fireplace, start it up. They had fire in cave-guy days, and something must have worked because we're all still here.)

- Wine (It's an easy way to add some class. For more on wine suggestions, see Chapter 22.)

For Starters

Appetizers set the stage for any meal or event, and that goes especially for date night. Rather than chips and dip, consider something almost as easy, but with some class. Here are some ideas.

Creamy Chicken Canapés

Prep time: 8 minutes • Cook time: 1 minute • Serves: 2 people as an appetizer

1 (5-oz.) can water-packed chunk chicken, drained

½ cup cream cheese, softened

½ cup mayonnaise

¼ cup shredded Parmesan cheese

1 tsp. Italian seasoning

½ tsp. salt

4 pieces bread, crusts removed, cut into 4 *triangles* per slice

Menu Manual

For an easy, classy way to slice bread, make **triangles.** Put a piece of sliced white or whole-wheat bread on a cutting board, cut off the crust, and cut the bread diagonally from each corner, making four triangles. You're done.

Preheat the broiler. Mix chicken, cream cheese, mayonnaise, Parmesan cheese, Italian seasoning, and salt in a bowl. Arrange bread triangles on a baking tray and broil on the high rack for 1 minute (watch carefully to avoid burning) or until bread begins to brown. Turn and toast the other side for another minute or less. Remove tray from oven, spread a spoonful of chicken mixture on each bread triangle, and arrange canapés on a serving plate.

Variation: In place of the bread, you can also use melba toasts (available at your grocery store) and skip the toasting requirement altogether.

Creamy Pumpkin Soup

Prep time: 5 minutes   •   Cook time: 20 minutes   •   Serves: 2 people plus leftovers

3 TB. butter or olive oil

1 medium onion (pool-ball size), peeled and cut into ½-inch pieces

1 (15-oz.) can chicken broth

1 (15-oz.) can solid-packed prepared pumpkin, not pumpkin pie filling

½ tsp. salt

½ cup heavy cream

Pinch ground black pepper

Heat butter in a large skillet over medium heat and cook onion, stirring, for 5 minutes or until onion has softened and becomes *translucent*. Add chicken broth, then stir in pumpkin and salt, stirring to a smooth consistency. Turn heat to low and cook for 20 minutes, stirring once in a while. Turn off heat, stir in heavy cream, and ladle into serving bowls, sprinkling a little bit of black pepper in the center of each bowl.

Variation: To make this soup even smoother, allow it to cool for a few minutes and run it through a food processor. This will be creamy and dreamy. Then heat it back up again and serve.

Menu Manual

Translucent means that the light shows through. When onions reach this stage, they are cooked enough to be soft and sweet.

Is It the Dish—or the Creamy Sauce?

Texture is a tremendous part of the appeal of a meal, and when it comes to date night, the right textures are smooth, creamy, and velvety.

Sole with Lemon Cream

Prep time: 5 minutes • Cook time: 10 minutes • Serves: 2 people

1 lb. fillet of sole	½ cup heavy cream
1 TB. fresh-squeezed lemon juice	3 TB. Parmesan cheese
Salt and ground black pepper	

End Run

My friend Sandy Richardson prepares this luxuriant dish for his wife a couple times a month. "If I can cook this," he says, "anybody can."

Preheat the broiler. Rinse fish under cold water and pat dry with paper towels. Sprinkle fish with lemon juice, salt, and pepper. Lay fish in a baking dish or baking tray in a single layer, pour heavy cream over it, and sprinkle with Parmesan cheese. Broil for about 5 minutes or until fish has turned white and flakes easily. Serve with lemon wedges, bread, and salad for a simple, delicious meal.

Cream Scallops

Prep time: 5 minutes • Cook time: 10 minutes • Serves: 2 people

3 strips bacon

1 lb. fresh bay scallops, or sea scallops cut into quarters

½ cup *mascarpone* or sour cream

Ground black pepper

Cook bacon in a large skillet over medium heat for 3 to 4 minutes per side or until crisp. Remove bacon to a plate covered with paper towels and turn the heat under the skillet to high. Add scallops to the skillet and cook in bacon fat, stirring, for about 2 minutes or until scallops are just opaque all the way through. Drain fat and turn the heat back to medium. Stir in mascarpone, heat for 1 minute, and spoon scallops with sauce to serving plates. Crumble bacon over scallops, sprinkle with black pepper, and serve.

Food Fumble

Cook scallops just until they turn white all the way through. They cook very quickly and will get tough if overcooked. A tough guy is okay; a tough scallop is not.

Menu Manual

Mascarpone is a thick, creamy, spreadable cheese, made originally in Italy but also now produced in the States. If you can't find it, use *crème fraîche* (another spreadable, creamy dairy product) or sour cream.

Mediterranean Lamb Loaf

Prep time: 5 minutes　•　Cook time: 1 hour　•　Serves: 2 people

1 lb. lean ground lamb

½ cup plain breadcrumbs

1 (7-oz.) can mushroom stems and pieces, drained

½ cup sun-dried tomatoes in oil (available in grocery stores; optional)

1 (4.25-oz.) can chopped black olives, drained

2 eggs, lightly beaten

1 TB. chopped garlic

1 tsp. ground cumin

1 tsp. Italian seasoning

½ tsp. dried rosemary

½ tsp. ground black pepper

4 slices provolone cheese

Parsley sprigs (optional, but nice)

Preheat the oven to 350°F. In a big bowl, thoroughly mix lamb, breadcrumbs, mushroom pieces, sun-dried tomatoes (if using), olives, eggs, garlic, cumin, Italian seasoning, rosemary, and pepper. The mixture should hold together. If it's too wet, add a few more bread crumbs. Place half of mixture in a greased loaf or baking pan. Lay ½ provolone slices across top. Spread rest of meat loaf mixture over cheese. Slide meat loaf into the oven and cook, uncovered, for about 1 hour. Remove, lay remaining cheese across top, and cook for another 5 minutes or until meat is cooked. (A meat thermometer will read 180°F.) To serve, slice with a butter knife and put pieces on serving plates. Put a sprig of parsley (if using) on top of each serving. Serve with fresh bread and salad.

Rich red Cabernet Sauvignon is a natural match with lamb dishes. (See Chapter 22 for more wine suggestions.)

End Run

If you've got single-serving size oven-safe bowls, it's a nice twist to prepare this loaf in personal-size containers. (Put the extra in a regular loaf pan.) If you do this, check for doneness at 40 minutes, as the smaller size loaves will cook more quickly. Pour off fat before serving, too.

Linguine with Clam Sauce

Prep time: 5 minutes   •   Cook time: 20 minutes, including water boiling time (while you show her your CD collection)   •   Serves: 2 people plus leftovers

½ (16-oz.) box (about ½ lb.) linguini

2 TB. butter or olive oil

2 TB. chopped garlic

1 (10-oz.) can water-packed baby clams

2 TB. heavy cream

1 tsp. Italian seasoning

Grated Parmesan cheese

Salt and ground black pepper

Boil water and start cooking pasta. Heat butter in a skillet over medium heat and cook garlic for 4 minutes, stirring, or until garlic just begins to tan. Pour in clams with water, cream, and Italian seasoning. Stir and turn the heat to low or simmer. Cover the pan and simmer for 15 minutes while pasta cooks. Drain pasta, put it in a serving bowl or on a platter, and pour clam sauce over. Serve with Parmesan cheese, salt, and pepper.

 End Run

If it's easier, cook the whole box of pasta and save the leftovers for another use, like dinner tomorrow.

Prosciutto Alfredo

Prep time: 5 minutes   •   Cook time: 20 minutes (pasta cooking time)   •   Serves: 2 people plus leftovers

½ lb. fettuccini or other pasta

½ cup heavy cream

½ cup light sour cream

1 cup shredded Parmesan cheese

½ cup diced prosciutto

½ stick (4 TB.) butter, melted

½ tsp. salt

½ tsp. ground black pepper

½ cup chopped fresh parsley (optional)

Cook and drain pasta and place it back in the cooking pot. Immediately add cream, sour cream, Parmesan cheese, prosciutto, melted butter, salt, pepper, and parsley. Mix thoroughly and serve. Candles, flowers, music, and white wine are good with this dish.

Variation: Use diced ham in place of the prosciutto.

Veal with Pepper Cream

Prep time: 5 minutes   •   Cook time: 10 minutes   •   Serves: 2 people plus leftovers

2 TB. butter

2 TB. olive oil

1 lb. veal leg cutlets (about 3 cutlets), pounded between two sheets of plastic wrap to a thickness of ¼-inch

Salt and ground black pepper

⅓ cup dry white wine

1 tsp. chopped garlic

½ tsp. salt

¼ tsp. ground black pepper

½ cup light sour cream

½ lemon, 2 thin slices cut for garnish, the rest saved for juice

Heat butter and olive oil in a large skillet over medium heat. Sprinkle veal with salt and pepper. Cook veal for 2 minutes per side or until done. (Cooking time will vary depending on veal thickness.) Remove veal to serving plates and cover with foil to keep warm for a couple minutes. Turn the heat under the skillet to high.

Food Fumble

Watch your delicate veal carefully as it cooks. Quick cooking is great, but overcooking is not.

Pour wine into the skillet and stir in garlic, salt, and pepper. Allow wine to boil for 1 minute. (It will reduce in volume.) Turn off the heat, add sour cream and lemon juice, and stir to mix thoroughly. With a rubber spatula, scrape every bit of this creamy elixir over veal servings. Lay a lemon slice on each serving and head to the table.

Basic Cheese Fondue

Prep time: 5 minutes • Cook time: 15 minutes • Serves: 2 people plus leftovers

1 cup dry white wine

2 tsp. chopped garlic

1 lb. shredded *Swiss* cheese

2 TB. cornstarch (or flour, if you don't have cornstarch)

1 TB. cooking sherry

½ tsp. nutmeg

Pinch ground black pepper

1 baguette crusty white or wheat bread, cut into 1-inch cubes

Heat wine and garlic in a saucepan over low heat until wine just barely begins to bubble. Put shredded Swiss cheese in a bowl and stir in corn-starch. A spoonful at a time, stir cheese into wine. Stir until spoonful melts, then add another. When cheese is all melted, stir in sherry, nutmeg, and pepper. Remove saucepan from stove and set it on a trivet between the two of you. Using forks or those cutesy little fondue forks, dunk bread cubes into cheese mixture to coat.

A salad and white wine make this meal complete.

End Run

If you have canned heat (those little cans with fuel) or even heating candles and the appropriate holder to hold the saucepan over the flame, that's a classy addition. Otherwise, if you need to, give the fondue a quick reheat on the stove to keep the mixture liquid enough to dunk.

Menu Manual

Fondue is a classic Swiss dish of melted cheese and white wine (among other things).

Swiss cheese, originally from Switzerland (no kidding), is now made across the world. It has a nutty, rich, slightly sour taste and those big bubble holes.

Far East Chicken and Broccoli

Prep time: 5 minutes • Cook time: 15 minutes • Serves: 2 people plus leftovers

1 small head broccoli, cut into 1-inch florets and stem pieces

3 cups cooked rice or 1½ cups uncooked (Brown rice works well with this dish, but it takes longer to cook.)

1 (5-oz.) can water-packed chunk white chicken, drained

1 TB. chopped garlic

3 TB. peanut butter

3 TB. water

2 TB. soy sauce

2 TB. sesame or canola oil

1 TB. sugar

Dash hot pepper sauce

Sesame seeds

Steam broccoli by adding an inch of water to a saucepan and bringing it to a boil. Insert a steamer insert if you've got one to hold broccoli over water, or if not, just put the broccoli in. Steam for about 5 minutes or until broccoli is crisp-tender. Cook rice in another saucepan.

End Run

Disclaimer: This recipe uses three pots—something we don't do much of in this book. But in my defense, your honor, the recipe is quick to prepare, and at least two of those pots will be easy to clean.

Meanwhile, stir together chicken, garlic, peanut butter, water, soy sauce, oil, sugar, and hot pepper sauce in a small saucepan on a third burner. Heat until just boiling and turn off the heat.

When broccoli and rice are done, distribute rice to serving plates. Scoop broccoli over rice (you might have some left over). Pour peanut sauce over each serving, sprinkle with sesame seeds, and serve.

Variation: Microwave broccoli in a microwave-safe bowl for 4 minutes covered with plastic wrap or until broccoli is crisp-tender.

Steak with Red Wine Sauce

Prep time: 5 minutes (not including marinating time)   •   Cook time: 10 minutes   •   Serves: 2 people plus leftovers

½ cup red wine

¼ cup olive oil

1 TB. chopped garlic

2 tsp. Italian seasoning

1 tsp. salt

½ tsp. ground cumin

½ tsp. ground black pepper

1 lb. beef tenderloin steak, T-bone, or your favorite

3 TB. butter

Thoroughly mix wine, oil, garlic, Italian seasoning, salt, cumin, and pepper in a large bowl. Place steak in the bowl, turning to coat. Cover and refrigerate for about 4 hours (enough time for you to get a haircut, do your laundry, and hide junk in the closet before she gets there).

When you're ready to cook, preheat your grill or broiler. Remove steak from its marinade and cook for 4 minutes per side or until done to your taste. (Cooking time will vary according to the cut of meat you're using.) Meanwhile, heat butter in a skillet over high heat and add remaining steak marinade. Rapidly boil marinade, stirring occasionally, for 5 minutes or until it reduces. Divide steak among serving plates, spoon sauce over it, and serve.

Food Fumble

Don't be tempted to skip the marinade-cooking step. This marinade has been in contact with raw meat, so the cooking is not just for taste—it's for *safety.*

Romance and Two Skillets

Sometimes she's worth a little extra effort. The following two recipes are intended to be cooked together for a coordinated meal. (The liquid used to cook the chicken is gradually also used to cook the risotto.) If you want, you can prepare this just before your date arrives, but it's fun to cook with your date there. You get to look like a chef, but all you're really doing is stirring. Add salad and wine, and you and that special someone can pretend you're on a piazza in Rome (Italy, not in upstate New York).

Chicken with Cream Sauce

Prep time: 5 minutes • Cook time: 45 minutes • Serves: 2 people

2 (14.25-oz.) cans chicken broth

2 (12-oz.) chicken breast halves, rinsed and patted dry on paper towels

⅓ cup sour cream

2 TB. olive oil

1 TB. fresh lime juice

Heat chicken broth in a large skillet until it begins to boil. Turn heat to between medium and low. Add chicken breasts and cook for about 10 minutes or until chicken is cooked and juices run clear. Put chicken breasts on a plate and cover with foil to keep warm. In a small bowl or cup, mix sour cream, olive oil, and lime juice. Scoop a spoonful of cream sauce on top of each breast when ready to serve.

This simple, creamy chicken dish pairs beautifully with the Asparagus-Cranberry Risotto (recipe follows). Start making it when you're waiting for the broth to boil.

Asparagus-Cranberry Risotto

Prep time: 5 minutes   •   Cook time: 20 minutes   •   Serves: 2 people

1 TB. butter

3 TB. olive oil

½ small onion (golf-ball size), peeled and chopped into ¼-inch pieces

½ cup *arborio rice*

½ lb. slender asparagus, washed, bottom inch of the stems removed, chopped into ½-inch pieces

½ cup dried cranberries

2 cups chicken broth, heated to a simmer

⅓ cup shredded Parmesan cheese

Heat butter and oil in a large skillet over medium heat and cook onion, stirring, for 3 minutes. Add rice, asparagus, and cranberries and cook for another 2 minutes, stirring to coat. Then add ½ cup hot broth and stir. Broth and *risotto* will bubble, and risotto will absorb the liquid over the course of a few minutes. Add another ½ cup broth and keep stirring. In total, you'll want to add about 2 cups broth, but you'll know it's done when rice is creamy but still has a bit of firmness. If risotto is too firm, add a little more broth. Stir in Parmesan cheese and you're done.

Serve risotto alongside Chicken with Cream Sauce and a bottle of white wine. The rest of the date is up to you.

Variation: Substitute white rice for arborio rice. Add rice along with asparagus, cranberries, and all of broth and cook for 15 minutes, stirring a couple times, or until rice is done. Stir in Parmesan and you're done.

Menu Manual

Risotto is a famous Italian rice dish made by browning **arborio rice** (a special kind of large-grain rice with a high starch content grown in Italy) in butter or oil, then slowly adding liquid to cook the rice, resulting in a creamy texture. It takes about 20 minutes to make, but it's easy (you're just gradually adding hot liquid) and delicious. You'll find arborio rice in the rice section of your grocery store.

A Sweet Ending

A simple, seductive dessert is the perfect end to a lovely dinner date. (For more on the sweet theme, see Chapter 10.)

Strawberries with Chocolate Sauce

Prep time: 5 minutes • Cook time: 10 minutes • Serves: 2 people plus leftovers

1 pint fresh strawberries, washed

1 cup bittersweet or semi-sweet chocolate chips

⅔ cup heavy cream

½ tsp. vanilla

Put strawberries in a presentable serving bowl. Put chocolate chips in a saucepan over low heat and stir until chocolate melts. Slowly stir in cream until it's all mixed in. Turn off the heat and stir in vanilla. Scrape sauce into a serving bowl, place it on the table next to the bowl of strawberries, and go for a dip.

The Least You Need to Know

- ◆ To add romance to a meal, use ingredients that are just a little indulgent, like cream, cheese, chocolate, and strawberries.
- ◆ Romantic does not have to mean time-consuming or complicated.
- ◆ Don't forget to set the stage: The surroundings are as important as the food.
- ◆ Just the fact that you went to the effort to create a special meal is going to earn you points!

Chapter 20

How Do You Like Your Eggs?

In This Chapter

- ◆ Breakfast—romantic and otherwise
- ◆ Classic egg dishes from over-easy to omelet
- ◆ Skillet delights from pancakes and French toast to home fries
- ◆ Speedy breakfast secrets and relaxed oven-baked favorites

Breakfast time is often overlooked altogether. But when we do think about it, our first thoughts are about "instant" options, such as cereals and breads. A hot breakfast doesn't make it onto the radar screen. The truth is, we often are in a rush so on a weekday, those "instant" foods are a necessity. But a hot breakfast is not hard and time-consuming, and it's perfect for any morning where you've got a few minutes and you want real flavor.

An added bonus of a cooked breakfast, by the way, is that it's often better for you, especially compared to sugar-loaded cereals and donuts. An egg breakfast, which would be my choice, is packed with nutrition and (if you're watching your girlish figure) is a great "low-carb" meal. Funny how eggs are back to being a health food.

Out of the Frying Pan: Eggs and More

Real men might not eat quiche, but they do eat eggs. Even my 9-year-old son (a *little* guy) begs for "egg on toast" just about every morning. (He doesn't always get it. There is such a thing as moderation.)

You can prepare eggs not just for breakfast but for any meal of the day as well. A quick dinner of egg on toast is sometimes just what we guys (9-year-olds and otherwise) need.

This section focuses on egg recipes that will get a delicious breakfast on the table—fast.

Fried Eggs

Prep time: 5 minutes   •   Cook time: 3 minutes   •   Serves: 2 guys or 4 regular people

3 TB. canola oil

4 eggs

Salt and ground black pepper

Heat oil in a skillet over medium heat. When a drop of water "dances" on hot oil, you're ready to cook. Crack 1 egg carefully on the edge of the skillet and, holding egg low over oil, open shell so egg drops into the skillet. Cook for about 1 minute or until egg white turns white about halfway to the surface. Carefully slide a spatula under egg and flip it in the skillet. Cook for another minute for *over-easy* or 1 minute longer for hard-cooked. Repeat with remaining eggs. Serve with freshly buttered toast and season with salt and pepper.

Menu Manual

An egg cooked **over-easy** is cooked on the outside but the yolk is still runny.

Scrambled Eggs

Prep time: 5 minutes • Cook time: 5 minutes • Serves: 2 guys or 4 regular people

4 eggs

¼ cup milk

3 TB. canola or olive oil

Salt and ground black pepper

Crack eggs in a bowl, add milk, and beat with a whisk or a fork. Heat oil in a skillet over medium heat. When a drop of water "dances" on hot oil, you're ready to cook. Pour eggs into the skillet, cook for 1 minute, then stir slowly to lift cooked parts from the skillet surface and let liquid parts cook. Cook to your desired consistency. (The more they cook, the drier they will get. Many people prefer less-cooked, creamy eggs.) Distribute to plates with toast and season with salt and pepper.

Variation: Add ½ cup shredded cheese (your favorite) to eggs in the bowl before you start cooking. Delicious!

End Run

Medium (or even low) heat is better than high heat for cooking scrambled eggs. Gradual cooking helps make a creamy, irresistible dish.

End Run

Scrambled eggs are very forgiving, and the possibilities for add-ins are endless. Chopped onion (cooked first in the skillet) is a natural. Shredded cheese? Of course. Chopped ham, cooked chicken, or cooked chopped beef? Why not? Leftover salsa? Throw it in! Many canned vegetables (mushrooms and sliced olives come to mind) are perfect, too. Experiment and make your favorite eggy mess!

Bacon and Swiss Eggs

Prep time: 5 minutes • Cook time: 8 minutes • Serves: 2 guys or 3 regular people

3 strips bacon

3 eggs

⅓ cup shredded Swiss cheese

⅓ cup milk

Salt and ground black pepper

Cook bacon in a large skillet over medium heat. While bacon is cooking, crack eggs in a bowl, add cheese and milk, and beat with a whisk or a fork. Remove bacon to a plate covered with paper towels and pour off most of bacon fat, leaving just enough to coat the bottom of the skillet. Pour eggs into the skillet, cook for 1 minute, then stir slowly to lift cooked parts from the skillet surface and let liquid parts cook. Crumble bacon into eggs. Cook to desired consistency. Distribute to plates with toast and season with salt and pepper.

Parmesan Cheese Omelet

Prep time: 5 minutes • Cook time: 3 minutes • Serves: 1 guy or 2 regular people (easily doubled)

2 eggs

2 TB. butter or olive oil

3 TB. shredded Parmesan cheese

Salt and ground black pepper

Crack eggs in a bowl and beat with a whisk or a fork. Heat butter in a small skillet (an omelet pan or nonstick skillet is best) over medium heat. When you're ready to cook, pour eggs into the skillet and cook for 1 minute. As they cook, carefully use your fork to loosen eggs around the edges from the skillet. When eggs are almost cooked through but still runny, sprinkle with Parmesan and carefully fold omelet over itself using the fork or a spatula. Lift the skillet over the serving plate and slide omelet out onto the plate. Serve, seasoning to taste with salt and pepper.

Note: Fillings that are great with scrambled eggs are just as good in omelets.

Scottish Salmon Eggs

Prep time: 5 minutes   •   Cook time: 5 minutes   •   Serves: 1 guy or 2 regular people, double as you like

2 TB. butter or canola oil for cooking, butter or margarine for toast

2 pieces white or whole-wheat bread, toasted

2 eggs

4 oz. thinly sliced smoked salmon (available in grocery stores)

Salt and ground black pepper

Heat butter in a skillet over medium heat. Toast and butter bread. When a drop of water "dances" on hot oil, you're ready to cook. Crack 1 egg carefully on the edge of the skillet and, holding egg low over oil, open shell so egg drops in. Cook for about 1 minute or until egg white turns white about halfway to the surface. Carefully slide a spatula under egg and flip it in the skillet. Add ½ smoked salmon to the skillet to heat as egg finishes cooking. Cook egg for another minute. Place toast on a serving plate, top toast with salmon, and place egg over salmon. Season with salt and pepper, repeat with remaining egg, and have breakfast in the Highlands.

Food Fumble

Take your own dietary concerns into account when eating eggs. Critics assert (correctly) that eggs are high in cholesterol and saturated fat. Fans counter (also correctly) that eggs are packed with nutrition and protein and are low in carbohydrates.

Bacon Home Fries

Prep time: 5 minutes • Cook time: 5 minutes • Serves: 2 guys or 4 regular people, double at will

3 strips bacon

1 medium onion (pool-ball size), peeled and chopped into ½-inch chunks

1 (15-oz.) can sliced white potatoes, drained

Salt and ground black pepper

Ketchup

Cook bacon in a large skillet over medium heat for 3 to 4 minutes per side. When crisp, remove to a plate covered with paper towels and pour off most of bacon fat, leaving just enough to coat the bottom of the skillet. Add onion and cook, stirring, for 5 minutes. Add potatoes and cook, stirring, for 4 minutes or until potatoes begin to brown. Distribute to plates, top with crumbled bacon, and season with salt and pepper. Ketchup goes well with these, too.

Egg Hammuffins

Prep time: 5 minutes • Cook time: 10 minutes • Serves: 4 guys or 8 regular people

3 TB. vegetable oil

8 split English muffins

Butter or margarine

8 eggs

½ lb. sliced honey ham

Salt and ground black pepper

Heat oil in a skillet over medium heat. Toast and butter English muffins. Crack 1 egg carefully on the edge of the skillet and, holding egg low over oil, open shell so egg drops in. Cook for about 1 minute or until egg white turns white about halfway to the surface. Carefully slide a spatula under egg and flip it in the skillet. Place a piece of ham in the skillet to heat as egg finishes cooking. Cook egg for another minute. Place English muffin half on a serving plate, top with ham, then add egg. Season with salt and pepper and top with other half of English muffin. Repeat with remaining eggs, ham, and muffins.

See if that beats the drive-thru!

Variation: Add a slice of cheese.

Pancakes

For a lot of us, pancakes and other flour-based breakfast foods hold a warm place in our memories. These are the things that relaxed weekend mornings are made of.

If you're a fan of instant mixes, I've started with a suggestion to improve on the boxed stuff. Making delicious pancakes and waffles from scratch is easy, though, and takes barely any more time than stirring the mix.

End Run

Invest an extra few minutes and make big batches. Those leftovers in the fridge become an instant delicious breakfast later in the week when there's no time to cook. Distribute cold pancakes to serving plates and reheat each serving for a minute or two in the microwave.

Pancake Mix Tune-Up

Prep time: 5 minutes • Cook time: 15 minutes • Serves: 2 guys or 4 regular people

½ cup small curd cottage cheese

2 TB. wheat germ

3 cups pancake mix (liquid already added per package instructions)

2 TB. butter, margarine, or cooking oil

Mix cottage cheese and wheat germ into pancake batter.

Heat butter in a large skillet over medium heat. Spoon batter (a ¼ cup measure is about the right size) into the skillet to make 3 or 4 pancakes, taking care to be sure pancakes stay separate. Cook until bubbles burst and stay open, then flip, cook for an additional minute, and serve or put in the oven on warm.

Serve with butter and syrup.

Food Fumble

Under the chronic guy "bigger is better" delusion, I am always tempted to make pancakes as big as the skillet. I'm warning you now—you'll have trouble flipping that monster, so make smaller ones instead. Don't say I didn't warn you!

Homemade Pancakes

Prep time: 5 minutes • Cook time: 15 minutes • Serves: 2 guys or 4 regular people

3 cups all-purpose flour	2 eggs
½ tsp. salt	2 cups milk
1½ tsp. granulated sugar	5 TB. canola oil
1½ tsp. baking soda	

Mix flour, salt, sugar, and baking soda in a large bowl. In a separate bowl, whisk eggs, milk, and 3 tablespoons oil. Stir egg mixture into flour until batter is mixed but still a little lumpy.

Heat remaining 2 tablespoons oil in a large skillet over medium heat. Spoon batter into the skillet to make 3 or 4 pancakes, taking care to be sure pancakes stay separate. Cook until bubbles burst and stay open, then flip, cook for an additional minute, and serve or put in the oven on warm.

Variation: Use half (or all) whole-wheat flour in place of all-purpose flour. It's better for you, and I find the cakes are more satisfying.

End Run

It's a nice touch to warm your serving plates and the syrup in the oven while you cook.

Got a sweet tooth at the breakfast table? Make those pancakes with chocolate chips! Hardly health food, but boy, are they good! (Banana slices, blueberries, and other berries are also classic.)

Finally, for a bit more health, substitute whole-wheat flour for an equal amount of the white flour. Start with 1 cup and see how it goes.

Toast the French Way

Take leftover bread, add delicious things (like eggs, milk, and spices), and cook it up in a skillet. It's sort of like making magic with ordinary ingredients, and that's a very good thing.

French Toast

Prep time: 5 minutes • Cook time: 15 minutes • Serves: 2 guys or 4 regular people

2 TB. butter or cooking oil

3 eggs

¾ cup milk

3 TB. sugar

8 slices white bread

Heat butter in a large skillet over medium heat. Whisk eggs, milk, and sugar in a large bowl and set the bowl next to the skillet. Dip a piece of bread into egg mixture and then move it to the skillet. Cook for about 2 minutes per side (longer if you're using thick bread slices) or until toast is nicely browned. Serve immediately or keep in a warm oven until cooking is complete.

Serve with butter or margarine and warm syrup.

End Run

French toast acts like a sponge, soaking up that egg and milk mixture. If you like your French toast lighter, only give it a quick turn in the egg. If you like rich, heavy French toast, submerge it in the eggs and let that sponge soak it all up. That's a slice that will stick to your ribs. Keep in mind, though, that you'll use up more of the eggs.

Healthful and Hearty French Toast

Prep time: 5 minutes • Cook time: 15 minutes • Serves: 2 guys or 4 regular people

2 TB. butter or cooking oil

3 eggs

¾ cup milk

8 slices whole-wheat bread

3 TB. wheat germ

Heat butter in a large skillet over medium heat. Whisk eggs and milk in a large bowl and set the bowl next to the skillet. Dip a piece of bread into egg mixture and move it to the skillet. Sprinkle top of cooking toast with wheat germ and cook for about 2 minutes, then flip and cook for another couple minutes or until toast is nicely browned. Serve immediately or keep in a warm oven.

Serve with butter or margarine and warm syrup.

Variation: Instead of syrup, use canned blueberries in syrup or another fruit that has been sliced or chopped with sugar in a food processor. In that case, it just seems natural to top your French toast with whipped cream.

Waffles

If you've got a waffle iron lurking in your kitchen, making waffles is as easy as pancakes. With waffles, you get fun shapes and lots of little craters to hold all that butter and syrup.

Easy Homemade Waffles

Prep time: 5 minutes   •   Cook time: 15 minutes   •   Serves: 2 guys or 4 regular people

1½ cups all-purpose flour

1 TB. granulated sugar

1 tsp. baking soda

½ tsp. salt

1 cup milk

3 eggs

3 TB. oil

Preheat the *waffle iron.*

Mix flour, sugar, baking soda, and salt in a large bowl. In a separate bowl, whisk milk, eggs, and oil. Stir egg mixture into flour until batter is mixed but still a little lumpy.

Spoon about ⅓ cup batter into the center of the waffle iron and close the top. Cook until waffles are crisp and browned, usually about 3 minutes, depending on the machine.

Serve with butter and syrup or fresh-cut strawberries and whipped cream.

Menu Manual

To make waffles, you need a **waffle iron.** You probably have one in your closet covered in dust, but if you don't, you'll find one at every kitchen-supply store and even in some grocery stores.

All-Day Waffles

Prep time: 5 minutes • Cook time: 15 minutes • Serves: 2 guys or 4 regular people

1 cup whole-wheat flour	1 cup milk
½ cup all-purpose flour	3 eggs
1 TB. sugar	⅓ cup sour cream
1 tsp. baking soda	3 TB. oil
½ tsp. salt	

Preheat the waffle iron.

Mix whole-wheat and white flours, sugar, baking soda, and salt in a large bowl. In a separate bowl, whisk milk, eggs, sour cream, and oil. Stir egg mixture into flour until batter is mixed but still a little lumpy.

Spoon about ⅓ cup batter into the center of the waffle iron and close the top. Cook until waffles are crisp and browned, usually about 3 minutes, depending on the machine.

Serve with butter and syrup. When you eat these for breakfast, you'll have no need for lunch.

Muffins and Bread

Although guys love them, muffins and breads fall into that category of intimidating foods that sound like they take a long time and are hard to make. Follow these recipes, and you'll learn the easy secrets.

George Ames's Blueberry Muffins

Prep time: 10 minutes • Cook time: 25 minutes • Serves: 6 guys or 8 regular people

6 TB. sugar

2 cups fresh blueberries, rinsed

4 cups all-purpose flour

6 tsp. baking powder

2 tsp. salt

2 eggs

2 cups milk

12 TB. melted all-vegetable shortening or melted butter

Preheat oven to 425°F. Mix sugar and blueberries in a bowl. Mix flour, baking powder, and salt in another bowl. In a large glass measuring cup or separate bowl, whisk eggs until they start to get foamy. Add milk and melted shortening (can be melted in the microwave). Make a crater in flour and pour in liquid mixture, mixing and stirring until combined but still lumpy. Stir in blueberries and spoon mixture into greased muffin pans. Bake for 25 minutes or until tops are golden brown.

 End Run

I included these traditional favorites in my book *The Complete Idiot's Guide to 20-Minute Meals*. These are not only great, but George was also the ultimate guy.

These muffins don't have a lot of sugar, and this is on purpose, so the blueberry flavor shines through. But feel free to add more to sweeten these up if you want.

Blueberry Breakfast Cornbread

Prep time: 5 minutes   •   Cook time: 25 minutes   •   Serves: 2 guys or 4 regular people

1 (15-oz.) can wild blueberries in syrup   1 egg

1 (15-oz.) box cornbread and muffin mix   ¼ cup milk

Preheat the oven to 400°F. In a bowl, mix blueberries with their syrup, muffin mix, egg, and milk. Add a little more milk if necessary to get a very thick, almost solid batter. (How much will depend on the amount of syrup with blueberries.)

Grease a small baking dish and scrape batter into the dish. Bake for 25 minutes or until top is browned and a toothpick inserted in the center comes out clean. Remove from oven and cut into squares with a knife. Serve with butter or margarine.

Variations: Other canned fruits, such as cherries, will work. Fresh fruits are also delicious, but in that case increase the amount of milk to achieve a thick batter.

The Least You Need to Know

♦ Egg dishes are fast and delicious.

♦ Scrambled eggs are the foundation, but you decide what to add. Vegetables, cooked meats, cheeses, and more are all fair game.

♦ Making pancakes and waffles from scratch is easy and quick.

♦ Make extra pancakes, waffles, or muffins. Those leftovers can be delicious survival rations during the week when there's no time to cook.

Chapter 21

Holidays and Dinner Parties

In This Chapter

- ◆ Presentation with a flourish
- ◆ Delicious, easy appetizers
- ◆ Main dishes that look great but still give you time to get ready
- ◆ Irresistible cream sauces
- ◆ Elegant seafood dishes

Every now and then a guy has to put on a big spread (holidays, celebrations, that kind of thing). Whether for family or friends, when guys cook, they want to do it right.

In this chapter, you'll find tips, recipes, and practical advice on how to "wow" your guests.

Look Good at the Big Dinner

When guests are coming, an unusual feeling comes over most guys: *stress*. But don't let it get to you. With just a bit of planning, you'll get it all done and wonder what all the fuss was about.

As you think about the meal, remember these quick tips to help you relax.

Go Easy on Yourself

Now is not the time to try some fancy, multi-step, all-day meal involving steamed yak milk and puréed cod bladders. Stick with simple, tasty recipes that don't take a long time to prepare.

> **End Run**
>
> For guests one night, I decided to make meat loaf. My wife wrinkled her nose until I told her I would make the Mediterranean Lamb Loaf (recipe in Chapter 19). It uses simple methods but slightly unusual ingredients—in other words, it's a twist on the familiar. The result? Everybody loved it! (Oh yeah, and it was no stress for me.)

Do the Work Ahead of Time

You can make many dishes from this book—think about stews, lasagna, meat loaf, baked chicken, even chili—in advance. By doing this, you have time to clean up the mess, and there's no stress. You also get extra credit when you hang out with your guests … and then casually whip out something that's already done. Smooth.

Any one of these recipes is perfect for making ahead of time:

- Stews and variations (Chapters 3, 7, 17, and others)
- Roast Beef (7)
- Chicken Zucchini (11)
- Lasagna (12)
- Sausage-Stuffed Peppers (17)
- Rosy the Pork (17)
- … and many others!

Stick With What You Know

Well, maybe not hot dogs, but after spending some time with this book, you should have something you're good at, whether it's grilled steak or pork chops or roast chicken or casseroles or whatever. Start with that concept, maybe come up with a slight twist to make it fun (even if it's simply a fun presentation), and you've got a crowd-pleasing meal.

Don't Go Too Crazy

If your favorite dinner is Molten Lava Chili (recipe in Chapter 16), pick something else (unless, of course, this dinner is for a bunch of the guys). Stick with something that has a good chance of being liked by most, if not all, of your guests.

Garnish

Some dishes look even more appetizing with snipped fresh chives, sliced scallions, a sprinkling of sliced almonds, or Parmesan cheese. Even when guys at the fire station sit down to a meal, there's a good chance their meat loaf will have a sprig of parsley on it.

... and Varnish

Think about the place where you're serving your food. How does it look? What about using music, some candles, and a tablecloth? Get out a good serving platter. A clean shirt is a good idea, too. All these things send a signal to your guests. You're telling them they are important to you—and that message goes a long way.

What If Guests Want to Help?

Let them! People like to feel involved and needed; it actually adds to the fun. Of course, don't forget our commandment: "Keep it simple!"

Appetizers

One way to get any gathering started off right is with an appetizer or two. People love these small bites with big flavor. They're easy and quick and can distract people if you're panicking in the kitchen. Try one of these ideas.

If you'd like more quick appetizer ideas, check out my book *The Complete Idiot's Guide to 5-Minute Appetizers*.

End Run

When purchasing cheese for appetizers, plan on *at least* 3 ounces per person. There is no harm in buying more.

Cheese Tray

Prep time: 2 minutes   •   Serves: 6 to 8 as an appetizer

Weights are approximate:

6 oz. aged Gouda (the "aged" part is important)

6 oz. Port Salut or Brie

6 oz. Roquefort or other block blue cheese

6 oz. sharp cheddar

1 baguette or other crusty bread, cut into ½-inch pieces

2 ripe pears, cut into slices

End Run

Cheese and fruit are as natural together as peanut butter and jelly. The same goes for bread and cheese. Crackers (the plain kind) also will work fine. Just watch out for flavored crackers because they'll hide the flavors of the cheese.

Find a decent large cutting board or platter. Set cheeses well apart, with at least two sharp knives for cutting, one near the blue and the other for the other cheeses. Arrange bread and pear slices around cheese.

If you've never had it, a bite of blue cheese with a slice of pear will be a "wow."

Note: Set cheeses out an hour in advance so they will come up close to room temperature. This brings out much more delicious cheese flavor.

Menu Manual

This simple, classy appetizer is always impressive. Head for your local grocery store cheese department (or cheese shop, if you've got one near you) and ask for these cheeses. After you've tried these, sample others. There's a world of cheeses out there.

Need some more ideas? I've got you covered (definitions adapted from my book *The Complete Idiot's Guide to 5-Minute Appetizers*):

◆ **Gouda** (Holland or the United States): The common variety is a mild cheese most popular (at least in my house) when it's "smoked" Gouda. Aged Gouda, on the other hand, is a buttery, nutty, smoky-tasting delicacy. It costs more—and it will be the first cheese to disappear from your tray.

◆ **Port Salut** (France): A creamy, rich, and irresistible cheese, similar to brie.

◆ **Brie** (France, with some good U.S. versions): A famous creamy, soft cheese with a soft, edible rind. Tasty with just about anything, from bread to fruit to nuts.

◆ **Roquefort** (France): The world-famous blue cheese made from sheep's milk.

Bruschetta

Prep time: 5 minutes   •   Cook time: 5 minutes   •   Serves: 6 to 8 as an appetizer

⅓ cup olive oil

1 TB. chopped garlic

1 *baguette*, cut into ½-inch slices

1 (14.5-oz.) can diced tomatoes, drained

⅓ cup shredded Parmesan cheese

Salt (optional)

Preheat the broiler and mix olive oil and garlic in a bowl. Spread bread slices on a baking tray and brush each with garlic olive oil (or spoon a little olive oil over each piece, spreading it with the back of the spoon). Broil for 1 minute or until bread begins to brown. Then flip and broil the other side. Bring out the tray and put a spoonful of tomatoes on each piece of bread. (You might have tomato left over.) Sprinkle Parmesan over each piece. Slide the tray back under the broiler for 1 minute, then put your bruschetta on a platter and serve, sprinkling with a little salt if necessary.

Variation: If you've got access to fresh tomatoes to chop up and use in place of the canned tomatoes, by all means go for it. Fresh (as in locally grown) tomatoes always have the best flavor.

Menu Manual

Bruschetta is bread grilled with garlic and olive oil, often with a topping or two, as in tomatoes and Parmesan cheese. Other toppings you can combine at will include the following:

- ◆ Artichoke hearts
- ◆ Cream cheese
- ◆ Fresh basil
- ◆ Goat's milk cheese
- ◆ Mozzarella slices

- ◆ Olives
- ◆ Prosciutto (and ham)
- ◆ Roasted red peppers
- ◆ Sun-dried tomatoes (drained and oil-packed are best; regular dried are tough)
- ◆ Sweet onion or scallions

A **baguette** is a long, skinny loaf of bread. The shape of the loaf gives you a lot more surface area than a loaf of similar weight in a standard stubby shape. Lots of surface area means lots of crust—a good thing for many purposes, such as appetizers, where a sturdy bread is better.

Warm Tuna Dip

Prep time: 2 minutes • Cook time: 2 minutes • Serves: 6 to 8 as an appetizer

1 (10-oz.) can or 2 (6-oz.) cans water-packed chunk white tuna, drained

1 (8-oz.) pkg. shredded cheddar cheese

1 cup mayonnaise

1 tsp. garlic salt

½ tsp. dried dill

Dash hot pepper sauce (optional)

Mix tuna (break up any large chunks), cheese, mayonnaise, garlic salt, dill, and hot pepper sauce (if using) in a microwave-safe serving bowl. Heat for 90 seconds or until dip starts to bubble. Stir and serve with wheat crackers or veggie sticks for dipping or slices of crusty bread for spreading.

Meats

These meaty dishes continue to be easy to prepare (like the rest of this book), but might just bring that extra appeal (or even "class") that you want to serve to guests.

Chicken Casserole

Prep time: 10 minutes • Cook time: 30 minutes (cooking time while you look for that clean shirt) • Serves: 4 guys or 6 regular people

4 to 6 slices bread

1 (15-oz.) can or 3 (5-oz.) cans water-packed chunk white chicken meat, drained

2 TB. minced dried onion

1 tsp. Italian seasoning

Dash hot pepper sauce

1 (14.5-oz.) can cut green beans, drained, or 1 (9-oz.) pkg. frozen cut green beans, thawed

2 (10.75-oz.) cans condensed cream of mushroom soup

½ cup breadcrumbs

1 (8-oz.) pkg. shredded cheddar cheese

Preheat the oven to 350°F. Lay bread pieces on the bottom of a baking dish in a single layer. (If it's a larger dish, use 6 pieces; if smaller, use 4.) Mix the chicken, onion, Italian seasoning, and hot pepper sauce in a bowl and spread this mixture over bread. Spread green beans over chicken. Pour soup (don't use extra water) over beans and then breadcrumbs over that and spread with the back of a spoon. Sprinkle cheese over the top and bake for 30 minutes or until casserole is bubbling.

 End Run

In the good old days, cream soups seemed to be the foundation of every meal. This casserole evokes those comfort food memories, as the cream of mushroom soup adds flavor and creamy texture.

Grilled Pork Tenderloin Medallions with Sherry Garlic Cream

Prep time: 10 minutes • Cook time: 30 minutes (cooking time while you pick up all your stuff off the couch and chairs) • Serves: 4 guys or 6 regular people

1 TB. chopped garlic	1 (1½-lb.) pork tenderloin, cut into ¾-inch slices
5 TB. olive oil	½ lemon
¼ cup cooking sherry (or cream sherry)	½ tsp. salt
⅓ cup sour cream	¼ tsp. ground black pepper

Preheat the grill. Sauté garlic in 3 tablespoons olive oil in a small skillet over medium heat for 3 minutes or until garlic starts to brown. Add sherry and cook until liquid is reduced by half, about 4 minutes. Turn off the heat under the skillet. Add sour cream and mix thoroughly.

Meanwhile, put tenderloin pieces in a bowl. Drizzle first with lemon juice, then with remaining 2 tablespoons olive oil. Turn pieces to coat and sprinkle with salt and pepper. Grill pork until just done, approximately 3 minutes per side.

Distribute tenderloin pieces to serving plates and divide the sauce between servings.

"Tarragarlic" Chicken

Prep time: 5 minutes   •   Cook time: 10 minutes   •   Serves: 4 guys or 6 regular people

2 TB. olive oil

2 tsp. crushed garlic

4 (about 1½ lb.) boneless, skinless chicken breasts, rinsed and patted dry on paper towels

Salt and ground black pepper

¼ cup white wine

¼ cup sour cream

Juice of ½ lemon, or 2 TB. lemon juice

1 tsp. dried tarragon

½ tsp. salt

Heat oil over medium heat in a large skillet. Cook garlic for 3 minutes, stirring. Sprinkle chicken breasts with salt and pepper on both sides. Cook for 4 minutes per side or until done and the juices run clear.

While chicken is cooking, mix white wine, sour cream, lemon juice, tarragon, and salt in a bowl.

Distribute chicken to plates. Pour sauce into skillet and heat for 2 minutes, but do not let it boil. Pour even portions over each piece of chicken.

End Run

One taste tester for this dish, which I adapted from my book *The Complete Idiot's Guide to 20-Minute Meals,* admitted licking his plate. That sounds like a good reason for including the recipe here.

One fail-safe meal to keep in mind for dinner parties is a ham. Just about everybody likes it. In fact, a case could be made for this being the perfect party food. Already cooked, it's just waiting to be served. A lot of hams even come with a glaze (a flavorful syrup). Heat that baby in the oven for an hour, and dinner is ready. Or serve it cold. Leftovers will keep you going for a week, too.

Seafood

Seafood dishes have a lot going for them. To start with, people see them as classy. Cooking can't take long because prolonged heat destroys flavor and texture. And for those of us keeping an eye on our health, seafood tends to be low in fat (or at least low in saturated fat) and packed with nutrition. Here are some of my favorite seafood dishes.

Pesto Shrimp Over Penne Pasta

Prep time: 10 minutes • Cook time: 20 minutes (mostly pasta cooking time while you try to find matching plates for the dining table) • Serves: 4 guys or 6 regular people

1 lb. uncooked penne pasta

3 TB. olive oil

2 TB. garlic

1 lb. (51 to 70 count) cooked shrimp, tail off and thawed

1 (7-oz.) tub prepared pesto sauce (available in grocery stores)

½ lemon

Grated Parmesan cheese

Cook and drain pasta. Return to the cooking pot to keep warm.

Heat oil in a large skillet over medium heat and cook garlic, stirring, for 3 minutes. Add shrimp and heat for 1 minute, stirring, and then add pesto sauce. Stir over heat for 3 minutes or until heated through. Distribute pasta to serving plates and top with big spoonfuls of the shrimp pesto sauce. Squeeze lemon juice over each serving, sprinkle with Parmesan cheese, and serve.

Variation: Sprinkle with toasted pine nuts (available at your grocery store). You can use tail-on shrimp; just break off the tails before adding to sauce.

Broiled Salmon

Prep time: 10 minutes • Cook time: 8 minutes • Serves: 4 guys or 6 regular people

3 TB. olive oil

3 TB. teriyaki sauce

2 lb. salmon fillets (2 fillets)

4 scallions, roots and dark green parts removed, rinsed, and sliced into very thin rings

Preheat the broiler. Mix olive oil and teriyaki sauce in a bowl. Rinse salmon under cold water and pat dry with paper towels. Set salmon in a baking dish, skin side down, and pour teriyaki mixture over. Turn to coat, ending up with skin side up. Broil for 4 minutes per side or until cooked. Distribute salmon to serving plates and sprinkle each serving with sliced scallion pieces.

Serve with fresh bread and salad or rice and buttered green beans.

Food Fumble _____

If you're not convinced that the fish at the market looks fresh, don't buy it. Cook something else. Fresh fish is great. Less than fresh is ... just plain fishy.

Poached Cod with Garlic Cream Sauce

Prep time: 10 minutes   •   Cook time: 20 minutes   •   Serves: 4 guys or 6 regular people

2 cups white wine

1 TB. plus 1 tsp. Italian seasoning

½ tsp. salt

2 lb. cod fillets (or other whitefish fillets)

2 TB. olive oil

2 tsp. chopped garlic

½ cup sour cream

1 TB. fresh lemon juice

1 bunch *watercress* for garnish, rinsed with stems discarded

Heat serving plates in the oven on warm.

Heat wine, 1 tablespoon Italian seasoning, and salt in a large skillet over high heat until boiling. Reduce heat to low and simmer for 10 minutes. Rinse cod in cold water. If you have a single-piece steamer insert for cooking vegetables, that's a good "basket" for your fish to keep it in one piece. Set cod in the basket and lower it into broth. Otherwise, set cod in broth and use a couple spatulas to carefully raise it out when it's cooked. (Don't worry if it breaks apart; a couple big pieces are fine.) If broth does not cover cod when you set it in the skillet, add some water until it does. Simmer for 10 minutes or until fish is just cooked (opaque all the way through).

Meanwhile, heat oil in a small skillet or saucepan over medium heat and cook garlic and remaining 1 teaspoon Italian seasoning for 3 minutes, stirring. Turn off the heat and stir in sour cream and lemon juice.

Lay watercress on each serving plate to cover an area a little bigger than the pieces of fish you're serving. When cod is done, lay a piece over watercress, spoon some cream sauce over, and serve. Wow!

Variation: If you can't find watercress, use another leafy vegetable such as baby spinach.

Menu Manual

To **poach** is to cook a food in simmering liquid, such as water, wine, or broth. The first time I used wine to poach fish, I hated the idea of "wasting wine." When I tried it, though, I changed my mind. The flavor comes through—and you might just have a new favorite meal.

Watercress, available in most grocery stores, is a spicy, crunchy, dark-green leafy vegetable. It is sold in bunches and is often in the veggie section near the fresh herbs. Its name comes from its love of growing in wet areas or in streams.

Seafood Stew

Prep time: 10 minutes   •   Cook time: 20 minutes   •   Serves: 4 guys or 6 regular people

3 TB. olive oil

1 TB. chopped garlic

2½ (15-oz.) cans tomato sauce

2 TB. tomato paste

2 tsp. Italian seasoning

½ tsp. crushed red pepper

¾ cup red wine

1 (16-oz.) pkg. assorted frozen scallops, shrimp, and calamari, or ½ lb. each fresh scallops and small shelled and deveined shrimp

½ lb. whitefish, such as cod, halibut, or haddock, cut into 1-inch chunks

Heat oil in a large skillet over medium heat and cook garlic for 3 minutes. Add tomato sauce, tomato paste, Italian seasoning, and crushed red pepper and simmer for 10 minutes. Add red wine, return to simmer, and add scallops, shrimp, calamari, and fish. Bring to a simmer and cook, stirring once in a while, for 10 minutes or until cooked (fish will be white all the way through).

Serve with fresh bread, a big salad, and a white or light-bodied red wine. Don't forget to put candles on the table.

 End Run

> If company's coming, don't just dump a bag of iceberg salad mix into a bowl. Dress it up with baby spinach leaves (they also come in bags) or a bag of "mixed greens." You can even grab one of those bags of sliced almonds (they're in the salad section of your grocery store) to sprinkle on top. Now, that's a salad! (For more salad ideas, check out Chapter 9.)

The Least You Need to Know

- Start your dinner with an appetizer or two. Conversation will heat up, people will have something to focus on while you get dinner going, and everything will be off to a good start.

- Control what's going on *around* your meal as well as what's *in* it. Presentation is everything, after all.

- Stick to recipes you know, and present your food with a flourish (even if it's just a nice platter and parsley). Your company will appreciate your effort to make things look good.

- Pick recipes that either cook quickly or can be put into the oven to give you time to get ready.

- Make things ahead of time to reduce stress when the doorbell rings.

Chapter 22

Food and Wine

In This Chapter

- ◆ Tips for matching food and wine
- ◆ Wine-friendly recipes
- ◆ Great taste for less than $10
- ◆ A sure-winner wine producer "cheat sheet"
- ◆ Wine and food pairing recommendations

If you're interested in wine and food (it's a tough hobby), you can have a lot of fun deciding just what wine goes best with salmon, baked chicken, or steak tips. That's what this chapter is about. Research can be fun. (Remember: It's not the destination, it's the journey.)

Matching Food with Wine

As a general rule for using wine with food, match "like with like." The logic is that a monster red wine would smother a delicate fish or shrimp dish. For that kind of seafood, a clean, refreshing white wine, such as a Sauvignon Blanc or Pinot Grigio, could do just the trick. On the other hand, for a rich beef dish, your light white wine will end up tasting like lemon water. This is the time for the monster.

One possible exception to this general rule is with spicy dishes such as curries, chili, and Thai food. In these cases, a cool, refreshing white with a bit of sweetness (like Gewürztraminer or Riesling) is a terrific match. (Beer is also great with these foods.)

For the purpose of deciding which wine goes with which food, I've listed several "types" of wine and the grapes (known as *varietals*) that generally fall into that category (with plenty of exceptions!):

- Light whites include Sauvignon Blanc and Pinot Grigio.
- Rich whites include American and Australian Chardonnay, Riesling, and Gewürztraminer.
- Light reds include Beaujolais (France), Chianti (Italy), Pinot Noir (some are rich, though), and some Merlot.
- Rich reds include many Côtes du Rhône reds (France), Cabernet Sauvignon, Shiraz/Syrah, and Zinfandel.
- Sweet wines include port, sauternes, sherry, and Madeira, among others.

Basic Food and Wine Matches

	Light Whites	Rich Whites	Light Reds	Rich Reds	Sweet Wines
Appetizers	X	X	X		
Light seafood	X	X			
Rich seafood	X	X	X		
White meats	X	X	X		
Rich meats				X	
Spicy foods		X (especially Gewürztraminer and Riesling)			
Dessert					X

End Run

If you want to do the right thing for your guests but don't want to spend a lot of time (like read this whole chapter), pick a red and a white from the recommended producers later in this chapter (or from one of the specific wines listed after that). A lot of people see themselves as "white wine people" or "red wine people." No matter what food you're serving, they'll go for that glass of white. So as long as you have the basic red/white choice, you're covered.

Food for White Wines

Since delicate seafood flavors are the traditional match for white wines, the following recipes are a good place to start. For others, look throughout this book not only at seafood, but also at many poultry- and pork-based recipes.

Quick Fried Scallops

Prep time: 5 minutes   •   Cook time: 5 minutes   •   Serves: 4 guys or 6 regular people

3 TB. butter

1 TB. chopped garlic

1 tsp. Italian seasoning

2 lb. bay scallops, or sea scallops, quartered

⅓ cup all-purpose flour

Salt and ground black pepper

Melt butter in a large skillet over medium-low heat and stir in garlic and Italian seasoning. While the skillet is heating, rinse scallops in cold water and pat dry on paper towels. Put scallops in a bowl and pour flour over them, stirring to coat. Spoon scallops into the skillet (leaving extra flour in the bowl) and cook, stirring, for about 3 minutes or until scallops are browned and cooked through. Serve with fresh bread and salad or over hot rice and season to taste with salt and pepper.

Asparagus and Shrimp Stew

Prep time: 5 minutes • Cook time: 25 minutes • Serves: 4 guys or 6 regular people

4 strips bacon

1 large onion (baseball size), peeled and chopped into ½-inch pieces

1 tsp. chopped garlic

½ tsp. ground cumin

½ tsp. ground thyme

4 (15-oz.) cans chicken broth

¼ tsp. ground black pepper

Dash hot pepper sauce

1 bunch (about 1 lb.) asparagus, bottom 2 inches discarded, chopped into 1-inch segments

½ lb. (20 to 40 count) cooked shrimp, tail off

¼ lb. (4 oz.) baby spinach, rinsed with stems discarded

¼ cup Madeira or sherry

Grated Parmesan cheese

Salt and ground black pepper

Cook bacon in a large pot over medium heat for 4 minutes or until crisp. Remove bacon to a plate covered with paper towels. Drain most of bacon fat, leaving enough to coat the bottom of the pot, and cook onion, garlic, cumin, and thyme for 4 minutes, stirring. Add broth, black pepper, and hot pepper sauce and bring to a boil. Add asparagus and cook for 10 minutes or until asparagus is just turning from crisp to tender. Stir in shrimp, spinach, and Madeira and cook for 3 minutes or until spinach has wilted and soup is just beginning to bubble again.

Serve to bowls, crumbling bacon over each serving, sprinkling with Parmesan cheese, and seasoning to taste with additional salt and pepper.

White or Red, Take Your Pick

Rich fish and light meats, such as salmon and pork, are very versatile when it comes to wine. Try one of these (or other recipes with these base ingredients) when you need a meal that can go both ways.

Skillet-Broiled Salmon with Vegetables

Prep time: 5 minutes • Cook time: 15 minutes • Serves: 4 guys or 6 regular people

2 lb. salmon fillets	2 TB. butter, cut into small pieces
1 TB. Italian seasoning	½ tsp. salt
½ tsp. ground black pepper	1 cup white wine
2 (14.5-oz.) cans diced tomatoes with juice	½ cup sour cream

Preheat the broiler. Rinse salmon under cold water and pat dry with paper towels. Place salmon in an oven-safe skillet or an aluminum baking pan, skin side down. Sprinkle salmon with Italian seasoning and pepper. Spread tomatoes over salmon, *dot* with butter, and sprinkle with salt. Slide skillet under the broiler and cook for 5 minutes, then turn over salmon. (Tomatoes will now be underneath.) Pour ½ cup wine over salmon and broil for another 5 minutes or until fish is done.

Put salmon onto a serving plate or platter and cover with foil to keep it warm. Put skillet with tomatoes and juices on the stove over medium heat. Add remaining ½ cup wine and cook, stirring, for 5 minutes. The liquid will reduce and thicken. Turn off heat. Stir in sour cream. Distribute salmon to individual serving plates and spoon chunky cream sauce over each piece. Serve with fresh bread, a salad, and your favorite wine.

Menu Manual

Dot means to spread small pieces of an ingredient around on top of a dish. In this case, the small pieces of butter dotted over the fish will evenly coat the fish as they melt.

Breaded Pork Chops

Prep time: 5 minutes   •   Cook time: 10 minutes   •   Serves: 4 guys or 6 regular people

½ cup sour cream

¼ cup milk

1 cup breadcrumbs

1 tsp. paprika

¼ cup canola oil

2 lb. thin-cut pork chops

Mix sour cream and milk in a small bowl. Mix breadcrumbs with paprika in a separate bowl. Heat oil in a skillet over medium heat. Dip pork chops into milk–sour cream mixture, roll in breadcrumbs, and cook for 4 minutes per side or until done.

These chops are delicious with applesauce.

Food for Light Red Wines

Here's one recipe that's perfect for light red wines. For others, look at the pasta and tomato-based dishes, salmon dishes, and chicken and pork recipes throughout the book.

Baked Chicken and Tomatoes

This is not only great wine food but also great comfort food.

Prep time: 5 minutes   •   Cook time: 25 minutes   •   Serves: 4 guys or 6 regular people

⅓ cup grated Parmesan cheese for rolling chicken, additional cheese for garnish

1 (.7-oz.) pkg. Italian salad dressing mix

1½ lb. boneless, skinless chicken breasts (about 6), rinsed and patted dry on paper towels

2 TB. olive oil

1 lb. uncooked pasta (your favorite)

1 (28-oz.) can stewed tomatoes

Preheat oven to 350°F. Mix cheese and ½ salad dressing mix on a plate. Drizzle chicken breasts with olive oil on both sides and roll in Parmesan mixture until completely coated. Place chicken in a baking dish and bake for 30 minutes or until done and juices run clear.

While chicken is cooking, cook pasta and prepare tomatoes by heating them in a saucepan and stirring in remaining dressing mix.

Distribute pasta to serving plates, lay a piece of chicken over pasta, and ladle generous amount of tomatoes over chicken. Sprinkle with Parmesan cheese.

Serve with a glass of Chianti or other dry red wine alongside and you've got a feast.

Food for Rich Red Wines

Got a Cabernet Sauvignon looking for a meal to go with it? Start with one of these tasty recipes. Other rich meats and stews throughout the book (especially those based on beef and lamb) are fair game, too.

Tenderloin Strips with Pepper Cream

Prep time: 5 minutes   •   Cook time: 10 minutes   •   Serves: 2 guys or 3 regular people

2 TB. butter or olive oil

1 lb. tenderloin steak, sliced across the grain into ½-inch–thick strips

1 tsp. ground cumin

½ tsp. salt

½ tsp. ground black pepper

Sour cream

Melt butter in a large skillet over medium heat. Sprinkle steak strips on both sides with cumin, salt, and black pepper and cook for 3 minutes per side or until cooked to your liking. Remove steak to serving plates, turn off the heat under the skillet, and stir in sour cream, mixing in remaining butter and seasonings from the pan. Scrape cream over steak strips and serve.

End Run

Looking for a quick choice for both a red and a white to go with dinner? Pick up a Sauvignon Blanc (the white) and a Shiraz (the red). You'll be covered, no matter your guests' preferences. For suggestions on wineries and specific wines, read on.

Grilled Lamb Chops

Prep time: 5 minutes   •   Cook time: 10 minutes   •   Serves: 4 guys or 6 regular people

2 lb. lamb loin chops, about ¾ inch thick

¼ cup olive oil

1 TB. chopped garlic

2 tsp. dried rosemary

1 tsp. ground black pepper

½ tsp. salt

Preheat the grill. Place chops in a bowl. Mix olive oil and garlic in a bowl and pour over chops, turning to coat. Sprinkle chops with rosemary, pepper, and salt, turning to coat all sides.

Grill lamb chops for 5 minutes per side or until done, drizzling with remaining olive oil from the bowl when turning.

Sure Winners: Producers

A number of subscribers to my *Wine Hotlist* newsletter have asked for not just specific recommendations (which are in each issue), but general guidance on reliable producers. This is my current list of favorites. Take this list with you on your next trip to your local wine shop. You'll find wines from quite a few of these producers on the shelves.

- Bogle (United States)
- Chateau Ste. Michelle (United States)
- Clos du Bois (United States)
- Coppola (United States)
- DuBoeuf (France)
- E. Guigal (France)
- Hogue (United States)
- J. Lohr (United States)
- Joseph Phelps (United States)
- Lindemans (Australia)
- Louis Jadot (France)
- Napa Ridge (United States)
- Penfolds (Australia)
- Rabbit Ridge (United States)
- Renwood (United States)
- Rosemount (Australia)
- Ruffino (Italy)
- Tyrrell's (Australia)
- Yellow Tail (Australia)

End Run

Don't feel the need to spend a ton of money on a bottle of wine. You can get a terrific, food-friendly wine for less than $15 and often less than $10.

The Wine Hotlist: Specific Wines to Buy

Here are some of my favorite wines from recent tasting. To make your search easier, I've listed them by country. (Wines are often listed by the country in wine stores.)

If you have trouble finding specific wines from this list, fall back to the list of sure-winner producers.

Prices listed were current at the time of this writing.

I tasted these wines with food, as the notes often reflect. The "grade" is a subjective measure of quality and price (I've only included here wines I highly recommend):

A = Yum. Worth *searching* for.

B = Very good. Worth buying again.

C = Fine, but not worth buying again.

Listings are in the following order:

Winery/producer

Region of origin

Varietal

Vintage

Country

Approximate price

Ongoing reviews and food and wine information are available on my website, www.tastingtimes.com. (Reviews © 2004 Tod Dimmick and TastingTimes.com; reprinted with permission.)

> **End Run** _____
>
> This list contains specific wines I've tasted over the past several months. By the time you read this, the vintage (the year a wine was made) might be 2004 instead of 2002. That's okay. The taste will not be exactly the same, but it should be similar.

> **Menu Manual** _____
>
> The **vintage** is the year in which the grapes were harvested and, usually, in which the wine was produced. A 2003 Shiraz means that the grapes were harvested in 2003.

South America Red

Caliterra, Colchagua Valley, Carmenere, 2000, Chile, $14: *Cherry liqueur, pepper, licorice. This is delicious stuff.* **A–**

Concha y Toro, Rapel Valley, Carmenere, 2001, Chile, $9: *An exotic floral bouquet, vanilla, blackberry, and tart plum flavors. Delicious with the inescapable Friday night pepperoni pizza and a steal for the price.* **A–**

Luis Felipe Edwards, Colchagua, Chile, Merlot, 2000, $7: *Cloves, strawberry, even almond, with a balancing acidity that gives the wine depth and pleasure. For the price, this is a real winner!* **B+**

France Red

Le Clos du Caillou, Côtes du Rhône, 1998, France, $12: *This is an example of what a Côtes du Rhône should be. Black cherry, clove, charcoal, and earth. It feels coarse and black on the tongue, in a very satisfying way, if you can imagine that. Delicious wine.* **A**

Château de Lavagnac, Bordeaux, 2000, France, $9: *Violets, blueberry, and earth. This is a delicious wine, especially for the price.* **A–**

> **End Run**
>
> It's not all about the wine. Enjoying a good bottle is a chance to visit another part of the world through something carefully, even lovingly, produced there. That "something" carries a bit of the countryside all the way to your table.

J & F Lurton, Vin De Pays d'Oc, Syrah, 2001, France, $7: *A medium-bodied wine with ripe plum and sweet fruit flavors.* **B+**

Château Plagnac, Médoc, 2000, France, $13: *Soft vanilla, earth, cinnamon stick, leaf mold (in a good way).* **B+**

Georges DuBoeuf, Vin de Pays d'Oc, Syrah, 1999, France, $6: *Ripe mulled cherry, mulled orchard fruits. A great match with pizza and an affordable weeknight wine.* **B**

France White

Château de la Chesnaie, Muscadet de Sèvre et Maine "Sur Lie," 2002, France, $9: *Mineral notes, lemon peel, and Granny Smith apple. A nice pair with garlic shrimp sauté … and talk about refreshing!* **A–**

J & F Lurton, Vin De Pays d'Oc, Sauvignon Blanc, 2001, France, $6: *How about butter, bitter orange, and mineral? Very tasty and perfect with seafood.* **B+**

Italy Red

Tomaiolo, Chianti Riserva, 1997, $11: *Warm earth, chocolate, and cherry. Wow, what a delicious wine!* **A**

Viticcio, Chianti Classico, 1999, Italy, $12: *Clove, earth, dried cherry, taut and sinewy.* **B+**

Bella Sera, Delle Venezie, Italy, Merlot, 2001, $7: *Bouquet of cherries and earth, flavors of black cherry, clove, coffee, and earth with mild tannins ("decent structure" in winespeak). For the price, this is one worth finding.* **B/B+**

Eco Domani, Delle Venezie, Italy, Merlot, 2001, $10: *An interesting wine that I might not have picked as a Merlot. Violets and clove on the nose, a sort of grapey Kool-Aid flavor (in a good sense, if you can believe it).* **B**

Italy White

Colterenzio, Alto Adige, Pinot Grigio, 2002, Italy, $11: *Flavors of grapefruit, vanilla bean, and (hold your skepticism!) hibiscus. Very tasty.* **B+**

Bigi, Orvieto Classico, 2002, Italy, $8: *Citrus and vanilla flavors, with a dusting of nutmeg. The gourmet match? Grilled sausages.* **B+**

New Zealand and Australia Red

Four Sisters, South Eastern Australia, Shiraz, 2000, Australia, $10: *Smells of violet. Flavors of pepper, anise, and vanilla. Delicious. This warrants inclusion on any affordable Shiraz list.* **A–**

Woop Woop, South Eastern Australia, Shiraz, 2002, $10: *Velvet soft, violet and plum flavors (or at least what I imagine a violet would taste like). Tasty.* **B+**

Penfolds, South Eastern Australia, Shiraz Cabernet, 2001, Australia, $13: *Super ripe raspberries and blueberries. A hint of tobacco (this is a good thing in wine). Cherry syrup. Ah.* **A–**

Rosemount, South Eastern Australia, Shiraz, 2002, Australia, $14: *Charcoal, lush spicy cherry, rich ripe fruits. This is the Shiraz that made the grape famous several years ago. Back then, it was a bit cheaper, but who can blame them for capitalizing on their reputation for reliable quality?* **A–/B+**

Yellow Tail, South Eastern Australia, Shiraz, 2002, Australia, $7: *Plush, lush, forward (meaning it's made for us Americans who like assertive flavors). Hint of violets and cloves. Blackberries. I was reminded why an earlier vintage of this wine, blinded at a tasting, won over wines many times the price.* **B+**

New Zealand and Australia White

Reynolds Vineyards, New South Wales, Chardonnay, 2001, New Zealand, $12: *Gardenia, rose petal, tangerine. Luscious tropical fruits. A delicious Chardonnay.* **A/A–**

Stonehaven, South Eastern Australia, Chardonnay, 2001, $9: *Floral notes, flavors of melon and grapefruit. A gorgeous Chardonnay.* **A–**

Reynolds Vineyards, New South Wales, Sauvignon Blanc, 2002, New Zealand, $12: *Peach, lemon essence, citrus.* **B+**

Spain and Portugal

La Vendimia, Rioja, Spain, 2001, $12: *A cornucopia of flavors, from charcoal (in a good way) and clove to cherry and hazelnuts. I know this mixes Mediterranean metaphors, but this Spanish beauty paired well with a Greek salad.* **A–**

Castano Solanera, Vinas Viejas of Monastrell, Yecla, Spain, 2001, $10: *Velvety black cherry, burnt toast. Hard to not have another delicious glass.* **A–**

Vinhos Sogrape, Douro, 2000, Portugal, $8: *Plum, earth, and jam. Good value for the money.* **B**

Spain and Portugal White

Mas de Caralt, Penedes, "Blanco Seco," 2002, Spain, $9: *Orange dry (remember that flavor?), tropical fruits in a clean, refreshing package.* **B+**

Spain and Portugal Rose

Ochoa, Navarra, Garnacha, 2002, Spain, $9: *Floral, with lemon and strawberry notes. A fun and tasty rose.* **B**

End Run

Chardonnay and Merlot are usually the trendy wines to order at bars and restaurants. Producers know this, so they make a lot of these wines (and some are not very good). Pick a different grape, and you'll likely spend less money—and maybe even get a better wine. For whites, try one of the many terrific Sauvignon Blancs out there. For reds, try a Shiraz, Petit Sirah, or one of the blends of different red grapes (many European wines are blends).

USA Red

Waterbrook "Melange," Columbia Valley, 2001, $12: *This mix of Sangiovese, Syrah, Merlot, and Cabernet Sauvignon is gulpably delicious, with rich flavors of black cherry, earth, plum, and ripe fruits. Delicious with grilled buffalo burgers.* **A**

HRM Rex-Goliath! Wines, Central Coast, Pinot Noir, 2001, $9: *Floral notes. Deep, luscious fruit, velvety cherry, opulent. Try this. You'll like it.* **A**

Jessie's Grove, Lodi, Zinfandel, 2001, $13: *A robust, rich wine with flavors of plum, cinnamon, and chocolate. Delicious.* **A**

Preston, Columbia Valley, Washington, Merlot, 1999, $15: *Bouquet of cocoa and coffee, flavors of toffee and chocolate. A little bit of bottle-age is a wonderful thing, even though I found this on the shelf in September. Delicious wine.* **A–**

Clos du Bois, Sonoma County, Shiraz, 2001, $13: *Fleshy, jammy fruit, ripe plums, a hint of smoke. Would I pick it out as a Shiraz? Uh, probably not. An example, perhaps, of the effect of different climate and technique.* **B+**

Bogle, California, Merlot, 2001, $12: *A mellow and easily drinkable wine, with soft tannins and flavors of cherry and faint clove. Yum.* **B+**

Columbia Crest "Two Vines," Columbia Valley, Washington, 2000, $8: *Ripe fruits, cherry, vanilla, a hint of nuts. Very tasty wine.* **B/B+**

Ravenswood, California, Merlot, 2001, $12: *Clove, cherry, and cinnamon. Good Merlot with distinctive character.* **B+**

Glen Ellen, California, Merlot, 2000, $7: *Don't give up on mass-produced wine for a weeknight glass. Glen Ellen offers earth, stewed cherry, and oak. Tasty for the price.* **B**

Hacienda, California, Merlot, 2000, $8: *Super-ripe cherries and strawberries, soft, vanishingly drinkable. Tasty and probably the wine they served you at that restaurant last weekend for $16 a bottle!* **B**

Pepperwood Grove, California, Merlot, 2000, $7: *Cedar, cinnamon, and plum flavors in this tasty, affordable wine. Pepperwood Grove is everywhere, so this is a sure bet.* **B**

Rabbit Ridge, California, Merlot, 2001, $11: *Clove, charcoal, and cherry. Tasty.* **B**

USA White

Villa San Maurice, Pinot Grigio, 2001, $10: *This is a wine to convert Pinot Grigio skeptics. Flavors of rich apricot and almond, mandarin orange, and a broad range of citrus flavors. Ah.* **A**

A to Z, Willamette Valley (Oregon), Pinot Gris, 2002, $15: *Tropical fruits. Apricot and honeydew. White pepper. This is a delicious wine.* **A–**

Estancia, Monterey County, Chardonnay, 2001, $12: *Grapefruit and vanilla flavors. Well made and tasty with roasted chicken.* **B+**

Pellegrini, Russian River Valley, Chardonnay, 2001, $10: *I was attracted to the "unoaked" claim on the label, and the flavor benefit is clear. Rather than overbearing wood and butter, this wine is clean, with mineral, citrus, and pineapple flavors. A good example of what Chardonnay fruit can be when not whacked with a wooden club.* **B+**

The Least You Need to Know

♦ Keep the concept of matching "like with like" in mind when planning wine to go with your meal.

♦ Don't stress over the perfect match at a dinner party. If you've got a decent red and a good white, you're covered.

♦ Remember that delicious, food-friendly wines are available for less than $15 and often less than $10 a bottle.

♦ Use this chapter's list of dependable producers as a "cheat sheet" to take with you to your local wine shop. Pick a wine from one of these producers or one of the specific wines from the detailed list, and you'll be ahead of the game.

Appendix A

Glossary

al dente   Italian for "to the tooth." Refers to pasta (or other ingredient, such as rice) that is neither soft nor hard, but just slightly firm against the teeth. This, according to many pasta aficionados, is the perfect way to cook pasta.

all-purpose flour   Flour that contains only the inner part of the wheat grain.

allspice   Named for its flavor echoes of several spices (cinnamon, cloves, nutmeg), allspice is used in many desserts and in rich marinades and stews.

almonds   Mild, sweet, and crunchy nuts that combine nicely with creamy and sweet food items. (Think of a cannoli!)

amaretto   A popular almond liqueur. A small drizzle works flavor-enhancing magic on fruit.

anchovies (also **sardines**)   Tiny, flavorful preserved fish that typically come in cans. The strong flavor from these salted fish is a critical element in many recipes. Anchovies are considered a traditional garnish for Caesar salad, the dressing of which contains anchovy paste.

arborio rice   A plump Italian rice used, among other purposes, for risotto.

artichoke hearts   The center part of the artichoke flower, often found canned in grocery stores and used as a stand-alone vegetable dish or as a flavorful base for appetizers or main courses.

arugula A spicy-peppery garden plant with leaves that resemble a dandelion and have a distinctive—and very sharp—flavor.

baguette A long, skinny loaf of bread. The shape of the loaf results in a lot of surface area (compared with a loaf of similar weight in a standard stubby shape). Lots of surface area means lots of crust—a good thing for many purposes, such as appetizers, where a sturdy bread is useful.

bake To cook in a dry oven. Baking is one of the most popular methods of cooking and is used for everything from roasts, vegetables, and other main courses to desserts such as cakes and pies. Dry-heat cooking often results in a crisping of the exterior of the food being cooked. Moist-heat cooking, through methods such as steaming, poaching, etc., brings a much different moist quality more appropriate to some foods than others.

baking pans Pans used for baking potatoes to chicken, cookies to croutons.

balsamic vinegar Vinegar produced primarily in Italy from a specific type of grape and aged in wood barrels. It is heavier, darker, and sweeter than most vinegars.

barbecue This is a loaded word, with different, zealous definitions in different parts of the country. In some cases it is synonymous with grilling (quick cooking over high heat); in others, to barbecue is to cook something long and slow in a rich liquid (barbecue sauce).

basil A flavorful, almost sweet, resinous herb delicious with tomatoes and in all kinds of Italian- or Mediterranean-style dishes.

beat To quickly mix substances.

blanch To place a food in boiling water for about 1 minute (or less) to partially cook the exterior and then submerge in or rinse with cool water to halt the cooking. This is a common method for preparing some vegetables such as asparagus for serving and also for preparing foods for freezing.

blend To completely mix something, usually with a blender or food processor, more slowly than beating.

boil To heat a liquid to a point where water is forced to turn into steam, causing the liquid to bubble. To boil something is to insert it into boiling water. A rapid boil is when a lot of bubbles are foaming the surface of the liquid.

bouillon Dried essence of stock from chicken, beef, vegetables, or other ingredients. This is a popular starting ingredient for soups as it adds flavor (and often a lot of salt).

bouquet The aroma or fragrance of a wine.

braise   To cook with the introduction of some liquid, usually over extended time.

bread flour   Wheat flour used for bread and other recipes.

breadcrumbs   Tiny pieces of crumbled dry bread. Breadcrumbs are an important component in many recipes and are also used as a coating on, for example, chicken breasts.

Brie   A creamy cheese, with a soft, edible rind. Tasty with just about anything, from bread to fruit to nuts.

broil   To broil is to cook in a dry oven under the overhead high-heat element.

broth   *See* stock.

brown   To cook in a skillet, turning, until the surface is brown in color, to lock in the juices.

brown rice   Whole-grain rice with a characteristic brown color from the bran coating; more nutritious and flavorful than white rice.

Cajun cooking   A style of cooking that combines French and Southern characteristics and has many highly seasoned stews and meats.

canapés   Bite-size hors d'oeuvres made up of any number of ingredients but prepared individually and usually served on a small piece of bread or toast.

caramelize   The term's original meaning is to cook sugar over low heat until it develops a sweet caramel flavor; however, the term is increasingly gaining use to describe cooking vegetables (especially onions) or meat in butter or oil over low heat until they soften, sweeten, and develop a caramel color. Caramelized onions are a popular addition to many recipes, especially as a pizza topping.

caraway   A distinctive spicy seed used for bread, pork, cheese, and cabbage dishes. It is known to reduce stomach upset, which is why it is often paired with, for example, sauerkraut.

casserole dishes   Primarily used in baking, these covered containers hold liquids and solids together and keep moisture around ingredients that might otherwise dry out.

cheddar   The ubiquitous hard cheese with a rich, buttery flavor that ranges from mellow to sharp. Originally produced in England, cheddar is now produced worldwide.

cheese boards or **cheese trays**   A collection of three or four mixed-flavor cheeses arranged on a tray, platter, or even cutting board. One classic example would be at least one cheese made from cow's, sheep's, and goat's milk. Often restaurants will offer a selection of cheeses as a "cheese flight" or course.

chickpeas (also **garbanzo beans**)   The base ingredient in hummus, chickpeas are high in fiber and low in fat, making this a delicious and healthful component of many appetizers and main dishes.

chili peppers (also **chile peppers**)   Any one of many different "hot" peppers, ranging in intensity from the relatively mild ancho pepper to the blisteringly hot habañero.

chili powder   A seasoning blend that includes chili pepper, cumin, garlic, and oregano. Proportions vary among different versions, but they all offer a warm, rich flavor.

chives   A member of the onion family, chives are found at the grocery store as bunches of long leaves that resemble the green tops of onions. They provide an easy onion flavor to any dish. Chives are very easy to grow, and many people have them in their gardens.

chop   To cut into pieces, usually qualified by an adverb such as "coarsely chopped," or by a size measurement such as "chopped into ½-inch pieces." "Finely chopped" is much closer to minced.

chorizo   A spiced pork sausage eaten alone and as a component in many recipes.

cider vinegar   Vinegar produced from apple cider, popular in North America.

cilantro   A member of the parsley family and used in Mexican cooking and some Asian dishes. Cilantro is what gives some salsas their unique flavor. Use in moderation, as the flavor can overwhelm.

cinnamon   A sweet, rich, yet spicy spice commonly used in baking or desserts. Cinnamon can also be used for delicious and interesting entrées.

cloves   A sweet, strong, almost wintergreen-flavor spice used in baking and with meats such as ham.

coat   To cover all sides of a food with a liquid, sauce, or solid.

cookie sheet   A large, thin, flat tray used for baking cookies and other foods.

core   To remove the unappetizing middle membranes and seeds of fruit and vegetables.

coriander   A rich, warm, spicy herb used in all types of recipes, from African to South American, from entrées to desserts.

cottage cheese   A mild, creamy-texture cheese made from curds from fresh cow's milk cheese. Curds vary in size; containers will indicate, for example, "small curd" or "large curd." In its low-fat and nonfat forms, cottage cheese is a useful component of low-fat dips, spreads, and other recipes.

count   On packaging of seafood or other foods that come in small sizes, you'll often see a reference to the count, or how many of that item compose a pound. For example, 31 to 40 count shrimp are large appetizer shrimp often served with cocktail sauce; 51 to 60 are much smaller.

croutons   Pieces of bread, usually between ¼ and ½ inch in size, that are baked, broiled, or fried to a crisp texture.

crudités   Fresh vegetables served as an appetizer, often all together on one tray.

cuisine   A style of cooking, typically reflecting a country or region (such as "Spanish cuisine"), a blending of flavors and cuisines (called "fusion"), or an updated style (such as "New Latin").

cumin   A fiery, smoky-tasting spice popular in Middle-Eastern and Indian dishes. Cumin is a seed; ground cumin seed is the most common form used in cooking.

curing   A method of preserving uncooked foods, usually meats or fish, by either salting and smoking or pickling.

curry   A general term referring to rich, spicy, Indian-style sauces and the dishes prepared with them. Common ingredients include hot pepper, nutmeg, cumin, cinnamon, pepper, and turmeric.

dash   A dash refers to a few drops, usually of a liquid, that is released by a quick shake of, for example, a bottle of hot sauce.

dice   To cut into small cubes about ¼ inch square.

Dijon mustard   Sharp, spicy mustard made in the French style of the Dijon region.

dill   A slightly sour, unique herb that is perfect for eggs, cheese dishes, and, of course, vegetables (pickles!).

dough   A soft, pliable mixture of liquid and flour that is the intermediate step, prior to cooking, for many bread or baked-goods recipes such as cookies or bread.

dredge   To cover a piece of food with a dry substance such as flour or corn meal.

dressing   A liquid mixture usually containing oil, vinegar, and herbs used for seasoning salads and other foods. Also the solid dish commonly called "stuffing" used to stuff turkey and other foods.

drizzle   To lightly sprinkle drops of a liquid over food. Drizzling is often the finishing touch to a dish.

dry   In the context of wine, a wine that has been vinified to contain little or no residual sugar.

dust   To sprinkle a dry substance, often a seasoning, over a dish. To do this, sprinkle, using your fingers or a spoon, from at least 6 inches above the dish to avoid unappetizing flavor clumping.

entrée   The main dish in a meal.

extra-virgin olive oil   *See* olive oil.

fennel   In seed form, a fragrant, licorice-tasting herb. The bulbs have a much milder flavor and a celerylike crunch and are used as a vegetable in salads or cooked recipes.

Feta (Greece and United States)   The white, crumbly salty cheese from Greek salad, this cheese is also tasty on its own and pairs beautifully with Kalamata olives.

fillet   A piece of meat or seafood with the bones removed.

fish basket   A grill-top metal frame that holds a whole fish intact, making it easier to turn.

fish poacher   A long, rectangular pan with a separate metal basket designed to hold a fish either above boiling water for steaming or in simmering liquid for poaching. Fish poachers come in varying sizes up to 24 inches, although an 18-inch version will cover all but the largest meals.

flake   To break into thin sections, as with fish.

floret   The flower or bud end of broccoli or cauliflower.

flour   Grains ground into a meal. Wheat is perhaps the most common flour, an essential component in many breads. Flour is also made from oats, rye, buckwheat, etc. Different types of flour serve different purposes. *See also* all-purpose flour, bread flour, and whole-wheat flour.

fondue   A classic Swiss dish of melted cheese and white wine (among other things).

fricassee   A dish, usually meat, cut into pieces and cooked in a liquid or sauce.

fritter   A food such as apples or corn coated or mixed with batter and deep-fried for a crispy, crunchy exterior.

fry   Pan-cooking over high heat with butter or oil.

garam masala   A famous Indian seasoning mix, rich with cinnamon, pepper, nutmeg, cardamom, and other spices.

garlic   A member of the onion family, a pungent and flavorful element in many savory dishes. A garlic bulb, the form in which garlic is often sold, contains multiple cloves. Each clove, when chopped, provides about 1 teaspoon garlic.

garnish   An embellishment not vital to the dish but added to enhance visual appeal.

ginger   Available in fresh root or powdered form, ginger adds a pungent, sweet, and spicy quality to a dish. It is a very popular element of many Asian and Indian dishes, among others.

Gouda (Holland or United States)   The common variety is a mild cheese most popular (at least in my house) when it's "smoked" gouda. Aged Gouda, on the other hand, is a buttery, nutty, smoky-tasting delicacy. It costs more, but it will be the first cheese to disappear from your cheese tray.

goulash   A rich, Hungarian-style meat-and-vegetable stew seasoned with paprika and other spices.

grate   To shave into tiny pieces using a sharp rasp or grater.

grill   To cook over high heat, usually over charcoal or gas.

grind   To reduce a large, hard substance, often a seasoning such as peppercorns, to the consistency of sand.

grits   Coarsely ground grains, usually corn.

Gruyère (Switzerland)   A rich, sharp cheese from the Swiss family.

handful   An unscientific measurement term that refers to the amount of an ingredient you can hold in your hand.

Havarti (United States and Denmark)   A creamy, mild cheese perhaps most enjoyed in its herbed versions (Havarti with dill).

hazelnuts (also **filberts**)   A sweet nut popular in desserts and in savory dishes to a lesser degree.

herbes de Provence   A seasoning mix including basil, fennel, marjoram, rosemary, sage, and thyme.

herbs   The leaves of flavorful plants characterized by fresh, pungent aromas and flavors, such as parsley, sage, rosemary, and thyme.

horseradish   A sharp, spicy root that forms the flavor base in many condiments, from cocktail sauce to sharp mustards. It is a natural match with roast beef. The form generally found in grocery stores is prepared horseradish, which contains vinegar and oil, among other ingredients. If you come across pure horseradish, use it much more sparingly than the prepared version, or try cutting it with sour cream.

hummus   A thick, Middle Eastern spread made of puréed chickpeas (garbanzo beans), lemon juice, olive oil, garlic, and often tahini (sesame seed paste).

Italian seasoning (also **spaghetti sauce seasoning**)   The ubiquitous grocery store blend, which includes basil, oregano, rosemary, and thyme, is a useful seasoning for quick flavor that evokes the "old country" in sauces, meatballs, and soups.

marinate   To soak meat, seafood, or other food in a seasoned sauce, called a marinade, which is high in acid content. The acids break down the muscle of the meat, making it tender and adding flavor.

marjoram   A sweet herb, a cousin of and similar to oregano, popular in Greek, Spanish, and Italian dishes.

medallion   A small round cut, usually of meat or vegetables such as carrots or cucumbers.

mince   To cut into very small pieces smaller than diced pieces, about ⅛ inch or less.

mushrooms   Any one of a huge variety of *edible* fungus. (Note emphasis on "edible"; there also poisonous mushrooms.) *See also* portobello mushrooms; white mushrooms.

nutmeg   A sweet, fragrant, musky spice used primarily in baking.

nuts   A shell-covered dry fruit rich in flavor and nutrition, and a critical component in many dishes. Many nuts are tasty on their own. *See also* almonds; hazelnuts; pecans; walnuts.

olive oil   A fragrant liquid produced by crushing or pressing olives. Extra-virgin olive oil is the oil produced from the first pressing of a batch of olives; oil is also produced from other "pressings" after the first. "Extra-virgin" olive oil is generally considered the most flavorful and highest quality and is the type you want when your focus is on the oil itself. Be sure the bottle label reads "extra-virgin."

olives   The fruit of the olive tree commonly grown on all sides of the Mediterranean. There are many varieties of olives but two general types: green and black. Black olives are also called "ripe" olives.

oregano   A fragrant, slightly astringent herb used in Greek, Spanish, and Italian dishes.

pan-broil   Quick cooking over high heat in a skillet with a minimum of butter or oil. (Frying, on the other hand, uses more butter or oil.)

paprika   A rich, red, warm, earthy spice that also lends a rich red color to many dishes.

parboil   To partially cook in boiling water or broth. Parboiling is similar to blanching, although blanched foods are quickly cooled with cold water.

Parmesan   A hard, dry, flavorful cheese primarily used grated or shredded as a seasoning for Italian-style dishes.

parsley   A fresh-tasting green leafy herb, used to add color and interest to just about any savory dish. Often used as a garnish just before serving.

peanuts   The nutritious and high-fat seeds of the peanut plant (a relative of the pea) that are sold shelled or unshelled and in a variety of preparations, including peanut butter and peanut oil. Some people are allergic to peanuts, so care should be taken with their inclusion in recipes.

pecans   Rich, buttery nuts native to North America. Their flavor, a terrific addition to appetizers, is at least partially due to high unsaturated fat content.

pepper   Biting and pungent, freshly ground pepper is a must for many dishes and adds an extra level of flavor and taste.

peppercorns   Large, round seeds that are ground to produce pepper.

pesto   A thick spread or sauce made with fresh basil leaves, garlic, olive oil, pine nuts, and Parmesan cheese. New versions are made with other herbs. Rich and flavorful, pesto can be made at home or purchased in a grocery store and used on anything from appetizers to pasta and other main dishes.

pickle   A food, usually a vegetable such as a cucumber that has been pickled in brine.

pilaf   A rice dish in which the rice is browned in butter or oil, then cooked in a flavorful liquid such as a broth, often with the addition of meats or vegetables. The rice absorbs the broth, resulting in a savory dish.

pinch   An unscientific measurement term that refers to the amount of an ingredient—typically a dry, granular substance such as an herb or seasoning—you can hold between your finger and thumb.

pine nuts (also **Pignoli**)   Nuts grown on pine trees, that are rich (read: high-fat), flavorful, and, yes, a bit pine-y. Pine nuts are a traditional component of pesto, and they add a wonderful, hearty crunch to many other recipes.

pita bread   A flat, hollow wheat bread that can be used for sandwiches or sliced, pizza-style, into slices. Pita bread is terrific soft with dips and baked or broiled as a vehicle for other ingredients.

pizza stone   Preheated with the oven, a pizza stone cooks a crust to a delicious, crispy, pizza-parlor texture. It also holds heat well, so a pizza removed from the oven on the stone will stay hot for as long as a half-hour at the table. A pizza stone is a versatile tool that can also be used for other baking needs, including bread.

poach   To cook a food in simmering liquid, such as water, wine, or broth.

Port Salut (France)   A creamy, rich, and irresistible cheese, similar to brie.

portobello mushrooms   A mature and larger form of the smaller crimini mushroom, portobellos are brownish, chewy, and flavorful. They are trendy served as whole caps, grilled, and as thin sautéed slices.

preheat   To turn on an oven, broiler, or other cooking appliance in advance of cooking so the temperature will be at the desired level when the assembled dish is ready for cooking.

presentation   The appealing arrangement of a dish or food on the plate.

prosciutto   Dry, salt-cured ham, rich and evocative of Italy. Prosciutto is popular in many simple dishes in which its unique flavor is allowed to shine.

purée   To reduce a food to a thick, creamy texture, usually using a blender or food processor.

quesadilla   A quesadilla is, at its most basic, two tortillas with something in between (sort of like a grilled cheese sandwich). The "what goes in between" is what makes all the difference. Cheese is a natural (start with Monterey Jack or cheddar; Swiss might not be what you would use first in Mexico, but it's still delicious); also use meats, vegetables, and of course, Southwest-style seasonings.

raclette   A famous cheese-intensive Swiss and French dish using raclette cheese (a richly flavored relative of Swiss cheese). The cheese is melted and combined with potatoes, pickles, and tiny onions and served with crusty dark bread.

red pepper flakes   Hot yet rich, crushed red pepper, used in moderation, brings flavor and interest to many savory dishes.

reduce   To heat a broth or sauce to remove some of the water content, resulting in more concentrated flavor and color.

refried beans (also **refritos**)   Twice-cooked beans—most often pinto beans—softened into a thick paste and often seasoned with peppers and spices. Most refried beans include lard, but many fat-free, lard-free versions are available.

render   To cook a meat to the point where its fat melts and can be removed.

reserve   To hold a specified ingredient for another use later in the recipe.

risotto   A popular Italian rice dish made by browning arborio rice in butter or oil, then slowly adding liquid to cook the rice, resulting in a creamy texture.

roasted red peppers   These beauties are in your grocery store in the international foods section. They come in jars and sometimes cans and will last as a secret weapon on your shelf (in your fridge after you open them) for a long time. Most people like them, but don't often eat them. When you serve them you get credit for being a good cook, when all you did was open a jar.

Roquefort (France)   A world-famous sheep's milk blue cheese.

rosemary   A pungent, sweet herb used with chicken, pork, fish, and especially lamb. A little of it goes a long way.

roux   A mixture of butter or another fat source and flour used to thicken liquids such as sauces.

saffron   A famous spice made from the stamens of crocus flowers. Saffron lends a dramatic yellow color and distinctive flavor to a dish. Only a tiny amount needs to be used, which is good because saffron is very expensive.

sage   An herb with a lemon-rind, fruity scent and "sunny" flavor. It is a terrific addition to many dishes.

salsa   A style of mixing fresh vegetables and/or fresh fruit in a coarse chop. Salsa can be spicy or not, can be fruit-based or not, can be served as a starter on its own (with chips, for example) or as a companion to a main course.

sauté   Pan-cooking over lower heat than frying.

savory   A popular herb with a fresh, woody taste.

scant   A measurement modification that specifies "include no extra," as in a scant teaspoon.

Scoville scale   A scale used to measure the hot taste in hot peppers. The lower the Scoville units, the more mild the pepper. Ancho peppers, which are mildly hot, are about 3,000 Scovilles; Thai hot peppers are about 6,000; and some of the more daring peppers, such as Tears of Fire and habañero, are 30,000 Scovilles or more.

scrapple   A sausagelike mixture of seasoned pork and cornmeal that is formed into loaves and sliced for cooking.

sear   To quickly brown the exterior of a food over high heat to preserve interior moisture (that's why many meat recipes involve searing).

sesame seeds   Originally from Asia, sesame seeds are shaped like watermelon seeds but are about $1/10$ the size. The most common form in our stores is a sort of tan color. These nutty seeds are popular in Asian dishes and on baked goods.

shallot   A member of the onion family that grows in a bulb somewhat like garlic and has a milder onion flavor. When a recipe calls for shallot, you use the entire bulb. (They might or might not have cloves.)

shellfish   A broad range of seafood, including clams, mussels, oysters, crabs, shrimp, and lobster. Some people are allergic to shellfish.

short-grain rice   A starchy rice popular for Asian-style dishes because it readily clumps for eating with chopsticks.

shred   To cut into many long, thin slices.

simmer   To boil gently so the liquid barely bubbles.

skewers   Thin wooden or metal sticks, usually about 8 inches long, that are perfect for assembling kebabs, dipping food pieces into hot sauces, or serving single-bite food items with a bit of panache.

skillet (also **frying pan**)   A generally heavy, flat metal pan with a handle designed to cook food over heat on a stove top or campfire.

slice   To cut into thin pieces.

slow cooker   An electric countertop device with a lidded container that maintains a low temperature and slowly cooks its contents, often over several hours or a full day.

soy sauce   A delicious dark Asian-style sauce made from fermented soybeans, grains, and salt. Soy sauce is delicious as a marinade by itself and as a component in many dishes.

steam   To suspend a food over boiling water and allow the heat of the steam (water vapor) to cook the food. Steaming is a very quick-cooking method that preserves the flavor and texture of a food.

stew   To slowly cook pieces of food submerged in a liquid. Also, a dish that has been prepared by this method.

sticky (or **glutinous**) **rice**   *See* short-grain rice.

Stilton (England)   The famous English blue cheese, delicious with toasted nuts and renowned for its pairing with port wine.

stir-fry   To cook food in a wok or skillet over high heat, moving and turning the food quickly to cook all sides.

stock   A flavorful broth made by cooking meats and/or vegetables with seasonings until the liquid absorbs these flavors. This liquid is then strained and the solids discarded. Stock can be eaten by itself or used as a base for soups, stews, sauces, risotto, or many other recipes.

stripe   To scrape the skin of a fruit or vegetable in lengthwise strokes, leaving a "stripe" of the skin between each scrape.

succotash   A cooked vegetable dish usually made of corn and peppers.

Swiss cheese   Originally from Switzerland (no kidding), but now made across the world, a style of cheese that results in a nutty, rich, slightly sour taste and those big bubbles.

Tabasco sauce   A popular brand of Louisiana hot pepper sauce used in usually small portions to season savory food. The name also refers to a type of hot pepper from Tabasco, a state in Mexico, that is used to make this sauce.

tarragon   A sour-sweet, rich-smelling herb perfect with seafood, vegetables (especially asparagus), chicken, and pork.

teriyaki   A sauce composed of soy sauce, rice wine, ginger, and sugar. It works beautifully with seafood as well as most meats.

thyme   Minty, zesty herb leaves that are used in a wide range of recipes.

toast   To cook something uncovered in an oven until it is browned and crisp.

toast points (also **toast triangles**)   Pieces of toast with the crusts removed that are then cut on the diagonal from each corner, resulting in four triangle-shape pieces.

translucent   Literally means "light shows through." When onion reaches this stage, it's a great sign that it is cooked enough to be soft and sweet.

twist   A lemon twist is simply an attractive way to garnish an appetizer or other dish. Cut a thin, about ⅛-inch–thick cross-section slice of lemon. Then take that slice and cut from the center out to the edge of the slice on one side. Pick up the piece of lemon and pull apart the two cut ends in opposite directions.

varietal   The type of grape used to make a wine, such as Cabernet Sauvignon, Merlot, or Chardonnay.

veal   Meat from a calf, generally characterized by mild flavor and tenderness. Certain cuts of veal, such as cutlets and scaloppini, are well suited to quick cooking.

vegetable steamer   An insert for a large saucepan. Also, a special pot with tiny holes in its bottom designed to fit on another pot to hold food to be steamed above boiling water. The insert is generally less expensive and resembles a metal poppy flower that expands to touch the sides of the pot and has small legs. *See also* steam.

venison   Meat from deer or other large wild game animals.

vindaloo   A famous, super-spicy Indian curry dish.

vinegar An acidic liquid widely used as dressing and seasoning. Many cuisines use vinegars made from different source materials. *See also* balsamic vinegar; cider vinegar; white vinegar; wine vinegar.

vintage The year in which the grapes were harvested and, usually, in which the wine was produced. A 2002 Sauvignon Blanc means that the grapes were harvested in 2002.

walnuts Grown worldwide, walnuts bring a rich, slightly woody flavor to all types of food. For the quick cook, walnuts are available chopped and ready to go at your grocery store. They are delicious toasted and make fine accompaniments to cheeses.

water chestnuts Actually a tuber, water chestnuts are a popular element in many types of Asian-style cooking. The flesh is white, crunchy, and juicy, and the vegetable holds its texture whether cool or hot.

whisk To rapidly mix, introducing air to the mix.

white mushrooms Ubiquitous button mushrooms. When fresh, they will have an earthy smell and an appealing "soft crunch." White mushrooms are delicious raw in salads, marinated, sautéed, and as component ingredients in many recipes.

white vinegar The most common type of vinegar found on grocery store shelves. It is produced from grain.

whole-wheat flour Wheat flour that contains the entire grain.

wild rice Wild rice is actually a grain with a rich, nutty flavor, popular as an unusual and nutritious side dish.

wine vinegar Vinegar produced from red or white wine.

wok A wonderful tool for quick cooking. Unfortunately, it is only suitable for use on a gas cooktop, unless you purchase an electric version, which might not have the important capability of rapid heating characteristic of a wok over a gas flame.

Worcestershire sauce Originally developed in India and containing tamarind, this spicy sauce is used as a seasoning for many meats and other dishes.

zest Small slivers of peel, usually from a citrus fruit such as lemon, lime, or orange.

zester A small kitchen tool used to scrape zest off a fruit. A small grater also works fine.

References

So you've caught the cooking bug. This appendix lists some of my favorite books, magazines, and websites on cooking. These are good places to start.

Books

Barrett, Judith. *From an Italian Garden*. New York: Macmillan, 1992.

Beard, James. *The New James Beard*. New York: Alfred A. Knopf, 1981.

Bittman, Mark. *The Minimalist Cooks Dinner*. New York: Broadway, 2001.

Brody, Laura. *The Kitchen Survival Guide*. New York: William Morrow, 1993.

Brooks, Barbara. *Crock-Pot Slow Cooker Cookbook*. Kansas City: Rival Manufacturing Company, 1979.

Brown, Alton. *I'm Just Here for the Food*. New York: Stewart, Tabori and Chang, 2002.

Cameron, Angus, and Judith Jones. *The L.L.Bean Game and Fish Cookbook*. New York: Random House, 1983.

Chalmers, Irena. *Good Old Food*. Hauppauge: Barron's, 1993.

Choate, Judith. *Meat and Potatoes*. New York: Simon & Schuster, 1992.

Cunningham, Marion. *The Fanny Farmer Cookbook*. New York: Alfred A. Knopf, 1990.

Dimmick, Tod. *The Complete Idiot's Guide to 5-Minute Appetizers*. Indianapolis: Alpha Books, 2003.

———. *The Complete Idiot's Guide to 20-Minute Meals*. Indianapolis: Alpha Books, 2002.

Fobel, Jim. *Casseroles*. New York: Clarkson Potter, 1997.

Gardiner, Anne, and Sue Wilson. *The Inquisitive Cook*. New York: Henry Holt, 1998.

Gorman, Donna, and Elizabeth Heyert. *The Artful Table*. New York: William Morrow and Company, 1998.

Gray, John, Ph.D. *Men Are from Mars, Women Are from Venus*. New York: Harper-Collins, 1992.

Green, Henrietta. *Farmer's Market Cookbook*. London: Kyle Cathie, 2001.

Harlow, Joan S. *The Loaf and Ladle Cookbook*. Camden: Down East Books, 1983.

Herbst, Sharon Tyler. *Food Lover's Companion*. Hauppauge: Barron's Educational Series, 2001.

Kropotkin, Igor, and Marjorie Kropotkin. *The Inn Cookbook*. Secaucus: Castle, 1983.

Loomis, Susan Herrmann. *Farmhouse Cookbook*. New York: Workman Publishing, 1991.

MacMillan, Diane D. *The Portable Feast*. San Francisco: 101 Productions, 1984.

McNair, James. *Pizza*. San Francisco: Chronicle Books, 1987.

Murphy, Margaret Deeds. *The Boston Globe Cookbook, Third Edition*. Chester: Globe Pequot Press, 1990.

Oliver, Jamie. *The Naked Chef*. London: Michael Joseph, 1999.

Ostmann, Barbara Gibbs, and Jane L. Baker. *The Recipe Writer's Handbook*. New York: John Wiley and Sons, 2001.

Richardson, Ferrier, ed. *Scotland on a Plate*. Edinburgh: Black and White Publishing, 2001.

Rosso, Julee, and Sheila Lukins. *The New Basics Cookbook*. New York: Workman Publishing, 1989.

Schulz, Phillip Stephen. *Cooking with Fire and Smoke*. New York: Simon & Schuster, 1986.

Seranne, Ann, ed. *The Western Junior League Cookbook*. New York: McKay, 1979.

Urvater, Michele. *Monday to Friday Cookbook*. New York: Workman Publishing, 1991.

Wells, Patricia. *Bistro Cooking*. New York: Workman Publishing, 1989.

White, Jasper. *50 Chowders*. New York: Scribner, 2000.

Wyler, Susan. *Simply Stews*. New York: HarperPerennial, 1995.

Magazines

Bon Appétit
www.bonappetit.com/

Cook's Illustrated
www.cooksillustrated.com/

Cooking Light
www.cookinglight.com

Fine Cooking
www.taunton.com/finecooking/index.asp

Food & Wine
www.foodandwine.com/

Saveur
www.saveur.com/

Wine Spectator
www.winespectator.com

Favorite Quick-Cooking Websites

Selected cooking-related web pages reviewed by Tod Dimmick in his e-mail newsletter for WZ.com. (© Copyright WZ.com Inc., reprinted with permission.)

My Meals

www.my-meals.com
This site includes a section devoted to recipes requiring 30 minutes or less. Some are very basic; others decidedly less so. Hot Carameled Apples with Pie Crust Dippers?

Simple Pleasures

www.allfood.com/mmeal.cfm
Minutemeals challenges the assertion that cooking quickly requires sacrifice of quality and taste. The listing of complete holiday menus is especially soothing.

Sam Cooks

www.samcooks.com
Longtime gourmet columnist for *Wine Spectator*, Sam Gugino has constructed a clean, information-packed site for the intelligent cook. Check out "Cooking to Beat the Clock."

General Cooking Sites

Allrecipes, All the time

www.allrecipes.com
Allrecipes draws on a massive database of recipes and provides advice on techniques, meal planning, and more. The "ingredient search" enables mix-and-match creativity; think shrimp and pasta or apples and cream. Type them in, the inspiration flows, and you can save your favorites to your personal recipe box.

Epicurious

www.epicurious.com

Epicurious claims more than 13,000 recipes, drawing from years of *Gourmet* and *Bon Appétit*, among other sources. Try visiting the search engine with random ingredients you have on hand that need a "common destiny." You'll be surprised what you come up with: ground turkey and sun-dried tomato meatloaf is a surprising delight I make every winter. Assemble your favorites and create your own personal recipe file.

Reluctant Gourmet

www.reluctantgourmet.com

Reluctant Gourmet is refreshing for its modesty. The site covers tasks simply and completely, from cooking techniques (how to braise) to a glossary of gourmet terms. I grin as soon as I see the photo on the home page. You'll see what I mean.

Southern Living

www.southernliving.com

Comfort food with a regional slant comes from *Southern Living*. Click on the "Foods" link. Tantalizing recipes throughout make it tough to decide where to start. Well, I guess it will be Apple Pancakes for me.

Cooking Light

www.cookinglight.com

Find tips, recipes, and themes (French, Italian, celebration menus, etc.) for those of us who want taste and quality, but who also might be concerned with what we eat. Who, me?

White Meat

www.eatchicken.com

This is a chicken-lover's paradise, with information from technique to recipes and poultry statistics. Follow the "show a little leg" link to Peruvian Grilled Chicken Thighs with Tomato Cilantro Sauce.

All Fins, All the Time

www.seafoodrecipe.com

This subset of the Allrecipes site has it all, organized by cooking method, ethnic origin, or specific undersea creature.

Eat Smart

www.usaweekend.com/food/carper_archive/index.html

A collection of articles from Jean Carper, the well-known columnist for *USA Weekend*, covers everything from vitamins and whole grains to avoiding carcinogens when grilling. I need those tips.

Cook's Thesaurus

www.foodsubs.com

The Cook's Thesaurus contains a truly massive gourmet glossary. Ever wonder where that cut of beef is from? Voilà! There it is, with diagrams. Each section provides guidance on substitutions—very useful if you cook with what's on hand.

Global Gourmet

www.globalgourmet.com

Global Gourmet will draw you in to articles on everything from "Holiday Helpers" to "I Love Chocolate (Let's Get to the Point Already)."

Food and Wine Sites

Start Simple

www.adwfoodandwine.com/index.asp

Here's a basic chart, courtesy of Clos du Bois, explaining matches that work and why.

EatDrinkDine

www.eatdrinkdine.com

What a great site! Sommelier Evan Goldstein offers a wonderfully complete, yet easy-to-use page that you can approach from "Start with Food" or "Start with Wine." Chicken cacciatore goes with …

Mondavi

www.robertmondavi.com/FoodWine/index.asp

Here is a friendly database of neatly organized menus with suggested wines. Butternut Squash Risotto with a friendly Merlot—it's a winner.

End Run

TastingTimes (www.tastingtimes.com) is the author's own site and offers a growing section on food and wine pairing, wine menus, and recipes. It also features a free e-mail newsletter, *The Wine Minute*, with recommendations under $15.

Wine and the Good Life

www.winespectator.com

Winespectator.com, one of the largest wine-related sites on the web, offers a mountain of information on wine, travel, restaurants, and more.

Wine Sauce

www.corkcuisine.com

A fun site for lovers of food and wine, you'll find history, recipes, and a wealth of wine and food tips.

Favorite Vendors

Here are a few of my favorite vendors.

Trader Joe's

www.traderjoes.com

This national chain offers an eclectic yet tempting array of ingredients helpful to the cook in a hurry.

King Arthur Flour

www.kingarthurflour.com

This mail- and Internet-order company provides a huge range of specialty flours and baking ingredients. Add a little buckwheat flour to quick pancakes, and you'll never go back to white.

Penzeys Spices

www.penzeys.com

Another mail- and Internet-order company with a huge selection of top-quality herbs and spices and a recipe-filled catalog to salivate over.

Your Local Farmer's Market

www.ams.usda.gov/farmersmarkets/map.htm

A farm stand is the place to go for the freshest, tastiest farm produce, key ingredients of healthful cuisine. This link takes you to a U.S. map where you can find the market nearest you.

Index

G

N–O

P

X-Y-Z

Check Out These
Best-Selling
COMPLETE IDIOT'S GUIDES®

More than
20 million
copies sold
since 1993!

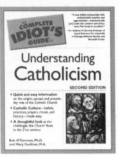

Understanding
Catholicism
SECOND EDITION

1-59257-085-2
$18.95

Learning
Spanish
THIRD EDITION

0-02-864451-4
$18.95

The
Bible
SECOND EDITION

0-02-864382-8
$18.95

Being a
Groom
SECOND EDITION

0-02-864456-5
$9.95

Grammar
and Style
SECOND EDITION

1-59257-115-8
$16.95

Playing the
Guitar
SECOND EDITION

0-02-864244-9
$21.95 w/CD

Personal Finance
in Your 20s & 30s
SECOND EDITION

0-02-864374-7
$19.95

Knitting and
Crocheting
SECOND EDITION
Illustrated

1-59257-089-5
$16.95

The Perfect
Resume
THIRD EDITION

0-02-864440-9
$14.95

Buying and
Selling a Home
FOURTH EDITION

1-59257-120-4
$18.95

Low-Carb
Meals

1-59257-180-8
$18.95

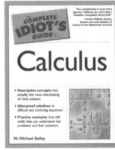

Calculus

0-02-864365-8
$18.95

More than *450 titles* in *30 different categories*
Available at booksellers everywhere

ALPHA